Reel Resistance –
the Cinema of Jean-Marie Teno

Reel Resistance –
the Cinema of Jean-Marie Teno

Melissa Thackway & Jean-Marie Teno

JAMES CURREY

James Currey
is an imprint of
Boydell & Brewer Ltd
PO Box 9, Woodbridge
Suffolk IP12 3DF (GB)
www.jamescurrey.com
and of
Boydell & Brewer Inc.
668 Mt Hope Avenue
Rochester, NY 14620–2731 (US)
www.boydellandbrewer.com

© Melissa Thackway & Jean-Marie Teno 2020

First published 2020
Paperback edition 2023

All rights reserved. No part of this book may be reproduced in any form, or by electronic or mechanical means, including information storage and retrieval systems, without permission in writing from the publishers, except by a reviewer who may quote brief passages in a review

The right of Melissa Thackway & Jean-Marie Teno to be identified as the author of this work has been asserted in accordance with sections 77 and 78 of the Copyright, Designs and Patents Act 1988

British Library Cataloguing in Publication Data
A catalogue record for this book is available on request from the British Library

ISBN 978-1-84701-242-5 (James Currey hardback)
ISBN 978-1-84701-349-1 (James Currey paperback)

The publisher has no responsibility for the continued existence or accuracy of URLs for external or third-party internet websites referred to in this book, and does not guarantee that any content on such websites is, or will remain, accurate or appropriate

'A tous les cinéastes inventifs et courageux, ceux qui créent un cinéma original, de fiction ou de documentaire, qui ne sont pas en lumière et qui continuent.'
Agnès Varda
(1928–2019)[1]

---

[1] Agnès Varda, inspirational filmmaker. Cannes Film Festival Palme d'Honneur 2015 acceptance speech, which Varda dedicated: 'To all the inventive and courageous filmmakers, those who create an original cinema, whether fiction or documentary, who are not in the limelight and who continue.' (See: 'Agnès Varda nous a quitté', Festival de Cannes, updated 17 April 2019, www.bit.ly/AgnèsVarda-Cannes, accessed 17 April 2019).

Contents

List of Photographs & Stills	ix
Preface	xi
Acknowledgements	xv
Introduction	1

PART I

1 Documentary Filmmaking in Africa: An Introduction	11
Defining Documentary	12
Documentary in Africa	14
Early African Cinema and the Documentary	18
Early African Documentary Practices .	21
Into the Eighties…	24
2 Critical Insights: Reading the Films of Jean-Marie Teno	29
A Film Style: Traits and Evolutions	32
Committed Cinema: A Poetics of Resistance	37
The Cinematic 'I': Subjectivity, Voice	56
(Hi)stories, Memory: Decolonial Readings of the Past	71
Reconstructing Archaeologies of Memory	74
Decolonizing the Archive	84
Spanning Borders in One Stride: Transnationality, Circulations and Exile	93
Conclusion: For a Decolonial Aesthetics?	109

PART II In Conversation

In the Beginning…	115
First Encounters, First Steps	125
First Films	136
Filming the Real	140
Documentary Practice	145
Experimentations, Assemblages	151
The Cinematic I	158

Journeys	168
(Hi)stories, Memory	170
Decolonizing the 'Colonial Library'	177
Endogenizing Film Language	185
Transmission	187
Circulations	196

PART III Appendices

Appendix 1 The Writings of Jean-Marie Teno — 201
Freedom: The Power to Say No — 201
Writing on Walls: The Future of African Documentary Cinema — 203
Filming Alone (extracts) — 209

Appendix 2 The Films of Jean-Marie Teno — 215
(List of works, their technical details & synopses)

Bibliography	223
Index	231

List of Photographs & Stills

(All images throughout this book are courtesy of Jean-Marie Teno / Les Films du Raphia)

Photo 1 Present in both *Hommage* and *Vacances au pays*, the shot of the path becomes a leitmotif, evoking a setting out and an invitation to journey. 7

Photo 2 Jean-Marie Teno on location filming *Vacances au pays*, Yaoundé, 1998. 27

Photo 3 On location in Yaoundé with the crew shooting *Mister Foot*, 1991. 32

Photo 4 On location filming the Sanaga River ferry sequence, *Vacances au pays*, 1999. 40

Photos 5a-b *Le Mariage d'Alex*. The body language betrays the tensions on the day Alex marries his junior wife. 45

Photos 6a-b *Lieux saints*. Abbo the public scribe; inside Bouba's ciné-club. 47

Photo 7 *Chef !* The tension and violence rapidly escalate. 50

Photo 8 *Bikutsi Water Blues*. The journalist character, Teno's avatar. 58

Photo 9 *Afrique, je te plumerai*. Teno embraces his now characteristic first-person voice. 64

Photos 10a-b-c-d-e-f *Afrique, je te plumerai*. The jarring transition from the nostalgic childhood sequence to the violence of the archive images of political repression. 68–9

Photo 11 *Le Malentendu colonial*. Bishop Kameta of the Namibian Lutheran Church. 79

Photo 12 *Une Feuille dans le vent*. Ernestine Ouandié delivers her powerfully raw testimony. 82

Photos 13a-b-c-d-e-f *Afrique, je te plumerai*. Subverting the authority of the colonial archives. 88–9

Photo 14 *Une Feuille dans le vent*. Kemo Samba's specially commissioned drawings in lieu of the missing images of Ernest Ouandié's execution. 91

Photos 15a-b-c-d-e-f On location shooting *Clando*, Douala, 1994. — 102–3

Photos 16a-b Naana Banyiwa Horne's enstoolment ceremony in Akwamufie, Ghana (*Chosen*). — 106

Photo 17 Jean-Marie Teno, c. 1993. — 111

Photos 18a-b The Wouri and Capitole cinemas in Douala and Yaoundé on the release of *Bikutsi Water Blues*, 1988–89. — 119

Photos 19a-b-c-d FESPACO 1983. — 126–7

Photos 20a-b-c On location shooting *Le Dernier voyage*, Limbe, 1990. — 139

Photo 21 Johan van der Keuken and Jean-Marie Teno, Perugia, Italy, 1999. — 147

Photo 22 Artist Pascale Marthine Tayou in *La Tête dans les nuages*, Yaoundé, 1994. — 152

Photo 23 Teno on location filming Naana Banyiwa Horne's 2010 return journey and enstoolment ceremony in Akwamufie, Ghana (*Chosen*). — 167

Photo 24 Plaza Cinema, Dakar. *Chef!* screening, 2000. — 178

Photo 25 Film historian Pierre Haffner with Jean-Marie Teno, Balufu Bakupa-Kanyinda, and François Woukouache, Switzerland, c. 1993/94. — 182

Photo 26 Jean-Marie Teno, post-screening Q&A. — 187

Photo 27 Teno at the world première of *Bikutsi Water Blues*, Tunisia, 1988. — 190

Photo 28a Ousmane Sembène and Teno, Milan, 1991. — 194

Photo 28b Souleymane Cissé and Teno, Germany, 2013. — 194

Photo 29 Teno on location filming *Chosen* in Awamufie, Ghana, 2010. — 198

Photo 30 Jean-Marie Teno and director of photography Mohamed Soudani shooting *Le Dernier voyage*, Yaoundé, 1990. — 209

Preface

A film critic whom I met at a social event once said to me that he found my films *romanesques*, or story-like. He never wrote a line about me though, ignoring my work as a form that had long been struggling to be accepted as 'Cinema': documentary. That is a tale long past, of course, and I shall not dwell on the hurdles that had to be jumped to reach today's recognition of documentary as an integral part of cinema. But the scope of officially sanctioned documentary is still proving to be slow in accommodating original and challenging non-fiction work from all over the world. It seems as if the space for documentary in Europe and in France in particular has become the space for selective indignation, and one that is increasingly occupied by bourgeois filmmakers who turn serious issues into a pretext for a contemplative approach to convey a distanced indignation that has the flavour of being politically engaged, without at any time challenging a social order within which they seem to be comfortable.

In such a context, and in today's global context, what space for minority expressions? Fight to be the 'acceptable and accepted Other' that legitimates the exclusion of the many? Mimetism and adherence to schools of thought and form that would have relegated me and my concerns to the backyard of history and memory were simply for me unacceptable.

In the early 1980s in Paris when my interest in cinema took off, the films I enjoyed watching were the European and Latin America avant-garde. When I began to make my own films, I could not help but make a cinema that was political in its form and content, and yet at the same time, I wanted to use cinema, in the words of Ousmane Sembène, as a tool for liberation. And the first step of this liberation was to deconstruct, in a comprehensive way, the mechanisms of oppression that continued to maintain the African continent in a state of chaos and poverty despite its abundance of intellectual and natural resources.

Did I oversimplify my process of making my films understandable to ordinary African people through a *romanesque* approach to the point that I lost part of the intellectual elite on the continent? I asked myself that question after attending the 'Penser et écrire l'Afrique aujourd'hui' colloquium, in which Alain Mabanckou brought together some of Africa's greatest thinkers and writers at the College de France in Paris on 2 May 2016, and after realizing that, in the

21st century, there was no mention of the work of African filmmakers in the process of deconstructing the 20th- and 21st-century colonial representations of Africa. Can one seriously think and write about Africa without addressing the filming of Africa as well? Particularly when one realizes the role that colonial propaganda films and visual ethnography occupied in the colonial process of domination, subjugation, predation, exploitation, and dehumanization. And, all the more so, when one considers how these shaped the representation of Africans by Europeans, then by Africans, and that the very first task that African filmmakers assigned themselves was precisely to challenge and to deconstruct those images and representations.

Seventy years of marginalizing and silencing political cinema have reduced the realities of the continent to slogans by Western humanitarian aid workers, while the pillage of the continent continues under the watch of autocratic presidents more concerned with safeguarding the devastating colonial system that leads today to the drowning in the Mediterranean of tens of thousands of young Africans fleeing poverty for a hypothetical better life in Europe.

How in this global mess do we represent uncomfortable realities?

My answer was to enter into formal resistance, away from the condescending response to the mimetic expressions by filmmakers who accept reproducing mainstream Western film codes, turning their faces away from their local realities to give agency to ready-made narratives that continue to assign Africa to a specific place in the global sphere.

The conversations I have had with audiences around the world while accompanying my films make me aware that more literature about Africa is needed alongside my films to put them into political, social, and even personal context, as my choice of the first-person narrative has often raised questions concerning the notion of autobiography. I have indeed long been thinking of writing my autobiography; a book in which I will elaborate on the relationship between my life and the genesis of each of my films. I started the first chapter of this future book one day in Amherst MA, while I was a Copeland Fellow, but set it aside when, after a discussion with Melissa Thackway, the idea of this present book on my work emerged.

The advantage of having a leading African cinema scholar theorizing my work and completing it with the intellectual and aesthetic processes that lead me to making the choices of my films seemed an attractive entry point to the understanding of my work. Melissa has taken the time to analyse and contextualize my films, to question me, but also to accompany me in the process of making new films. We have spent long hours discussing the history of African cinema during the writing of this book and Melissa's academic input in the theoretical analysis of my films is, I believe, a great complement to my work, past, present and hopefully future. Working together has certainly provided me with the rare opportunity as a filmmaker to step back and review my path, evolving creative processes, motivations, and at times trials and doubts. I hope that this will transpire from these pages for the reader. I hope too that this book will re-kindle the conversation about a cinema in Africa that is more focused on its people, their lives and realities at a time when they are being stripped of almost everything, rather than a cinema chasing chimeras and pipe dreams.

Jean-Marie *Teno*
Mèze, 2019

Acknowledgements

This book came to being after a long period of gestation that my late father, John Thackway, kick-started into action after most unfairly extorting a promise from me on his deathbed: that I write 'that book'. It was a promise that he knew very well I could hardly refuse – the twinkle had not yet gone out in his eye – but my thanks go first to him for the welcome push and for his loving support throughout my life. While he is no longer here to read this, I am sure that his spirit, somewhere out there, possibly among the stars for which he always taught me to reach, or in the waters where he rests, is contented at last.

Thanks equally to my mother, Frances Thackway, for the unwavering encouragement and support, which has at times been material too, for this book was written outside of any institutional funding framework and amounted often to what I can only describe as a juggling act. A model in many ways, and not least my first inspiration as a feminist, thanks for all you have taught me and for just being you.

My deep thanks to Wendy Everett, my most inspirationally passionate university tutor, later PhD supervisor, to whom I quite naturally turned, many years down the line, to be the first reader of this book. My thanks for that precious close reading and feedback, consistent warm encouragement, but also for being the first, many moons ago, to kindle my burgeoning interest in film into a passion.

To my publisher, Lynn Taylor, with whom I already had the pleasure to work on my first book, *Africa Shoots Back*, and whose enthusiastic welcoming of the idea of the present, and unwavering patience while it was in the making, was another great motivation.

To my film colleague-friends / friend-colleagues Sada Niang and Odile Cazenave for agreeing to review this book, and for the precise and insightful comments and feedback. To Anjali Prabhu, for our invaluable early discussion when the book was first an idea, a conversation that proved decisive in helping me determine its form. To them and to Frieda Ekotto, Kenneth W. Harrow, Rachel Gabara, Daniela Ricci, Olivier Barlet and Michael Witt for the academic invitations, stimulating film conversations, and the laughter over the years.

My thanks and respect, too, to the inspirational women thinkers in Paris whose brilliance, creativity, and critical minds carry me forward, stimulate my own thought, and keep me questioning, always. They form for me a kind of intellectual community to whom I have often had the incredibly good fortune to listen, exchange with, and/or share friendship as I have been writing and who have directly, indirectly, and laterally nourished this present work: Françoise Vergès, Seloua Luste Boulbina, Paola Bacchetta, Nacira Guénif-Souilamas, Nadia Yala Kisukidi, Fabiana Ex-Souza, Myriam Dao, Maboula Soumahoro, and Anna-Louise Milne.

To my daughter, Zélie, whose soulful and militant presence has accompanied me throughout this writing process like a breath of fresh air and a beacon of light.

And last, yet foremost, to Jean-Marie Teno, thanks to whom, and with whom I have travelled many paths.

It is, as the saying goes, not the destination, but the journey that matters.

Melissa Thackway
Paris, 2019

Introduction

There is this Native Indian poem that has been with me in my heart for some time: 'We want what is real. We want what is real. Don't deceive us.'

The history of colonization, imperialism is a record of betrayal, of lies and deceits. The demand for what is real is a demand for reparation, for transformation.

bell hooks[1]

In 1994, two years after the film's release, I watched Jean-Marie Teno's *Afrique, je te plumerai* in a tiny, packed cinema at the Images d'Ailleurs Festival in Paris.[2] At a time when, in the early stages of my PhD research, I was viewing all the African films I could access, it was the first work by Jean-Marie Teno that I stumbled across, unprepared and unsuspecting. To this day, I remember the bombshell that was the film. During the final scenes, I was aware in the darkness of the cinema of a presence standing waiting in the aisle. As the lights came up after the final credits, this presence took the stage for the Q&A: Teno. In all honesty, I remember little of the ensuing discussion, reeling as I was from this stark awakening to chapters of colonial history completely unbeknown to me at the time, delivered, what is more, from a radically different perspective that pulled no punches. Stunned as I was too by the force and originality of the film's completely unorthodox form, which resembled nothing I had ever seen before. A documentary? Every facet of the film could only be described as challenging. And I love nothing more in cinema than to be challenged.

My passion for Jean-Marie Teno's work was born.

This passion accompanied me throughout my PhD and the subsequent writing of my book, *Africa Shoots Back*, in which I devoted considerable space to discussing *Afrique, je te plumerai* and Teno's later fiction film, *Clando*. It is a passion that has not left me since as I have continued over the years to

---

[1] hooks, *Talking Back*, 3.
[2] Throughout the book, I shall use the original language titles of Teno's films whose English titles, in chronological order, are: *Homage*; *Africa, I Will Fleece You*; *Head in the Clouds*; *The Colonial Misunderstanding*; *Chief!*; *Trip to the Country*; *Alex's Wedding*; *Sacred Places* and *Leaf in the Wind*. The French title of the originally English-titled *Chosen* (used here) is *Le Futur dans le retro*.

assiduously follow and focus on Teno's work as I write, give papers in seminars and conferences, and teach. Over the past ten years, ours has become a close friendship and a collaboration: I accompanied Jean-Marie Teno when he filmed *Chosen* in Ghana, interested to observe his filmmaking process at first hand. Our discussions while he was editing *Une Feuille dans le vent* and *Chosen* led him generously to credit me as Assistant to the directing of both films. I have translated several of Teno's films' subtitles, and read projects in gestation. In strictly academic terms, therefore, I have crossed a scientific line; that of detached exteriority. I do not purport to an objective, disengaged distance from Teno's work, then; on the contrary, I claim and embrace the subjectivity and proximity of my critical gaze and position. This should not, I believe, be a barrier to meaningful analysis, just as in a cinematic form long believed to be objective, Teno embraces the subjectivity of his own 'position of enunciation', to cite the late Stuart Hall.[3] Moreover, I have only ever written about the films that I critically value and enjoy; why on earth otherwise spend long hours poring over them? In *Africa Shoots Back*, in the early 2000s, I earnestly and understatedly wrote that the films selected in the book for analysis reflected 'a degree of personal preference'. Today, older, bolder, I can unmitigatedly say that I critically value and love the films about which I write here; it is indeed from, and based on, that value and cinematic pleasure that I wish to write and to share.

But, of course, my personal taste alone would not suffice to justify an in-depth study of Jean-Marie Teno's oeuvre that today comprises two documentary shorts, ten feature-length documentaries, and one fiction feature film.[4] This is warranted by the fact that, in the thirty or so years that this filmmaker has, against the odds and with painstaking commitment and resilience, been filming, analysing and critiquing Cameroon and postcolonial Africa in his films, his evolving formal and thematic explorations have consistently found themselves at the vanguard of, and in remarkable resonance with, some of the period's most fascinating and challenging social, political, intellectual and artistic debates, from postcolonial, subaltern and decolonial theory to debates in documentary filmmaking. Focusing on Cameroon, Teno's cinema is at the same time outward-looking, internationalist and cosmopolitan. Constantly pushing back the aesthetic boundaries and modes of documentary film-making too, resisting fads and fashions, his practice is marked by its freedom: its freedom of form, its defence of freedoms, and its claiming of the freedom to speak out in a tone that is often irreverent, dissenting, ironic, yet never devoid of hope. Teno's cinema is indeed like Teno: an unconventional free spirit. From

---

[3] Hall, 'Cultural Identity and Cinematic Representation', 68.
[4] At the start of his career, Teno also directed several little-known fictional shorts, which are listed in Appendix 2.

both an African and world perspective, he is a major filmmaker of our times. His award-winning works are widely taught and screened in North American, European and African universities and festivals, and Teno was made a member of the Academy of Motion Picture Arts and Sciences in 2017. This first in-depth study of his cinema is, then, a timely recognition of Jean-Marie Teno's path.

In the same way that Teno's work eschews stylistic and genre boundaries and borders, this book is at once a work of Film Studies, African Studies, a monograph of this prolific Cameroonian director's oeuvre, and a critical dialogue between a filmmaker and scholar. Addressing common themes and issues, the complementary analysis and interview in Parts I and II reverberate and weave together to form an intertextual dialogue of their own. Convinced of the importance of testimony, of voice, our long conversation is an 'interview' in the etymological sense, derived from the French *entrevue*, itself derived from *s'entrevoir*, 'to see one another'. It is, then, both a coming together to share our respective perspectives and ways of seeing, a joint dialogic work that combines both the written and spoken word. By including this extended interview, this book not only echoes the interview format common to the documentary form on which it focuses, but also seeks to give the artist behind the works the space to articulate his own thoughts on his creative process, as a speaking subject, just as he imposes himself thus in his films. Indeed, given Teno's long experience of presenting and discussing his work with cinema and festival audiences, in universities and in conferences around the world, and having been an active player in, and witness of, the African film world since the 1980s, his testimony is a rare and precious one. It is certainly one that is worth listening to, for, in the words of Jean-Luc Nancy, '[i]f "to hear" is to understand the sense ... "to listen" is to be inclined towards possible meaning'.[5] But above all, aware of the asymmetry of our respective positionalities – White British female scholar from the global North / Black Cameroonian male artist from global South – it is also a political stance, an attempt to redress an imbalance; it is an attempt on my part not to speak *about* – or worse, *in the place of* –, but rather *to* and *with*; it is an attempt to avoid this work on Jean-Marie Teno being the space of his absence, to borrow bell hooks' expression.[6]

---

[5] Nancy, *À l'écoute*, 19. I thank Julie Lorimier for bringing this quotation to my attention in her paper 'Une redéfinition du documentaire par le film-griot : *Parlons Grand-mère* de Djibril Diop Mambéty' at the *Documentary Filmmaking Practices in Africa* conference, University of Toronto, 19-20 January 2017.
  Unless otherwise stated, all the translations from the French are mine. For the benefit of French speakers, I have provided the original French in the notes throughout. ['*Si "entendre", c'est comprendre le sens ... "écouter", c'est être tendu vers un sens possible.*'].

[6] hooks, 'Marginality as a Site of Resistance', 343.

Presenting and contextualizing Teno's cinema in its entirety, identifying and analysing its stylistic and thematic traits, examining the individual films and the collective oeuvre, this book will trace the connections, intersections, and liaisons present and highlight the evolutions of its film language and concerns. It will take the reader on a journey through Teno's multifaceted on-going filmic reflection on contemporary and past Cameroon, on the African continent, on its political systems, culture, history, memory and people; in short, a cinematic reflection that restores complexity.

Questioning the documentary form itself, tracing the emergence and development of documentary in Africa as first introduced by the European colonial powers and later adopted and developed by African filmmakers after Independence, Part I, Chapter 1, **Documentary Filmmaking in Africa: An Introduction**, considers notions of the real, of representation, and their specificity in the colonial and postcolonial African contexts. Divided into subsections – *Defining Documentary, Early African Cinema and the Documentary, Early African Documentary Practices, Into the Eighties…* – the chapter situates and contextualizes Teno's work within the fields of documentary filmmaking in general, and within African cinema.[7]

Chapter 2, **Critical Insights: Reading the Films of Jean-Marie Teno**, is the core analytical part of this book. It focuses on what I non-exclusively identify as the most striking and salient themes and characteristics that intertwine and overlap throughout all of Teno's films, illustrating these with filmic examples. Divided into four sections, this chapter seeks both to fully explore and analyse Teno's cinema, complementing and shedding light on issues discussed in our later critical conversation, and vice-versa.

Considering the notion of political commitment in art, and of art as a form of resistance, *Committed Cinema: A Poetics of Resistance* contextualizes what

---

[7] The term 'African cinema' has been the object of much comment and debate over the years. While the term is an undeniably essentializing one, my own understanding and use of it does not preclude the obvious plurality, hybridity, diversity and diversification of filmmaking practices in an approximately 30.4 million km^2 continent comprising 55 countries (as currently recognized by the African Union). While this book focuses predominantly on the cinema of West and Central Africa, and, more specifically, for reasons both cinematic and historical, to what is also problematically referred to as 'Francophone Africa' – a term that neither reflects the linguistic diversity of this zone, nor the predominant usage of many of its peoples, not to mention its problematic on-going centring of the former colonial metropolis (ties which, certainly in France's case, remain remarkably (neo)colonial), I use the term 'African cinema' in the Pan-African collective spirit still expressed by numerous filmmakers from the continent. I use it, finally, in reference to films that, in the words of Olivier Barlet, 'seek a just gaze and rhythm to testify, from within, to the intimacy of the African experience and question the world' (*Contemporary African Cinema*, 40).

Kenneth W. Harrow describes as Teno's 'cinematic politics'.[8] It considers his filmmaking in relation to the debates that animated the first-generation West and Central African filmmakers of the 1960s and 1970s regarding the nature and role of filmmaking in Africa; debates that have left a lasting trace. Looking at the ways in which Teno seeks to question Cameroonian, and more generally African societies in his works, it considers his own cinematic and political stance towards these questions. It identifies and explores the predominant committed socio-political and historical themes in these works, such as violence, power, struggle, memory, gender, trauma and exile, and considers his constant focus, both thematically and in his filmmaking choices, on forms and instances of resistance.

The Cinematic 'I': Subjectivity, Voice focuses on Teno's signature recourse to a first-person narrative voice, now a trademark of his films and one of their defining characteristics. Both a personal and collective 'I', and a looking, questioning 'eye', Teno's embracing of subjectivity is contextualized within the documentary tradition and also in the postcolonial moment as a decolonial gesture. It is examined, then, in terms of its aesthetic and political impact as it centres the African subject and reclaims voice in a vital on-going postcolonial process of reconstruction and self-affirmation.

(Hi)stories, Memory: Decolonial Readings of the Past considers the centrality of the notions of history and memory in the works of Jean-Marie Teno and their relevance in the postcolonial African context. Divided into further subsections, *Reconstructing Archaeologies of Memory* considers the evolution in filmic approaches to the question, from the uncovering of hidden histories and restoring of missing chapters, to writings 'from below' and the corollary questions of situated, logocentric perspectives, to the questioning of the very epistemes of historiography itself. Not a nostalgic celebration of the past, Teno's readings of history are shown, like in the region's oral (hi)story-telling practices, to translate the lessons of the past in terms of the present. A form of resistance, they are shown to be part of an effort to reconstruct postcolonial identities, and an attempt to understand the current state and future perspectives of Africa's postcolonial societies. *Decolonizing the Archive* focuses specifically on the ways in which Teno has, since his earliest works *Hommage* (1985) and particularly *Afrique, je te plumerai* (1992), revisited colonial archives, reworking and reinterpreting this material from an African perspective to tell a different story, creating a subversive counter-memory in the process.

Finally, *Spanning Borders in One Stride: Transnationality, Circulations and Exile* highlights the transnationality of Jean-Marie Teno's cinema. While living in a constant exilic to-ing and fro-ing between continents, Teno consistently

---

[8] Harrow, 'Manthia Diawara's Waves and the Problem of the "Authentic"', 7.

turns his lens to Africa's spaces, and journeying, migration and return are both constant themes in, and central to, the narrative structures of his work. Focusing on the questions of circulations, in-betweenness, deterritorialization, and belonging, this section explores the ways in which the filmmaker's own interior-exterior position affects his film work and filmic gaze. It also examines the aesthetic crossings and traversing of genre boundaries that Teno undertakes in his works.

Part II, **In Conversation**, is our in-depth dialogic journey through Jean-Marie Teno's life and work. Structured under the following sub-headings – *In the Beginning…*; *First Encounters, First Steps*; *First Films*; *Filming the Real, Documentary Practice*; *Experimentations, Assemblages*; *The Cinematic I*; *Journeys*; *(Hi)stories, Memory*; *Decolonizing the 'Colonial Library'*; *Endogenizing Film Language*; *Transmission* and *Circulations* – the interview offers Teno's personal perspective on the themes and ideas analysed and developed in Part I.

Finally, to offer further insight into Jean-Marie Teno's evolving reflections on cinema in Africa, **Appendix 1** offers a selection of three essays written by him, commissioned for and previously published in film journals, compendiums, or festival catalogues: 'Freedom: The Power to Say No' (1995), 'Writing on Walls: The Future of African Documentary Cinema' (2010) and 'Filming Alone' (2016). Of interest in their own right, these texts are also chosen for their particular resonance with the issues explored and discussed in Parts I and II.

Appendix 2 comprises a complete list of Teno's films – notably *Hommage* (1985), *Bikutsi Water Blues* (1988), *Afrique, je te plumerai* (1991), *La Tête dans les nuages* (1994), *Clando* (1996), *Chef !* (1999), *Vacances au pays* (2000), *Le mariage d'Alex* (2003), *Le Malentendu colonial* (2004), *Lieux saints* (2009), *Une Feuille dans le vent* (2013), *Chosen* (2018) – their synopses and technical details.

So, without further ado: 'Let us go, then, you and I…'[9]

---

[9] T.S. Eliot, *The Love Song of J. Alfred Prufrock*.

Photo 1 Present in both *Hommage* and *Vacances au pays*, the shot of the path away from Teno's family compound becomes a leitmotif, evoking a setting out and an invitation to journey.

Part I

Documentary Filmmaking in Africa: An Introduction

Tous les grands films de fiction tendent au documentaire, comme tous les grands documentaires tendent à la fiction.
Jean-Luc Godard[1]

Before looking specifically at Jean-Marie Teno's work, it is useful to start with a word or two about documentary filmmaking in general, and its particular development – and at times complex representational issues – in the African context. While some existing studies have focused on documentary films made *in* Africa, mostly in the colonial era,[2] and numerous articles, chapters and some rare books have focused on individual documentary films or filmmakers,[3] at present, African documentary filmmaking per se remains a relatively uncharted domain, even if there are clear signs of growing academic and critical interest in it.[4] This introduction does not purport to fill that gap. It does not aim either to give an exhaustive historical presentation of the documentary, multiple

---

[1] 'All great fiction films tend towards documentary, just as all great documentaries tend towards fiction'. *Jean-Luc Godard par Jean-Luc Godard*, 181-2.
[2] See, for example, Peter J. Bloom, *French Colonial Documentary: Mythologies of Humanitarianism*, or Nwachukwu Frank Ukadike's chapter, 'The Documentary Tradition', in his book *African Cinema: Narratives, Perspectives and Poetics*. Rachel Gabara's article 'War by Documentary' also focuses on both colonial and postcolonial African documentary.
[3] See, for example, Henri-François Imbert's book on Samba Félix Ndiaye; Anjali Prabhu, 'Jean-Marie Teno' or Ken Harrow's 'Cameroonian Cinema' on Jean-Marie Teno's works; or Sheila Petty's analysis of *Clando*. For full references and further examples, see the Bibliography at the end of this book.
[4] The first international conference devoted exclusively to the field entitled *Documentary Filmmaking Practices in Africa* was, for example, organized by Suzanne Crosta, Sada Niang and Alexie Tcheuyap at the University of Toronto on 19-20 January 2017. The conference was followed by their publication of the first English-language academic issue devoted specifically to African documentary: 'Documenting the African Experience', *Critical Interventions* 11, issue 3, 2017. Rachel Gabara has also published in-depth articles on African documentary cinema (see Bibliography), and is currently preparing a book on the subject. In French, see also Fronty and Kifouani's *La diversité du documentaire de création en Afrique*, which focuses on African documentary filmmaking in the digital era (the 2000s); and Cazenave and Célérier (eds), 'Le Documentaire francophone africain et afro-diasporique'.

excellent studies of which already exist,[5] nor specifically of African documentary, which would require a book of its own. It simply seeks to offer a frame, or a context in which to situate Jean-Marie Teno's work.

Defining Documentary

Answering the what might at first appear simple question of what defines a documentary has long proven to be notoriously slippery, as Patricia Aufderheide illustrates.[6] Not only are there multiple types of documentary, but its boundaries and forms have shifted and evolved since the invention of cinema in 1895, often thanks to on-going technological evolutions. Aufderheide offers a useful broad definition, notwithstanding, describing documentaries as 'portraits of real life, using real life as their raw material'.[7] Bill Nichols adds, 'documentaries address *the* world in which we live rather than *a* world imagined by the filmmaker'.[8] But perhaps it is the three pioneering filmmakers of the 1920s considered the 'fathers' of documentary – Robert Flaherty (USA), John Grierson (Scotland) and Dziga Vertov (Russia) – who, in their respective claims to film 'truthfully' *and* to be artists, best captured the inherent elusiveness of the form's boundaries. They captured too the tensions within a form that is never more than a *reproduction* of reality, with all the possible manipulations that this infers.[9] Grierson's famous definition of documentary as the 'artistic representation of actuality' is perhaps the most usefully enduring one, then. Or, as Toni de Bromhead puts it well, documentary, 'by its very nature … looks two ways … cinema on the one hand and concrete reality on the other'.[10]

By virtue of film's ability to capture movement and to appear to faithfully record and reproduce reality – or at least an impression, if not to say an illusion, of it – there have always been degrees of confusion concerning the verisimilitude of film. From early audiences' mythically reported alarm at the shots of a locomotive advancing towards the camera and thus seemingly at them in Louis Lumière's 1895 film *L'Arrivée d'un train en gare de la Ciotat*, to debates about Flaherty's direction of his protagonists in *Nanook of the North* (1922) and his staging and filming of defunct customs as if they were still in practice, to

---

[5] See, for example, the works of Patricia Aufderheide, Bill Nichols and Toni de Bromhead, or Guy Gauthier's *Le documentaire : un autre cinema*.
[6] Aufderheide, *Documentary Film: A Very Short Introduction*, 1.
[7] Ibid., 2.
[8] Nichols, *Introduction to Documentary*, xi.
[9] For more details on Flaherty and Grierson's predominantly realist approach to documentary, and Vertov's predominantly formalist one, see Aufderheide, *Documentary Film*, 26-44.
[10] de Bromhead, *Looking Two Ways*, 11.

public realization after the Second World War in particular of film's potential to manipulate and spread political propaganda and ideology, questions concerning the relationship between film images and the 'real life' they capture have always arisen, and continue to arise, as do the questions of ethics, objectivity, manipulation and truthfulness that they infer.

Although practised from the outset, as Flaherty's work reminds us, mise-en-scène and reconstitution were long deemed suspect and inauthentic in documentary filmmaking, and documentary has often been described as 'a window on the world'. As Aufderheide reminds us, however, perhaps obviously but still nonetheless necessarily: 'Documentaries are *about* real life; they are not real life'.[11] All documentaries, whatever their style, manipulate information in the choosing of their subject, their shooting style, editing, mixing, and so forth. Likewise, there are no hard and fast boundaries between documentary and fiction. As Bill Nichols states: 'Some documentaries make strong use of practices or conventions, such as scripting, staging, reenactment, rehearsal, and performance, for example, that we often associate with fiction', just as, '[s]ome fiction makes strong use of practices or conventions, such as location shooting, the use of non-actors, hand-held cameras, improvisation, and found footage (footage not shot by the filmmaker) that we often associate with non-fiction or documentary'.[12] Going further still, filmmaker and theorist Trinh T. Minh-Ha has challenged the reification of cinema into 'a corpus of traditions', rejecting the Cartesian division between documentary and fiction film altogether. Hence her uncompromising declaration: 'There is no such thing as documentary – whether the term designates a category of material, a genre, an approach, or a set of techniques ... despite the very visible existence of a documentary tradition.'[13] Disputing the notion that documentary cinema captures the real ('so real that the Real becomes the one basic referent – pure, concrete, fixed, visible, all-too-visible'),[14] or the truth, Minh-ha recalls that these are never neutral, nor objective, but rather – like meaning – are produced, and this according to regimes of power:

> Truth, even when "caught on the run", does not yield itself either in names or in filmic frames ... Truth and meaning ... are likely to be equated with

---

[11] Aufderheide, *Documentary Film*, 2
[12] Nichols, *Introduction to Documentary*, xi.
[13] Minh-Ha, 'Documentary Is/Not a Name', 76. In her later work, *Looking Two Ways*, Toni de Bromhead refutes the argument that there is no significant difference between fiction and documentary, even if both do share forms, modes and sometimes styles. Conceding, however, that the differences are 'complex and multi-levelled', sensed rather than clearly articulated, de Bromhead rather equivocally argues that this difference 'has to do with that delicate relationship between the film and its source material', 131.
[14] Minh-Ha, 'Documentary Is/Not a Name', 80.

one another. Yet, what is put forth as truth is often nothing more than *a meaning*.'[15]

Also recalling that 'the whole of filmmaking is a question of manipulation, whether 'creative' or not',[16] Minh-ha suggests that a more useful distinction is whether this manipulation is visible or concealed, whether or not what is accepted as non-factual (namely, aesthetics) is excluded, or whether a film is 'aware of its own artifice' and 'understands the mutual dependence of realism and 'artificiality' in the process of filmmaking'.[17]

What ultimately and convergingly emerges from these viewpoints are the limitations and limitedness of a rigid, unchanging or universally applied fiction/documentary binary in defining an evolving, multifarious filmmaking practice that, furthermore, exists across geographic or temporal borders. If we can most likely agree that 'real life' is indeed at the core of what is commonly defined as documentary film – even if, again, this is not exclusive to this form – perhaps, then, it is the anxiety of categorization that we would do well to relinquish, looking simply, on the screen, to the cinema.

Documentary in Africa

Until the digital era of the 2000s, which saw a significant and lasting take-off of documentary practice across Africa and the emergence of ever more documentary filmmakers, documentary filmmaking in the early post-Independence years remained what might be described as the poor relation of African cinema.[18]

---

[15] Ibid., 76.
[16] Ibid., 88.
[17] Ibid., 89.
[18] Among notable documentary filmmakers to have emerged in Africa in the 2000s are (in alphabetical order): Aïcha Boro (Burkina Faso), Angèle Diabang (Senegal), Mamadou Sellou Diallo (Senegal), Taghreed Elsanhouri (Sudan), Jihan El-Tahri (Egypt), Hassen Ferhani (Algeria), Dieudo Hamadi (Democratic Republic of the Congo [DRC]), Delphe Kifouani (Congo), Leila Kilani (Morocco), Hajooj Kuka (Sudan), Osvalde Lewat (Cameroon), Aïcha Macky (Niger), Sani Elhadj Magori (Niger), Idrissou Mora-Kpaï (Benin), Katy Léna Ndiaye (Senegal), Khady Sylla (Senegal), Rama Thiaw (Senegal), Michel Zongo (Burkina Faso). Among the diaspora filmmakers are Isabelle Boni-Claverie (France/Ivory Coast), Alice Diop (France/Senegal), Mati Diop (France/Senegal), and Pascale Obolo (France/Cameroon). Some already confirmed fiction filmmakers have also made documentaries in the 2000s, for example Jean-Pierre Bekolo (Cameroon), Dani Kouyaté (Burkina Faso), Mahamat-Saleh Haroun (Chad), Zeka Laplaine (DRC), and Moussa Touré (Senegal), and veteran filmmaker Souleymane Cissé (Mali) returned to the documentary format of his beginnings with his 2015 documentary, *Oka*. Other filmmakers' already burgeoning documentary careers truly took off in the 2000s, notably Nadia El Fani (Tunisia), Khalo Matabane (South Africa), Ousmane William Mbaye (Senegal), Monique Mbeka Phoba (DRC), or François Woukoache (Cameroon). See also Olivier Barlet's *Les cinémas d'Afrique*

While paradoxical, given the prevalence of realism in early African fiction films, this is no doubt best explained by the highly specific and profoundly marking representational context in which, with the notable exception of 1920s-born Egyptian cinema, African cinema was born.

When African filmmakers predominantly from the West, Centre and North of the continent first appropriated the film medium in the wake of Independence in the 1960s, they were faced with the legacy of the ways in which the West had depicted Africa and its people on screens for over sixty years. Cinema was indeed invented just ten years after the 1884-85 Berlin Conference at which the European imperial powers divided the African continent between them. These new colonial powers were quick to realize the potential of film as a powerful propaganda medium that could be used to promote and justify colonial expansion and assert European hegemony. The famous French explorer and empire-builder Colonel Marchand indeed described cinema as 'quite clearly the perfect weapon for conquering Africa'.[19] Later in 1932, a French Ministry of Political Affairs report on 'the need to adopt a "film policy" in the colonies' stated: 'The importance, in the war, taken by propaganda relayed through films ... has drawn governments' attention to the resources that cinema offers in the dissemination of ideas to be conveyed, teachings to be propagated and the vulgarization of concepts.'[20]

Like the British, who created the Colonial Film Unit in 1937, the French Ministry of Colonies' Intercolonial Information and Documentation Services started producing films in the 1930s to celebrate the strength and success of the 'colonial pact'. Like most documentaries of the time, these films carried what is commonly referred to as a 'voice-of-God' off-screen commentary that explained and interpreted the images seen; omniscient, disembodied, this authoritative, male voice assumed the power/knowledge to speak. Construed as neutral, objective, these commentaries of course constructed and conveyed colonial ideology and propaganda. Infused with notions of white supremacy, staging the gratitude and fidelity of the colonized peoples, these films insisted

---

des années 2000 / Contemporary African Cinema and François Fronty and Delphe Kifouani (eds.), *La diversité du documentaire de création en Afrique* for further details. Betti Ellerson also references the works of women documentary filmmakers predominantly from the Anglophone African countries, in her article 'African Women and the Documentary: Storytelling, Visualizing History, from the Personal to the Political'.

[19] Cited in Thackway, *Africa Shoots Back*, 31 ['de toute évidence, l'arme de conquête de l'Afrique'].

[20] Report signed Gaston Joseph. Cited by Odile Goerg, *Fantômas sous les tropiques*, 73 ['L'importance prise, pendant la guerre, par la propagande effectuée à l'aide de films ... a ... attiré l'attention des gouvernements sur les ressources offertes par le cinématographe pour la diffusion des idées à répandre, des enseignements à propager, des notions à vulgariser'].

on the benevolence of a 'Mother France' portrayed as bringing 'modern advances' to the colonies, notably building schools, hospitals, and roads, and educating and 'civilizing' the natives.[21] The 1931 French propaganda documentary *Promenade en AEF* (*Promenade in French Equatorial Africa*), for example, typically lauded the construction of the Congo-Ocean railway, and boasted the setting up of health services in French Equatorial Africa, relaying the European imperial myth of its so-called 'Civilizing Mission'. Naturally, it, like other such works, painted a falsely bright picture of life in the colonies, omitting its far more brutal realities: the use of forced labour to build such infrastructures in life-threatening conditions; the acute shortage of health centres and schools; forced conscription; exactions and punishment for failing to pay colonial taxes; the violent repression of any form of social or political protest; the predation of resources; the exploitation of the labour force. These works also systematically erased any mention of African resistance or revolt, and never gave Africans a voice.[22] Simultaneously, colonized Africans were denied access to filmmaking processes. In the French colonies, for example, the 1934 Laval Decree, which stipulated that all film crews shooting in the French colonies receive prior authorization – an authorization never granted to colonial subjects – gave the colonial authorities control of who shot what in the colonies.[23]

The colonial era also saw the development of ethnographic documentary filmmaking, which also undoubtedly played a significant role in many early African filmmakers' reticence towards the form. As early as 1935, French ethnographer Marcel Griaule pioneered using film as a means to record his field research in the Dogon region of Mali. With the increasing availability of light-weight 16 mm film cameras and synchronous sound recording equipment in the 1950s, other ethnographers – and notably Griaule's student, Jean Rouch,

---

[21] Just to give one example of the abyss between this civilizing discourse and reality, by 1957, only 10% of school-age children on average actually attended colonial schools in French West Africa. See Pascale Barthélémy, 'L'enseignement dans l'Empire colonial français : une vieille histoire ?'. I thank Odile Goerg for the reference.

[22] For further discussion of the construction and representation of Africa in the Western imagination and cinema, see Thackway, *Africa Shoots Back*, 30-36 and Gabara, *War by Documentary*.

[23] On the very rare occasions that filmmakers strayed from what they had been authorized to shoot – for example, the young French filmmaker René Vautier, who was commissioned in 1949 by the Ligue française de l'enseignement to make a film about the French colonial education effort, but who started shooting the atrocities he discovered in French West Africa – their footage was seized and/or censored. Having managed to smuggle a third of his footage back to France before the destruction of the film's negatives was ordered by the Bobo-Dioulasso colonial tribunal, Vautier completed his 19-minute anti-colonial film, *Afrique 50*. The film was immediately censored, however, and remained so until 1996. Vautier was condemned to one year in prison for violation of the Laval Decree.

who founded the Comité du Film Ethnographique at the Musée de l'Homme in Paris in 1952 – continued to develop this practice in Africa.[24] As direct, or observational cinema emerged in the United States and Canada, advocating 'fly-on-wall' approaches to filming that sought not to disturb, or to intervene as little as possible in the situations filmed so that the filmed subject, and the spectator, would 'forget' the presence of the camera, in France, Rouch and Edgar Morin in particular developed the similar, but not identical practice of *cinéma vérité*. Inspired by Dziga Vertov's 1920s *Kino-Pravda*, and by Flaherty, *cinéma vérité* filmmakers sought to capture fragments of reality as they appeared, but then, through their montage, to objectively unveil 'truths' and hidden realities invisible to the naked eye. While the sympathies and intentions of these ethnographic filmmakers may have diverged from those making colonial propaganda works, ethnographic cinema was (is) nonetheless marked by what Paula Amad terms 'colonial structures of seeing'. Whether unwittingly or not (the road to hell being paved with good intentions, as Teno reminds us in *Lieux saints*), it thus perpetuated the violence and asymmetrical power of non-reciprocity, or 'the right to look without being looked at'.[25] Indeed, the roots of ethnography itself are profoundly colonial. A study of people and cultures that was initially born out of European exploration and mapping in the 18th century, ethnography – 'the handmaiden of colonialism', as Zoe Todd comments –[26] pointed a unidirectional European gaze at 'exotic' Others in the spaces that the imperial nations sought to govern, drawing up a knowing of them, and failing to position them as thinking subjects with epistemologies of their own. Moreover, with its focus on what it defined as 'authentic', uncontaminated, 'traditions', rituals and ceremonies, this ethnographic gaze also contributed to constructing and conveying the essentializing European preconception that precolonial African societies and cultures were age-old, unchanging and 'traditional', when they were in reality fluid, flexible and open.[27]

---

[24] See Gabara, *From Ethnography to Essay*, 362, for more on other bodies in France that also funded ethnographic film.
[25] Paula Amad, 'Visual Riposte: Looking Back at the Return of the Gaze as Postcolonial Theory's Gift to Film Studies', 50. Here Amad draws notably on a 1973 review by literary critic Jacques Leenhardt and on Michel Foucault's *Discipline and Punish* in her reflection on the power inherent to viewing relations, seeing and being seen; she also posits looking back into the camera as a possibility of resistance or agency.
[26] Todd, *The Decolonial Turn 2.0: the reckoning*.
[27] The familiar description of African societies, cultures and practices as 'traditional' is a construction, as Terence Ranger argues in his seminal chapter, 'The Invention of Tradition in Colonial Africa'. Here, Ranger describes the processes by which European colonialists and Africanists, who drew on their own models and references and transposed them to practices that did not necessarily have an equivalent, invented African traditions for Africans. Misreading local customs, multiple identities and belongings, which, in the 19th century tended to be flexible and changing, Europeans 'set about to codify

While Jean Rouch's early works were conventionally ethnographic, in the mid-1950s, Rouch became increasingly experimental in his approach, aware of the imbalance of power that necessarily stemmed from the looking relations of ethnography. In *Moi, un noir* (1957) in particular, Rouch thus adopted a more interactive, participatory practice, embracing mise-en-scène, role-playing, enactment and improvisation, calling on his actor-subjects to contribute to the making of works, and partially including their voices in an attempt to create what he called 'shared anthropology', or an 'anthropological dialogue'.[28] While still narrating these later 'ethno-fiction' films, Rouch's voice became, Gabara argues, 'less authoritative and more speculative' as he attempted to no longer make Africans purely the object of his works.[29] This 'reflexive turn', as Matthias De Groof describes it, did not completely redress the imbalance, however, or entirely rid Rouch's films made in Africa of their colonial vision.[30]

Early African Cinema and the Documentary

The emergence of Africa's own filmmakers could only but challenge some of the underlying principles and beliefs around documentary, questioning the real, truth, and their representation – a reflection? a construction? – and notions of objectivity.[31] As hitherto suppressed viewpoints and voices emerged in Africa, they, like elsewhere, naturally questioned and subverted existing hegemonic voices. Notions such as *cinéma vérité* begged the question of 'whose truth?' or even 'whose reality?' By virtue of their very existence, these alternative voices also posed the question of *who* is speaking, thereby exploding notions of objectivity and forcing the recognition of the importance of situated speech, thinking and knowledge.

In the African context, documentary had, as described above, broken the implicit 'pact' of reproducing reality faithfully; European colonial documentary did not capture life in Africa as it was, but rather constructed it as it needed it to be seen in the colonizing process. Having been on the receiving end of such

---

and promulgate these traditions (partly through a desire to document, partly through a desire to control), thereby transforming flexible custom into hard prescription' (598). Henceforth, in the African context, the term 'traditional' erroneously purveys the notion that Africa and its cultures are static and unchanging, a vision still widely circulated today. I shall return to the vacuity of the notion of 'authenticity' in Chapter 2.

[28] Cited by Aufderheide, *Documentary Film*, 112.
[29] Gabara, *From Ethnography to Essay*, 363.
[30] De Groof, *Rouch's Reflexive Turn*, 112-16.
[31] Other non-hegemonic emerging cinemas worldwide, such as women's filmmaking, queer cinema, or Latin American or Asian film movements, similarly questioned and challenged these notions.

misrepresentations, African filmmakers were highly aware of these representational constructions and the proximity of – and fluidity between – documentary and fiction, undoubtedly making them all more wary of claims to documentary objectivity and truth. Sada Niang goes as far as to suggest that, as a result, many early African filmmakers had a 'distinct aversion' to the documentary form, which they considered 'a tainted tool, an antecedent to and accomplice of the creation' of negative representations of African peoples and their realities.[32] Indeed, early African filmmakers by and large tended to favour works of fiction. Yet, their fiction works were clearly infused with realism and marked by social realist filmmaking practices. These 'documentarized fictions', to cite Rachel Gabara, indeed generally used non-professional actors, improvisation, natural settings, and 'real-life' scenarios. Like the post-war Italian Neorealist works that were clearly an inspiration,[33] pioneering African fiction works, such as Paulin Soumarou Vieyra, Mamadou Sarr and the Groupe africain du cinéma's *Afrique sur Seine* (France/Senegal, 1955), Ousmane Sembène's *Borom Sarret*, *La Noire de...* and *Mandabi* (Senegal, 1962, 1966 & 1968), or Oumarou Ganda's *Cabascabo* (Niger, 1968), were thus deeply rooted in the lives and spaces of the people they sought to portray and were, in Niang's words, 'branded with [the] semiotic features of documentary'.[34] Portraying African realities from an African point of view, these filmmakers both responded to and challenged existing demeaning representations of Africa. They also questioned, raised awareness and contributed to the building of their newly independent nations, re-imagining African societies and redefining identities. In the spirit of the liberation theorists such as Frantz Fanon, Amilcar Cabral, or Kwame Nkrumah, who all saw culture as a powerful weapon in the liberation process and effort to, as Ngũgĩ wa Thiong'o describes, decolonize minds, the pioneering filmmakers were indeed convinced that film could play a key socio-political role.[35] In this, their work also resonated with other international film movements of the time, such as Latin American 'Third Cinema',[36] Brazilian 'Cinema Novo' and Glauber Rocha's famous

---

[32] Niang, 'Fiction and Documentary African Films: Narrative and Stylistic Affinities', 228.
[33] See Gabara's enlightening examination of the impact of Neorealism on early African filmmaking, '"A Poetics of Refusals": Neorealism from Italy to Africa', 204.
[34] Niang, 'Fiction and Documentary African Films', 229.
[35] See Ngũgĩ wa Thiong'o's landmark 1986 work, *Decolonising the Mind: the Politics of Language in African Literature*.
[36] Developed in Latin America in the Sixties, 'Third Cinema' was inspired by the 1959 Cuban revolution, Brazil's Cinema Novo and certain aspects of Italy's Neorealist cinema, notably the latter's use of non-professional actors, real locations, lack of Hollywood-style polish, and portrayals of the quotidian realities of ordinary characters. 'Third Cinema', whose goals were defined in two manifestos – Octavio Getino's and Fernando Solanas' *Towards a Third Cinema* (1969), and Julio Garcia Espinosa's *For an Imperfect Cinema* (1970) – rejected the codes and conventions of both dominant mainstream 'First Cinema', epitomized by Hollywood studio productions, and the politically impotency of predominantly

'aesthetics of hunger', and his slogan 'a camera in the hand, and an idea in the head'. It resonated too with the broader political agendas of internationalist, anti-imperialist solidarity movements, such as the 1955 African-Asian Bandung Conference, the 1966 Havana Tricontinental Conference, or the Pan-African movement.

Favouring realist fiction in his own works, it is interesting that Ousmane Sembène, commonly referred to as the 'Father of African Cinema', repeatedly attacked the influential works of Jean Rouch. Despite the widespread veneration in French and certain Francophone African circles for Rouch and his Africa-based films, which remain a reference for many today,[37] and for his role as a mentor – Rouch having worked with certain early African technicians and filmmakers, notably Oumarou Ganda and Safi Faye – Sembène remained fiercely critical. When publicly asked by Rouch why he did not like Rouch's 'purely ethnographic films, those in which traditional life is shown, for example', Sembène famously answered: 'Because they show, they enact a reality but without showing its evolution. What I object to ... is that they look at us like insects.'[38] Perhaps more interesting and revealing, however, is the exchange earlier in the conversation, when Rouch asserted:

> I have what is both an advantage and a disadvantage: I bring an outsider's eye. The very notion of ethnology is based on the following idea: before a culture that is foreign to him, a person sees certain things that people within that very same culture don't see'.

Sembène answered:

European, *auteur* 'Second Cinema'. Essentially a counter-cinema in both thematic and aesthetic terms, the South American purveyors of 'Third Cinema' defended the notion of progressive, socially and politically motivated film, calling for the medium to be used as both a tool of liberation from all forms of oppression and imperialism, whether colonial, neocolonial, cultural or political, and a tool for change. An alternative cinema for liberation, 'Third Cinema' thus embraced the notion that formerly subjugated subjects could redefine their realities and identities and reappraise their historic and collective memories in film. This conception clearly echoes with that set out in the Pan-African Federation of Filmmakers' (FEPACI) 1975 Algiers Charter, to which I shall return later.

[37] In France, the Musée de l'Homme's annual Festival International continues, for example, to honour the legacy of its founder Jean Rouch. I personally cannot count the number of times in France that people answer my telling them that I teach African cinema with a heartfelt 'Ah, Rouch!', manifestly the first 'African' filmmaker that comes to their minds...

[38] Extracts of a confrontation organized in 1965 by Albert Cervoni. First published in *France Nouvelle*, 1033, August 1965. 'Tu nous regardes comme des insectes', Derives TV website, www.derives.tv/Tu-nous-regardes-comme-des, accessed 27 July 2017. [Rouch: 'mes films purement ethnographiques, ceux dans lesquels on montre, par exemple, la vie traditionnelle'; Sembène: 'Parce qu'on y montre, on y campe une réalité mais sans en voir l'évolution. Ce que je leur reproche ... c'est de nous regarder comme des insectes.']

> You say you see. But in the domain of cinema, it isn't enough to see; you need to analyse. What interests me is what is before and after what we see. I'm sorry but what I don't like in ethnology is that it isn't enough to say that a man we see is walking, we need to know where he's coming from, where he's going.[39]

Sembène's words thus sharply capture a fundamental difference of intention; for him and for a number of early African filmmakers, cinema, be it fiction or non-fiction, was not simply an observational tool, but a tool of analysis and understanding.

Early African Documentary Practices

A few African filmmakers did begin making documentaries in the 1960s and 1970s, notwithstanding. Again, I do not aim here to provide an exhaustive panorama of those filmmakers, nor to focus in depth on their work. I would like simply to mention the few key figures who precede Jean-Marie Teno to better grasp the filmmaking context in which his works emerged in the mid-1980s to early 1990s.[40]

Among the earliest documentary filmmakers in West and Central Africa were Thérèse Sita Bella (1933-2006), Cameroon's first female journalist, whose one 1963 short documentary about the Cameroonian national dance troupe's tour of France, *Tam-Tam à Paris*, was also the first film by an African woman; and Benin-born, Senegalese-by-adoption filmmaker, Paulin Soumarou Vieyra (1925-87), who was also one of the first African film historians and critics.[41] Of Vieyra's filmography of some twenty or so works, only a few shorts, including *Afrique sur Seine*, and one feature-length film, *En résidence surveillée* (1981), were classified as fictions or docu-fictions. The first African student to train at

---

[39] Ibid. ['Je dispose d'un avantage et d'un inconvénient à la fois, j'apporte l'œil de l'étranger. La notion même d'ethnologie est basée sur l'idée suivante : quelqu'un mis devant une culture qui lui est étrangère voit certaines choses que les gens qui sont à l'intérieur de cette même culture ne voient pas.' ; 'Tu dis voir. Mais dans le domaine du cinéma, il ne suffit pas de voir, il faut analyser. Ce qui m'intéresse, c'est ce qui est avant et après ce que l'on voit. Ce qui me déplaît dans l'ethnographie, excuse-moi, c'est qu'il ne suffit pas de dire qu'un homme que l'on voit marche, il faut savoir d'où il vient, où il va.'] For other critiques made of Rouch by various African filmmakers, including Paulin S. Vieyra, Med Hondo and Safi Faye, see Matthias De Groof, *Rouch's Reflexive Turn*, 117-18.

[40] For a more in-depth study of some of these early documentary filmmakers, see notably Henri-François Imbert's book *Samba Félix Ndiaye, cinéaste documentariste africain* and Rachel Gabara's article *War by Documentary*, or her chapter *From Ethnography to Essay*.

[41] Vieyra notably published *Le Cinéma africain des origines à 1973* (Paris/Dakar: Présence Africaine, 1975).

France's prestigious IDHEC national film school (the present-day FEMIS), Vieyra returned to Senegal in 1956 to work for the Ministry of Information, becoming head of the Actualités sénégalaises state news agency in 1960. One of the very few filmmakers of his generation to make documentaries, many of which were short documentary news reports, or *actualités*, shown in cinemas before the main bill in the days before the widespread introduction of television, his best-known works from the pioneering period are the short films *Une nation est née* (1961), produced by the Ministry of Information to celebrate Senegal's Independence; *Lamb* (1963), presenting Senegal's national sport, wrestling, its rules and ceremonial practices; and *Môl* (1966), a docu-fiction about a young fisherman who dreams of motorizing his fishing dugout, symbolizing the quest for progress – a concept that the film does not question – and portraying local fishing communities and their economic mutations. In his capacity as head of the Actualités sénégalaises, Vieyra also accompanied and filmed all of President Senghor's official visits until the late 1970s. While Vieyra's documentaries clearly reflect a desire to portray Senegalese society and culture from within, Vieyra largely adopted existing documentary conventions and codes, his works at times adopting markedly ethnographic tones, notably in their omniscient voice-of-God narrative commentaries. It was not truly until the 1980s, after leaving the Actualités sénégalaises, that Vieyra's final short documentary portraits of Ousmane Sembène during the shooting of *Ceddo* – which Vieyra produced, along with several of Sembène's earlier works – of artist Iba Ndiaye, and of poet and writer Birago Diop (respectively *l'Envers du Décor*, 1981; *Birago Diop, Conteur*, 1981; and *Iba Ndiaye, Portrait d'un peintre*, 1982), definitively moved away from this typically ethnographic approach, while otherwise remaining conventional in form.

After Paulin S. Vieyra came Senegal's Samba Félix Ndiaye (1945-2009), who, with a corpus of fifteen or so documentary works of varying lengths filmed from 1974 until his death, remains one of the most recognized, and certainly the most prolific of Africa's pioneering documentary filmmakers. Focusing on the everyday lives of ordinary Senegalese people, Ndiaye's early films, such as *Perantal* (1974), a film about the ritual massage and care given to babies in Senegal, and *Geti Tey* (1978) on local fishing, were both descriptions of Senegalese realities that adopted an un-situated, descriptive third-person narrative voice that nonetheless at times veers into more political appeals to not lose local cultures. Other works, such as the five films that made up the *Le Trésor des poubelles* (1989) series on the art and skill of transformation and recuperation, adopted an uncommented, purely observational register. By and large, Ndiaye's early works remained predominantly within existing documentary codes, albeit obliquely infusing these with an African perspective. In the words of Henri-François Imbert, who devoted a book to Ndiaye's work,

Ndiaye's early films can be characterized as 'at the same time ethnographic and political, militant and informative'.[42] In the 1990s, however, Samba Félix Ndiaye's work took a less conventional, more reflexive, non-linear, and at times even impressionistic introspective turn. From *N'Gor, l'esprit des lieux* (1995) onwards, his narrative voice notably became more personal as he for the first time adopted first-person address. Ndiaye continued this personal approach in his following works, including *Lettre à Senghor* (1998), which, as the title indicates, is a cinematic epistle, or filmic travel diary, addressing Ndiaye's relation to the complex and contradictory figure of Senegal's first President; *Rwanda pour mémoire* (2003), a work of memory that, after accompanying ten writers to Rwanda in 2000, breaks the silences surrounding the 1994 genocide; and finally Ndiaye's final film, *Questions à la terre natale* (2007), which retrospectively appears as a testimonial work in which Ndiaye invokes an array of African intellectuals to ask the question of where hope lies in a post-Independence Africa that failed to fulfil its promises. Throughout Ndiaye's career and its evolutions, then, observing and testifying to African realities from within remained at the core of his documentary approach, for, as he put it himself: 'It is from ourselves, from what we are, from what we know, that we can testify to the world'.[43]

Finally, Safi Faye, born in 1943 in Senegal, is one of Africa's first women filmmakers and, to my mind, the least conventional of the pioneering documentary filmmakers. A schoolteacher in Dakar when she met Jean Rouch during the Festival Mondial des Arts Nègres in 1966, Faye played a role in his 1969 film *Petit à petit*. Although also later critical of the work itself,[44] Faye nonetheless acknowledged that she learned *cinéma vérité* techniques from Rouch during the shoot, thereby encouraging her to use cinema as an ethnographic tool when she later went to study ethnology at the Sorbonne and EHESS social sciences graduate school in Paris. Yet, while documenting daily life in her family village in the Serer region of Senegal, Faye's own first feature documentary, *Kaddu Beykat* (*Letter from My Village*, 1975) departs from the typical ethnographic filmmaking mode on many counts. Introduced by Faye herself in a voice-over letter to the viewer in which, quite radically at the time, Faye adopts an autobiographical first-person voice, she situates herself very much within the community she

---

[42] Imbert, *Samba Félix Ndiaye*, 146 ['un cinéma documentaire à la fois ethnographique et politique, militant et informatif'].

[43] Speaking during a masterclass at the first edition of the Dakar Film Festival (FIFDAK) in 2008. Cited by Aboubacar Demba Cissokho, 'Samba Félix Ndiaye: "Dites simplement la vérité"', Le grenier de Kibili blog, November 2010, https://legrenierdekibili.wordpress.com/2015/11/06/samba-felix-ndiaye-dites-simplement-la-verite, accessed 22 January 2018 ['C'est à partir de nous, de ce que nous sommes, de ce que nous savons, que nous pouvons témoigner du monde'].

[44] See, for example, 'Jean Rouch jugé par six cinéastes d'Afrique noire', propos recueillis par Pierre Haffner, *CinémAction* 17 (1982), 63-64.

films. Although she remains off-screen, her presence is fully acknowledged both by her voice, and the direct-camera address of many of the film's protagonists. Eschewing the habitual ethnographic position of the omniscient and distant external male observer – for the ethnographic voice-of-God narrative was exclusively a male one – Faye creates a non-hierarchical relation with her filmed subjects. Likewise, Faye does not attempt here to capture so-called 'traditional' lifestyles; the rural world she films is a complex evolving one, totally connected with Senegal's urban centres as characters to-and-fro between the interpenetrating spaces, returning to the village from Dakar, or even France, and as the radio and the newspaper keep villagers in touch with the wider world. Manufactured utensils, Western clothes and even the cigarettes that the protagonist introduces on his return from the city are also seen to be present in the village, symbolizing these connections. More importantly still, Faye gives the villagers, habitually ignored by those in the urban seats of power, a space in which to express themselves, voicing their grievances and concerns. Going well beyond simply observing and capturing reality, the film was a deliberately militant gesture. The villagers' direct criticism of the State's on-going monoculture policy indeed led the film to being censored by the Senegalese government of the time. Striking too in *Kaddu Beykat* and Faye's work in general is her blurring of documentary and fiction. Her documentaries contain fictionalized scenes rooted in reality, just as her fiction feature *Mossane* (1995) is infused with documentary moments. Indeed, Faye has repeatedly claimed that such categories and divisions have no meaning for her. It is, to conclude, Faye's adopting, but above all adapting and disrupting of documentary conventions and her at the time radical subjective positioning that gives her work the closest affinity with what would later emerge as Jean-Marie Teno's practice.

Into the Eighties...

In 1985, Jean-Marie Teno made his first 13-minute documentary, *Hommage*, heralding a resolute and determined rupture with existing documentary codes. While having studied audiovisual communication at university in France, and while at the time working as a television editor for France 3, as a director Teno was self-taught. This perhaps in part accounts for the liberty he took from the start with prevailing documentary codes. Disrupting the predominantly observational style of many Direct Cinema and *cinéma vérité*-inspired or -infused works of the time, Teno audaciously mixed footage shot in his family's home region in Western Cameroon, still photos of his father's funeral celebrations, painting, and archive footage from the Cameroonian Independence period to weave together a part-fictionalized, part-true tale of two local characters, one of whom is returning to his home village, and one who has never left. Through their off-screen dialogue, the film addresses the situation of postcolonial Cameroon, the questions of exile, return, belonging and, as we finally realize at the end of the film, pays homage to Teno's late father. Interestingly, as Anjali Prabhu observes in her perspicacious close reading of the film, this both explosive, amusing and poignant short work already contains many seeds of issues explored in Teno's subsequent works and elements of his characteristic stylistic experimentation and playful – and at times mocking – rule-breaking and dissensus.[45] Like in Faye's earlier work, Teno blends fiction and documentary in this film and, like Faye, has expressed his disinterest in rigid genre categorization: 'What matters most is … to let oneself be transported by an emotion, a line of thought [rather] than trying to work out whether a scene is enacted or not.'[46] While undoubtedly in part a reflection of the filmmaker's disruptive refractoriness to codes and rules, this is perhaps also characteristic of the holistic, rather than compartmentalized nature of his, and other African filmmakers' endogenous belief systems and cultures. Indeed, numerous African cultures make no absolute binary distinctions between the worlds of the living/visible and the worlds of the dead/invisible, nor between the natural and supernatural. Frontiers between them are most often porous, with local religions and rituals centred on maintaining harmony, equilibrium and symbiosis between them all. Similarly, art – carving, sculpture, music, dance, storytelling – is often both aesthetic or ornamental and also an integral part of daily life and activities, playing a functional/socio-educational role. Equally, there are often no rigid boundaries between art forms either: song and dance are frequently woven into storytelling, for example, playing a fundamental role in the narrative development. In cinema, this is reflected in the imbrication of form and content – rather than a privileging of cinematic formalism – and in the fluidity and frequent generic blending that caused Teshome Gabriel to aptly dub African film a 'nomadic cinema', unfettered by genre boundaries.[47]

With *Hommage*, then, Teno confirmed the fluidity present in earlier African documentary works such as Faye's, and took formal experimentation to new,

---

[45] See Prabhu, 'Jean-Marie Teno. Creating an African Repertoire', in *Contemporary Cinema of Africa and the Disapora*, 187-215.

[46] Cited in Thackway, *Africa Shoots Back*, 98. Interestingly, like Faye's *Mossane*, Teno's feature fiction *Clando* (1996) is also marked by its clearly documentary moments. This also resonates with Samba Félix Ndiaye's stance, as Niang recalls in 'Fiction and Documentary African Films' (232). Ndiaye indeed insisted that not only were documentary and fiction in Africa 'aesthetically close', but 'also cross-fertilize[d] each other', the frontier between them being 'very fine'.

[47] See Teshome Gabriel, 'Thoughts on Nomadic Aesthetics and Black Independent Cinema: Traces of a Journey'. For an in-depth discussion of the influences of orature on film, see the chapter 'Screen Griots: Orature & Film' in Thackway, *Africa Shoots Back*, 49-92.

exciting levels. In so doing, he heralded a spate of new documentary works by a range of filmmakers in the 1990s that confirmed a more creative, hybrid, and at times militant approach to the documentary form. Some adopted what Bill Nichols has qualified as the 'reflexive mode' of documentary filmmaking: namely works about historical or social issues that draw attention to the filmmaking process, engaging actively with issues of realism and representation.[48] Others were more what Nichols terms 'performative', namely often autobiographical works in which the filmmaker draws on personal experience to help understand the processes at work in society.[49] Most, like Teno's works, blended more than one mode at different moments, and can be usefully described as 'essay films'. A reference to the essay literary genre popularized by the 16th-century French philosopher Montaigne, José Moure indeed defines the *film essai* as an open, heterogeneous ensemble situated in, and embracing, the indeterminate zone between non-fiction and fiction, using collage to advance its argument, discourse or reflection, and characterized by its freedom, experimentation, spontaneity and formal hybridity; a definition that echoes resoundingly with these works of the 1990s, which fall outside the existing cinematic nomenclature.[50] Other notable examples in Africa include David Achkar's *Allah Tantou* (1991), Raoul Peck's *Lumumba, The Death of a Prophet* (1990), Abderrahmane Sissako's *Rostov-Luanda* (1997) and *Life on Earth* (1998), Mahamat-Saleh Haroun's *Bye Bye Africa* (1999), Anne-Laure Folly's *Les Femmes aux yeux ouvertes* (1994) and *Les Oubliées* (1997), and the iconoclastic diasporic films of British-Ghanaian John Akomfrah working in the 1980s and 1990s with the London-based Black Audio Film Collective.

---

[48] Bill Nichols, *Introduction to Documentary*, 125.
[49] Ibid., 130.
[50] José Moure, 'Essai de définition de l'essai au cinéma', 25.

Photo 2 Jean-Marie Teno on location filming *Vacances au pays*, Yaoundé, 1998.

Critical Insights: Reading the Films of Jean-Marie Teno

> *The world is like a Mask dancing.*
> *If you want to see it well, you do not stand in one place.*
> Chinua Achebe[1]

Faced with the question of how most usefully to broach a corpus of a dozen films, made over a period of approximately thirty years, I have opted here to focus less on each work individually than on Jean-Marie Teno's work as a repertoire, to borrow Anjali Prabhu's term.[2] Perspicacious close readings and analyses of Teno's individual films already exist in an array of articles (see Bibliography), and in my own earlier work, *Africa Shoots Back*. Here then, I want, rather, to take the opportunity that this monographic format presents to step back and analyse this oeuvre in its entirety, as an ensemble. Taken individually, each of Teno's films is a journey unto itself; collectively, they weave a fascinating bigger journey into Cameroonian society, its history, realities, predicaments and complexities, into postcolonial North-South relations, and into Pan-African relations more generally. Here, I want to highlight what seem to me to be some of the most salient and enduring stylistic and thematic characteristics and threads that traverse both the individual films and collective corpus like leitmotifs, or arcs, to the point of becoming trademark signatures of Jean-Marie Teno's cinema.

Imagined as both a complement to, and in dialogue with our subsequent critical conversation, this part of the book is divided into sections and further sub-sections, each of which seeks to identify a defining trait of Teno's work as a possible lens through which to read his films. It seeks, too, to frame and contextualize these characteristics within the theoretical and socio-political debates that both inform them, and which the films articulate. Indeed, Teno's cinema, like all art forms, is not isolated from the socio-political sphere from which it stems, and which is an integral part of it. The aesthetic, *le sensible*, conveys human experiences; poetics and politics intertwine; the text exists

---

[1] Achebe. *Arrow of God*, 46.
[2] Prabhu, *Contemporary Cinema of Africa and the Diaspora*, 187.

within a context. This contextualizing approach will at times take us back to debates and issues that are assuredly not new, and which have at times been addressed in existing writings and works on African cinema, including my own. Yet, as this present book addresses a body of filmmaking that stretches back to the mid-1980s, it strikes me as important not to lose sight of the context in which they were made, and thus to recall the preoccupations and debates of their time. But more importantly still, many of these broader socio-political and theoretical debates remain at the fore, or have, along with certain figures such as Frantz Fanon, strikingly resurfaced in recent times in both African and the decolonial circles that I am personally informed by in France, re-actualizing issues that Teno explored some years back, and confirming the on-going pertinence of his films today.[3] Judging too by the more contemporary works of both Teno and an array of other African filmmakers, some of the earlier issues that traversed African cinema also manifestly remain on the cinematic agenda, albeit in actualized forms, making these issues impossible to ignore; indeed, contemporary African cinema is indubitably marked as much by continuities as it is by ruptures. Revisiting, as opposed, I hope, to rehashing these contexts and debates will at the same time help trace the not necessarily antinomic constants, shifts and evolutions within both African cinema generally, and within Teno's corpus of works. Without doubt, this re-visitation is a journey too, a trajectory more interested in what Mary Ellen Higgins calls 'tanglings' in her focus on cinematic 'winds', rather than 'waves', and which she aptly describes as 'not successive but concurrent', 'multifarious and polymorphous, like the formation of dunes transformed by the wind', '[swelling] from a place, but … not necessarily anchored in that place'[4], thereby salutarily moving away from the rather sterile binary oppositions often heard today in the field between 'old' and 'new'.

Indeed, contemporary scholarship and critique of African cinema has often been framed in oppositional terms since African video film produced principally, but not exclusively, in Nigeria, since the 1990s – what is now referred to as the ubiquitous and hugely successful Nollywood – caught the academics' eye in the 2000s. This originally cheaply, quickly made and efficiently distributed commercial form that is easily accessible to, and popular with, wide African audiences is often pitted against the supposedly elitist auteur or arthouse films made hitherto, but again not exclusively, in the Francophone African world. The latter, which certain scholars and critics have – usually disparagingly – dubbed

---

[3] Fanon's return to the fore was recently analysed by Alice Cherki in the *Mobiliser Fanon* edition of *Politique africaine* 143, 2016. See also the Frantz Fanon public conference on 2 February 2017, at ~~La Colonie~~, Paris, featuring Roberto Beneduce, Simona Taliani and Françoise Vergès.
[4] Higgins, 'The Winds of African Cinema', 81

'embassy films', 'FESPACO films', and 'festival films', are indeed, like all arthouse cinema around the world, not necessarily viewed primarily by local audiences, when it is actually accessible to them, many countries' cinemas having closed down, and African auteur films often remaining badly distributed.[5] These binary oppositional arguments are, to my mind, sterile and reductive, however, as if Africa alone were not permitted the multiplicity of cinematic forms that coexist, rather than compete, everywhere else in the world. They also elide questions of the transnationality of many films around the world in terms of funding, production and thus necessarily of distribution and audience. They eclipse, too, the long-standing existence of more classically popular comedies within the essentially Francophone African auteur model (for example, the films of Cameroonian Daniel Kamwa in the 1970s, of the Ivoirian Henri Duparc in the 1980s, or even the satirical comedies of 'serious' Ousmane Sembène), and ignore the popularity of 'serious cinema' among local audiences when given access to them (the films of Sembène in Senegal, of Cissé in Mali, or of Gaston Kaboré and Idrissa Ouedraogo in Burkina Faso, for example).[6]

Revisiting such contextualizing debates, then, and stepping back to consider Teno's works not individually, but as an ensemble, I hope also to point both to

---

[5] Like much independent cinema around the world, African auteur films find one of their main spaces of distribution and circulation in international film festivals. Lindiwe Dovey offers a fascinating analysis of the importance of such festivals for such films' visibility in *Curating Africa in the Age of Film Festivals*.

[6] Such simplistic oppositions also tend to overlook the ideology and social messages at play even in works primarily considered to be entertainment. Furthermore, as Lindiwe Dovey writes in her article 'African Film and Video: Pleasure, Politics, Performance', '[s]uch oppositions are being rendered obsolete by, first, the diversification that has occurred in terms of the mediums in which African filmmakers are working ... and, secondly, the diversification in terms of the kinds of films that festivals are screening (FESPACO, for example, now has categories devoted to films made on digital media)' (2). I would also add that, since Dovey's article, the divide has lessened even more, with the shift of numerous Nigerian filmmakers away from lower-quality Nollywood DVD production and local distribution to high-quality digital cinema produced for, and distributed in, the cinemas and multiplexes that have reopened in Nigeria in recent years, but also now overtly seeking wider international distribution. Some works are also now breaking into the international festival circuit – see, for example the Toronto International Film Festival's 2016 focus on Nigerian films, or director Kunle Afolayan's discussion of trying to break into the Cannes Film Festival at the Paris Nollywood Week festival in 2015 – marking a significant shift from Nollywood's classic mantra of being '100% by Africans for Africans'. While such 'New Nigerian cinema' – or 'New Nollywood' works, as they are now referred to, by filmmakers including Kemi Adetiba, Kunle Afolayan, Mahmood Ali-Balogun, Chineze Anyaene and Biyi Bandele – remain within a predominantly commercial cinema model, more typically arthouse Nigerian films are now emerging, for example, Kenneth Gyang's *Confusion Na Wa* (2013); Abba Makama's *Green White Green* (2016); Izu Ojukwu's '76 (2016); C.J. Obasi's *Ojuju* (2014) and *Hello, Rain* (2018), or Daniel Emeke Oriahi's *Oko Ashewo/Taxi Driver* (2015), with veteran filmmaker Tunde Kelani in a category of his own, at the junction of the two.

its continuities, constants, and to the thematic and stylistic shifts, evolutions, and diversification at play in this work over the years.

A Film Style: Traits and Evolutions

Stylistically first, Teno's films collectively and at times overlappingly have indeed evolved from what may loosely be described as his early non-linear, multi-layered 'assemblage films' – notably *Hommage*, *Bikutsi Water Blues* and *Afrique, je te plumerai* – which freely and innovatively mix registers and forms, ranging from typical documentary 'talking-head' interview sequences, to footage of daily life captured spontaneously as it unfolds (notably street and market shots, shots of city and rural landscapes), to photographs, newspaper titles, and illustrations that Teno's camera tracks over or zooms in on, to fictionalized scenes, and archive footage. Next came a series of more linear works whose narrative structures revolve around happenstance. Already present in the resolutely non-linear *Afrique, je te plumerai*, and recurrently a narrative device in many of Teno's more recent works too, unplanned, serendipitous

Photo 3 On location in Yaoundé with the crew shooting the short film *Mister Foot*, 1991.

encounters or incidents serve here as a trigger, setting the film in motion, or steering it off onto a previously unanticipated tack. In the more linear works, in particular, one idea or theme leads to the next, as if stringing beads to carefully craft a tale-like narrative, such as in *Chef!*, *Le Mariage d'Alex* and *Lieux saints*.

In terms of film content too, a recent shift can be detected from Teno's predominantly 'ideas-based' films that articulate strong socio-political and/or historical themes – whether the formally innovative *Afrique, je te plumerai,* or the more linear, expository *Le Malentendu colonial* – or the more autobiographical, yet linear 'road-trip' journey of *Vacances au pays*, to more character-based works, first evidenced in the still linear and ideas-based personalized reflection on the state of African cinema and artistic creation in *Lieux saints* (here foregrounding the video parlour owner Nanema Boubakar, aka Bouba, the drum-maker Jules César Bamouni, and Abbo, the whimsical, quasi-mystical 'public writer'). Indeed since, Teno's latest two films, *Une Feuille dans le vent* and *Chosen*, have developed this character-based approach to focus on, and give voice to individuals, or interestingly, so far always to women. While these character-based testimonial films still branch out from the personal, the individual, to explore wider collective socio-political or historical themes, they do so from the angle of the impact that these have on people; in short, their human cost.

After a long period of more conventional, linear narratives structures, Teno appears too, and notably since *Une Feuille dans le vent*, to have returned to greater formal innovation and mixing of registers. Typically a 'happenstance film', Teno's desire in the film to posthumously contextualize his protagonist's personal history within a still little-told chapter of Cameroon's colonial and postcolonial history, few images of which exist, forced him to find other ways to represent the unrepresented, notably by mixing media again (contemporary footage, archives and specially commissioned black-and-white ink illustrations). In *Chosen* too – a film again triggered by a chance encounter – Teno again embraces non-linear, non-chronological narrative in a desire to mirror the way in which the protagonist's complex story unfolded fragmentedly to him.

Structured rhizomatically as one idea leads the filmmaker to the next, and as thoughts, words, images or thematic threads that initially seem unrelated cross and intersect, Teno's films all blend different modes of documentary representation. In them, one may notably identify what Bill Nichols describes as the performative mode, which engages the director as author and participant, constructing subjective perspectives as an entry to understanding wider social processes, offering greater creative freedom; the reflexive mode, in which attention is drawn to the filmmaking process, form, and to the fact that film is a construction; and the participatory mode, in which the filmmaker interacts with his/her subjects, rather than unobtrusively observing them, often through interviews;[7] or what Toni de Bromhead classifies as episodic and hybrid documentary narrative structures.[8] According to de Bromhead, the episodic mode presents a situation, character, or state by juxtaposing a series of disparate scenes ordered around, or linked by one dominant theme or idea. Hybrid modes may, according to the author, combine both the 'linear (the journey) and episodic (unconnected adventures that occur along the way)' (121) as the narrative is 'built up around what happens to the film-maker during the period of shooting' (82). These descriptions strike me as describing well Teno's own centrality in all his works, his acknowledgement of his extra-diegetic presence (sometimes a subjective camera point of view, often his voice) and the fact that his films are often a form of physical or intellectual journey, as shall be discussed later. But most of all, these modes overlap and shift from one to another in Teno's works, making rigid classification impossible.

Teno's documentaries are not journalistically informative; they are critical, subjective, not least due to his own presence in all his works (see later). They are also, and above all, cinematic, both formally and stylistically. Literally, first, Teno's works have all been destined for theatrical-release, only some having also been released on television, and specifically the Franco-German cultural television channel ARTE, namely: *Afrique, je te plumerai, La Tête dans les nuages*, the fiction feature *Clando, Vacances au pays* and *Le Malentendu colonial*. Most are feature-length (sixty-minutes or more; sometimes seventy minutes, sometimes ninety), rather than conforming to the standard television slot lengths (either twenty-six or fifty-four minutes in France), giving Teno greater creative freedom. In this sense, Teno's work is indeed no doubt best described as what in France is called *documentaire de création* (creative documentary); that is, the predominantly publicly funded works loosely defined by the Centre national de la cinématographie (CNC) as a 'a documentary by an auteur that combines the subjectivity of a viewpoint and the experience of the real, and seeks a pertinent artistic accord between the form and content'.[9]

But perhaps most of all, Teno sees documentary as a form of storytelling that intricately weaves together layers of image and sound to captivate the

---

[7] See Nichols, *Introduction to Documentary* for his well-known description of six documentary 'modes' that may overlap in an individual film.

[8] In *Looking Two Ways*, Toni de Bromhead focuses more on the cinematic qualities of documentary, its use of creative devices, its expression not just of opinion or ideas, but also of emotion. She identifies four sub-genres of documentary to describe their narrative structures, defining narrative as 'the structure that gives order and meaning to the material in hand' and that makes the material interesting and involves the spectator (5).

[9] 'Scénariothèque documentaire', CNC website, www.cnc.fr/web/fr/scenariotheque-documentaires, accessed 11 July 2018 ['documentaire d'auteur, qui allie la subjectivité d'un regard à l'expérience du réel, et cherche un accord artistiquement pertinent entre un fond et une forme'].

audience. In it, montage plays an essential creative role, reinforcing the cinematic quality as it crafts together what initially appear to be disparate ideas and themes. Associations and patterns of ideas, images, words and sounds thus emerge, creating connections and motifs. Leitmotifs are indeed particularly central to Teno's work, their repetition little by little conferring structure, coherence and meaning to the often intricate, multi-layered ensembles. In *Lieux saints*, for example, the fifty-year-old Abbo's daily writing on walls finally emerges at the end of the film as a metaphor for the fifty-year-old African cinema's speaking out 'pour réécrire son histoire sur les murs de la ville ou sur les écrans plats de nos case et de nos villas pour continuer d'avancer, recommencer à espérer, et partager nos rêves' ('to re-write our history on the city walls or the flat screens of our huts and villas in order to continue to advance, to start to hope anew, and share our dreams'), just as Jules César's craftsmanship emerges as a leitmotif and a metaphor for the craft of the filmmaker. In *Une Feuille dans le vent*, to take another example among many, the leaf-shot leitmotifs that repeat at the start, during and at the end of the film take on their symbolic meaning when we finally understand them to be a metaphor for Ernestine, an uprooted leaf in the wind (the English title of the film). Similarly, the same archive footage of trees being felled that in itself links *Afrique, je te plumerai* and *Une Feuille dans le vent* – both films addressing the history of the crushing of the UPC (Union of the Peoples of Cameroon) party's struggle for true Independence – repeats in the latter. First seen at the opening of the film just after Ernestine's as yet unidentified voice-over evokes the impossibility for a leaf without a stalk to live, and then heard over the ink illustrations of Ernest Ouandié's execution to evoke the felling of this hero, the leaf/tree metaphor and leitmotif thus also connect father and daughter, and is picked up again in Teno's voice-over's repeated references to the forest.

Teno also accords a foremost place to sound design in all his works, crafting both the diegetic and extra-diegetic sounds' expressive rather than realistic qualities. From work to work, he creates distinct, at times autonomous, layers that, like his voice-over commentaries, are complementary, rather than subordinate to, dependant on, or purely illustrative of the images. Music, too, plays an expressive, rather than simply illustrative role. At the end of *Lieux saints*, for example, when the owner of the small, artisanal Ouagadougou video parlour, whose simple workings have been shown in the film, visits a town-centre electronics store dreaming of purchasing a brand-new, widescreen TV he manifestly cannot afford, the mismatched, over-inflated, histrionic symphony music seems to gently tease his delusions of grandeur. At the same time, this being the kind of music one might typically associate with Hollywood, it is perhaps too a nod to 'the dream-machine', bring us back to the film's reflection on cinema, as if to say what could be more legitimate for both this cinephile entrepreneur and filmmakers like Teno than to want to dream, bettering the lives of their people? Elsewhere, old hit songs familiar to both Cameroonian and wider African audiences not only immediately conjure bygone eras – for example, the Ghanaian highlife in *Une Feuille dans le vent* that Teno chooses to accompany the ink illustrations of Ernest Ouandié and Regina Kwedu's meeting in Accra in the late 1950s – their lyrics, which commonly carry morals and messages of their own, also add extra layers of meaning to the films too. Heard over shots of pathways and villagers walking or riding into the distance in *Hommage*, for example, the opening lines of André-Marie Tala's 1972 hit song *Je vais à Yaoundé*, whose chorus repeatedly asks, 'Où vas-tu, paysan?' ('Where are you going, farmer?'), not only resonates with the two characters' voice-over dispute over whether or not it is better to leave or stay in the village; those knowing the rest of this famous song (even if it is not heard in *Hommage*) will know and understand the allusion to its final moral: 'Cherche ton bonheur dans la vie quotidienne, chaque instant, chaque jour, là où Dieu t'a placé' ('Seek your happiness in daily life, every instant, every day, there where God set you down'). Or again, in *Une Feuille dans le vent*, to take a final example, the tender melody and final words of another highlife song that plays in an interlude in Ernestine Ouandié's account between her being taken away from her abusive aunt's house and returning to live with her mother – 'She run for home to say hello to Mum, and her Mum go say "My darling, darling come home to me"' – lure us into mistakenly thinking, as the young Ernestine did herself at the time, that she is now safe, rendering her immediately following disclosure of her mother's displeasure and continuing ill-treatment of Ernestine both more brutal and more tragic.

Committed Cinema: A Poetics of Resistance

> *Créer c'est résister ; résister c'est créer*
> Stéphane Hessel[1]
>
> *For a responsible, free and committed cinema*
> FEPACI[2]

The above epigraph of the 1975 Pan-African Federation of Filmmakers' (FEPACI) Algiers Charter serves as a highly fitting epigraph to the works of Jean-Marie Teno too. Perhaps the first most striking and enduring characteristic of Teno's work is indeed its commitment to exploring socio-political issues. In this, it has consistently remained in resonance with the aims of the pioneering African filmmakers' Charter, which went on to stipulate that 'the cinema has a vital part to play because it is a means of education, information, and consciousness raising, as well as a stimulus to creativity'. While the first-generation African cinema has regularly been described, or even decried, as having been politically committed at times to the point of didacticism, the Charter, which also described African filmmakers as 'creative artisans at the service of their people', whose 'freedom of expression' was 'a prerequisite', is a salutary reminder that the notions of freedom and creativity were always at the fore in the works by these pioneering filmmakers. Indeed, the aesthetic experimentations of the 1960s and 1970s works of filmmakers such as Ousmane Sembène, Souleymane Cissé, Oumarou Ganda, Med Hondo, Sarah Maldoror, Safi Faye, Djibril Diop Mambéty, Jean-Pierre Dikongue-Pipa, Ababacar Samb Makharam or Desiré Ecaré, to cite but a few, remain incredibly innovative and ground-breaking even today, as highlighted, for example, in recent returns among African cinema scholars to the formal characteristics of some of their works,[3] and as is acknowledged by several recent international initiatives to restore and revalorize these early works.[4]

---

[1] Hessel, *Indignez-vous !*, 13 ['To create is to resist; to resist is to create'].
[2] 'The Algiers Charter on African Cinema, 1975', in Bakari & Cham, *African Experiences of Cinema*, 25.
[3] See, for example, Anjali Prabhu's reading of Sembène's *La Noire de…* in *Contemporary Cinema of Africa and the Diaspora* (22-26), or Manthia Diawara's reading of Sembène's *Mandabi* in *African Film* (33-44).
[4] See Martin Scorsese's Film Foundation World Cinema Project's restoration of Sembène's *La Noire de…* and *Borom Sarret*, and Djibril Diop Mambéty's *Touki Bouki*; the restoration to date by the African Film Heritage Project (a partnership between FEPACI, Scorsese's Film Foundation, UNESCO and the Cineteca di Bologna to restore fifty African

Likewise, Teno's filmmaking is unquestionably committed in its themes, ever evolving, and consistently cinematographically experimental. As Anjali Prabhu comments, his engagement and filmic creation cannot be separated, and committed and/or political content is not antithetical to aesthetics.[5] Kenneth W. Harrow, too, invites us to move away from looking at African cinema 'as either failed political thought or failed art', drawing on the works of Jacques Rancière to revisit the typically Western 'art/politics binary' that originally stemmed from the Renaissance, notions of Fine Art, 'high culture and beauty', and later 'art for art's sake'.[6] Here, then, commitment and creativity are the inextricable faces of the same coin, and Teno strives in all his films to find the forms that best convey his ideas and reflections.

Arising from the already much-discussed and charged colonial and postcolonial socio-political contexts in which African cinema was born, at least in West and Central Africa, the committed approach to cinema formulated by the first-generation FEPACI filmmakers has left a lasting – although necessarily shifting – legacy on perceptions of the medium on the continent. Their vision of cinema as a way of telling one's own stories and of speaking out against all forms of domination and oppression remains a preoccupation according to declarations of an array of contemporary filmmakers of different ages and provenances –unsurprisingly so, given the on-going bias of mainstream Western representations of Africa and the asymmetrical access to image-making and distribution – even if this often manifests itself in a variety of actualized forms. It remains the case irrespective of whether directors' predominant filmmaking styles leans towards serious, auteur, arthouse, entertainment, mainstream or commercial modes, and despite cinematic diversifications and evolutions – and despite the corollary need to keep adjusting one's analytical lens too.[7]

---

classics) of Med Hondo's *Soleil O*, Jean-Pierre Dikongue-Pipa's *Muna Moto*, Mohammed Lakhdar-Hamina's *Chronique des années de braise* and Timité Bassori's *La Femme au couteau*; the Berlin Arsenal's restoration of Sarah Maldoror's *Monangambé* and Assia Djebar's *La Zerda ou les chants de l'oubli*; and the University of Glasgow's Africa's Lost Classics project (Dr Lizelle Bisschoff, Dr Stefanie Van de Peer, Professor David Murphy), which has restored Safi Faye's *Mossane*, Ingrid Sinclair's *Flame* and Selma Baccar's *75 Fatma*.

[5] Prabhu, *Contemporary Cinema of Africa and the Diaspora*, 197.

[6] Harrow, *Trash: African Cinema from Below*, 31.

[7] In his earlier 2007 work *Postcolonial African Cinema*, for example, Kenneth Harrow rousingly called for 'a revolution in African film criticism. A revolution against the old tired formulas' in the hope of 'shaking to pieces' the 'truisms' and 'sacred cows' of much critical thought on African cinema (xi-xv). While I thoroughly agree with Harrow's call to constantly reappraise our thinking, and while I particularly agree with his demolition of some of the earlier underlying assumptions of much critique – and notably the problematic notion of authenticity (see 115-16) – I remain wary of the way in which some scholars and critics have leapt, rather, on Harrow's call for a 'space clearing' to simplistically and

In this respect, Prabhu rightly argues that contemporary African and diaspora cinema's 'sustained commitment to rethinking meanings, destinies and futures for African peoples', its 'idea of newness, of revolution, and imaginative change', continue to strongly link it to the *methods*, if not to the *moment*, of Third Cinema in its dedication 'to rescuing the many possibilities from the missed opportunities and the tragic destruction of human potential and celebrating and promoting the [often obscured] human successes'. This remains a relevant agenda, then, rather than a worn-out old paradigm.[8]

Moreover, I have already argued elsewhere and continue to argue here that this enduring conception of a socially responsible filmmaking is inseparable from, and thus needs to be situated within, these filmmakers' various specific cultural contexts, and notably their often similar perceptions of the role of the artist and of the arts as an integral part of daily life, unseparated from the functional.[9] The influences of local oral literature and theatre on African film have already been much documented too, as has the fact that many early and contemporary filmmakers alike drew – and continue to draw – inspiration from, and directly liken their role to, that of the storyteller griot, guardian and transmitter of collective memory, history, culture and mores.[10] 'Father' of African cinema and key purveyor of its socially and politically committed vein, the late Ousmane Sembène famously argued, for instance, that 'the artist must in many ways be the mouth and ears of his people. In the modern sense, this corresponds to the role of the griot in traditional African culture'.[11] Interestingly, Teno, who over the years has also discussed the stylistic inspirations that he has drawn from the narrative structures of the tales listened to in his childhood,[12] directly returns to address this heritage in his 2009 film *Lieux saints*. Following the daily workings of a local Ouagadougou video parlour, drawing an analogy between the craftmanship of drum-making and cinema in order to question the role, place and pertinence of African cinema today, the film ends with quotations of Sembène and Djibril Diop Mambéty likening their roles as filmmakers to that of the griot: the 'memory and conscience of the people'

---

ever-binarily write off the 'old' and sing the praises of the 'new' by simple virtue of its (not actually always very new) newness.
[8] Prabhu, *Contemporary Cinema of Africa and the Diaspora*, 203.
[9] See, for example, my 'Screen Griots: Orature and Film' chapter in Thackway, *Africa Shoots Back*, 49-92
[10] Ibid. See, also, Manthia Diawara's 'Oral Literature and African Film'.
[11] Sembène, 'Filmmakers and African Culture', 80.
[12] See our 1997 interview in Thackway, *Africa Shoots Back*, 208; and Part II of this volume, *In Conversation*.

Photo 4 On location filming the Sanaga River ferry sequence, *Vacances au pays*, 1999.

(Sembène)[13] and 'messenger of his time' (Mambéty).[14] Excavating and revisiting this original linking at a time when the continent's filmmakers are struggling to connect with their audiences, reasserting this earlier conception as a possible way forward, Teno appears, then, to echo the words of his character Sobgui in the fiction feature *Clando*: 'If you reach the point where you don't know where to go anymore, retrace your steps and start again. Come back to the source and grow.'

In Teno's cinema, this drawing inspiration from orature is not backward-looking or nostalgic, nor has it anything to do with essentializing notions of a purported 'authenticity' – a highly problematic concept in itself when referring to cultures[15] – any more than it was for earlier cineastes; on the contrary, for Mambéty, the griot was above all 'a visionary and a creator

---

[13] Sembène, cited by Françoise Pfaff, 'The Uniqueness of Ousmane Sembene's Cinema', 15 ['la mémoire vivante et la conscience de son peuple'].
[14] In June Givanni, 'African Conversations: An Interview with Djibril Diop Mambety', 30-31.
[15] What, say, to take my own example, is 'authentic' British culture? How can it be determined and defined? To what 'original', 'pure form' might it refer? Celtic? Roman? Anglo-Saxon? Viking? Norman? Which culture has been left untouched by contact with

of the future'.[16] It is, rather, as Olivier Barlet states, a way of avoiding 'imitation and mimesis', of asserting 'a new aesthetic to break with the dominance of the spectacular and consumerism', a strategy 'of filmmakers who resist standardization and uniformity'.[17] It is, then, more a question of infusing cinema with local storytelling codes and purposes; a vernacularization that seeks to make works more relevant to, and connected with, their local context; it is a third way that neither succumbs to the depoliticised and depoliticising professionalizing aestheticism advocated in the past decade by certain Western festivals and funders, nor to the neo-liberal consumerist ideology that infuses Hollywood-leaning cinemas.

Given the damaging hegemonic representations of the African continent and its people that have long been constructed and conveyed in film and the media, the question of and commitment to representational issues – representation understood as playing not just a reflexive, but rather a *constitutive* role, as Stuart Hall argued[18] – has long been an urgent one for Africa's filmmakers, including Teno. Back in 1997, he reasoned:

> 'It is important for individuals to be able to identify with people who are like them, to be able to see their reality on the screen, so that they feel they exist, especially for people who have been colonized, because colonization amounts to reducing the other to a non-being'.[19]

While again not a new debate, the desire to portray one's own realities, in all their multiplicity and complexity, to speak in one's own name and to tell one's own stories, remains a burning one in both African, diasporic and Afropean circles. Numerous filmmakers indeed continue to refer to how their representations of their experiences and environments, how the images that they convey still matter to them. This is hardly surprising given the enduring colonial stereotypes conveyed in the majority of contemporary Western representations, themselves a reflection of the still resolutely un-decolonized attitudes towards colonization in many European countries. In Britain, for example, in a YouGov survey carried out in 2014, 59 per cent of respondents declared that the British Empire 'is something to be proud of', and in a 2016 survey, 43 per cent that it was 'a good thing'.[20] In France, a law was adopted on 23 February 2005 imposing the teaching in schools of the 'positive role of French overseas pres-

---

other cultures over the history of humankind and human migration? What, if anything, in this instance does 'authentic' actually mean?
[16] Givanni, 'African Conversations', 30-31.
[17] Barlet, *Contemporary African Cinema*, 287.
[18] Hall, 'New Ethnicities', *Black Film, British Cinema*, 27.
[19] Thackway, *Africa Shoots Back*, 205.
[20] Dahlgreen, 'The British Empire is "something to be proud of"', YouGov, 'Survey Results'.

ence';[21] conversely, protest was sparked when the then presidential candidate Emmanuel Macron called colonization 'a crime against humanity' on Algerian television on 15 February 2017.[22] As for mainstream Western representations, it would be quicker to cite those that *do not* purvey colonial imagery. Just to take two recent examples completely at random, however, one may cite Sean Penn's reworking of the White Saviour-cum-humanitarian aid worker trope in *The Last Face* (USA, 2016), or Taylor Swift's *Out of Africa*-inspired colonial nostalgia *Wildest Dreams* pop video staging an Africa of wild animals, beautiful sunsets and savanna, but glaringly devoid of Africans.

The on-going commitment to offering alternative representations no doubt also remains strong given that, with the exception of the Nigerian 'Nollywood' film industry – the world's second biggest movie producer after Bollywood, with a production of some 1000 to 2000 movies a year – film production remains sporadic in many African countries.[23] With both local and international distributions circuits relatively closed to the alternative visions that African cinema has to offer, not to mention the limited number of cinemas operational today in many African countries – even if, after the dearth of the 1990s to early 2000s, new cinemas and multiplexes are gradually opening, and some old cinemas being reopened after renovation[24] – the possibilities of countering

---

[21] After protest initiated by French historians (see the signature by 1038 historians of a petition against an official history of colonization following the publication of the tribune' Colonisation: non à l'enseignement d'une histoire officielle' published by seven leading historians in *Le Monde* newspaper on 25 April 2005, www.lemonde.fr/societe/article/2005/03/24/colonisation-non-a-l-enseignement-d-une-histoire-officielle_630960_3224.html, accessed 6 July 2018. Article 4 paragraph 2 of the law was finally repealed by the government a year later, removing the 'positive role' reference. According to a CSA-Le *Figaro* opinion poll carried out on 30 November 2005 during the controversy, 64% of French people declared themselves to be 'favourable to the law stating that school programmes recognize the positive role of French colonization' (see www.nouvelobs.com/politique/20051202.OBS7372/les-francais-approuvent-le-role-positif.html, accessed 6 July 2018).

[22] Macron's declaration provoked indignation on the right and extreme right. Right-wing presidential candidate François Fillon notably attacked 'this detestation' of French history, 'unworthy of a Presidential candidate'. See Roger, 'Colonisation : les propos inédits de Macron font polémique'.

[23] While Nigeria's Nollywood is the biggest and best-known of Africa's video film industries, others do exist, most notably Ghana's 'Ghallywood', or 'Gollywood'. See Garritano, *African Video Movies and Global Desires: A Ghanaian History*.

[24] Since 2004, for example, the Silverbird Group has, to date, opened six multiplexes in Nigeria, two in Ghana and one in Liberia (Nigeria having the continent's second largest pool of cinemas and multiplexes (29), after South Africa (84). 2017 figures). Since 2016, Canal Olympia (Canal+ Vivendi) has, to date, opened cinemas in Niamey, Dakar, Ouagadougou, Conakry, Lomé, Cotonou, Douala and Yaoundé, and is due shortly to open cinemas in Mali, DRC and Congo. Before the Canal Olympia openings, Cameroon had no longer had any functioning cinema since 2009. Since 2015, Majestic Cinemas has opened three cinemas in Abidjan. In 2011, the Normandie Cinema, closed since the mid-1980s,

the continuingly distorted dominant representations remain limited, and undoubtedly all the more so today in an increasingly homogeneous late-capitalist global world that tends to steamroller non-mainstream cinematic expressions. In this context, then, today as in the past, African filmmakers like Teno are still confronted with what Kobena Mercer aptly described as a burden to represent: 'represent', as in 'depict', of course, but also 'to speak on behalf of', or to give voice to the many who are not given a platform to speak. [25] It is, judging by the themes and form of his films, a 'burden' that Teno remains committed to carrying.

Over the decades, then, Teno's films have addressed an intricate array of often interrelated social and political themes, with one film often segueing on from where the previous one left off, or certain themes and issues resurfacing in later works from new angles and perspectives. While specific to Cameroon's contemporary situation, these themes often have wider resonance not only for Africa, but for the world. As Teno has explored, questioned and challenged these complex situations over the years, he has often been remarkably in tune with the issues of his times. Certain themes run through these works with a striking unifying consistency. Of those most frequently explored, history, memory, colonialism, its on-going legacies, violence, freedom, justice, political repression, and trauma are at the heart notably, but not exclusively, of *Hommage, Afrique, je te plumerai, Clando, Le Malentendu colonial, Une Feuille dans le vent*, and *Chosen*, all of which shall be discussed further in this chapter. Power, its abuse, gender dynamics and power relations, authoritarianism, democracy, local economies, development (or lack thereof), and modernity are also explored in *Bikutsi Water Blues, La Tête dans les nuages, Chef !, Vacances au pays, Le Mariage d'Alex*, and *Chosen*.

In *Bikutsi Water Blues*, for example, Teno addresses the health and socio-economic problems caused by the Cameroonian state's failure to provide the basic amenity of clean water. Fictionalized sequences in which a child tells his family about the clean water campaign in his school – the classroom scenes then unfolding in flashback – are juxtaposed with real day-to-day footage relating to sanitation that speaks for itself (shots of rubbish-strewn gutters, women washing laundry in rivers, etc.). To these are added fictionalized sequences of the sanitation engineer, Kana, on the radio introducing interviews that Teno in reality filmed, showing ordinary Cameroonians talking about their lack of access to water. The musician who accompanies Kana's campaign is none

---

re-opened in Chad after a state-funded renovation, and in 2013, the renovated Magic Babemba Cinema reopened in Bamako. Most of these cinemas bill mainstream international movies, and ticket prices target middle- to upper-class audiences.

[25] Mercer, 'Recording Narratives of Race and Nation', 9.

other than the real-life guitarist Zanzibar of Cameroon's famous Têtes Brûlées band, whose songs are also woven into the film, playing on the fictional radio show. Finally, footage of real village primary health awareness campaigns, and footage of a women's group who pool their resources in a *tontine* (community fund) to build a well – organizing themselves rather than waiting for the incompetent state to remedy the problem – weave together, the multiple threads and registers all exploring this same theme.

In the later film *Chef !*, to take another example – after happening across a scene of popular justice after an adolescent is caught stealing chickens in Teno's hometown of Bandjoun the day after he films festivities organized for the inauguration of a monument to the town's former *Fô 'A-Djo* ('king', 'chief') Kanga Joseph III, and after further discovering the 'Husband's Domestic Rules' on the back of a local calendar (Article 1 reads: 'The husband is always right'; Article 2: 'The husband is always the head of the family', and so forth) – Teno sets out to meet an array of different characters: newly-weds; a women's rights campaigner; political opposition activists; writer Mongo Beti; newspaper editor Pius Njawe, thrown in prison for ten months after writing an article questioning President Biya's health. Through their activities, actions and voices, Teno seeks to examine and understand the authoritarian power relations prevalent in Cameroon, from the home, to the local chieftaincies, to institutions inherited from the colonial era, all the way up to the head of state.

Or finally, in *Le Mariage d'Alex*, Teno unveils both the gender dynamics and fraught, ruthless domestic power relations at play in a polygamous family after his neighbour, Alex, convinces the unwilling Teno to film his second marriage. While filming the joyful celebrations in Josephine, the beaming new junior bride's family home, Teno reveals the barely disguised tensions as he films the tense, bowed, set face of Elise, Alex's senior wife of eighteen years, and mother of their six children. The festive moment that is meant to be 'chargé de promesses heureuse' ('full of joyful promise'), Teno ironically tells us, gradually descends into a vicious tragi-comedy in the second half of the film when Josephine arrives in Alex's home, where the maliciously vengeful Elise reigns, her stature and statute restored as she makes painfully clear who is in charge to the now-forlorn bride. Capturing the body language, facial expressions, the silences, the sidelong glances, the muttered verbal sparring, and the territorial vying, Teno adroitly reveals and denounces the psychological violence and tensions that polygamy can provoke.

Colonial cultural genocide, assimilation, acculturation, cultural syncretism, and their on-going legacies are key themes in *Afrique, je te plumerai* and *Vacances au pays* (as discussed later), and cultural practices and craftsmanship in *Lieux saints*. In the latter, for example, during the 2007 FESPACO (Pan-African Film and Television Festival of Ouagadougou) in Ouagadougou, a friend invites

Photos 5a-b *Le Mariage d'Alex*. The body language betrays the tensions on the day Alex marries his junior wife: senior wife Elise is counselled by her mother-in-law during the wedding celebration at her new junior wife's home; Alex and his co-wives back in the marital home, where Elise reasserts her primacy.

Teno to discover a modest neighbourhood in the city centre: St Léon. Here, filming the workings of Bouba's 'ciné-club', or local video parlour where the film-loving entrepreneur screens mainly bootlegged DVDs of predominantly Hollywood action movies – although he does screen local filmmaker Idrissa Ouedraogo's hit *Yaaba*, still popular twenty or so years after its release – before packing away the benches and equipment to turn the premises into a local mosque at prayer time, Teno's montage underlines the incongruous passage from some of the DVDs' less than 'sacred' content. Twenty-five years after coming to the FESPACO for the first time and before the rumours of 'the death of African cinema', Teno seeks what remains of the pioneering African filmmakers' dream of, and debates on, cinema as both means of mass education and entertainment; discussions that the filmmaker tells us he first followed in Ouagadougou.

Via Bouba's ciné-club, which is totally integrated into the daily life of the neighbourhood as the many shots of the inhabitants going about their daily lives suggest, Teno raises questions about the state of African cinema today, the place and tastes of African audiences, the question of developing locally adapted film economies and notably distribution systems, the role of the filmmaker – 'Qui parle, pour dire quoi, à qui?' ('Who speaks, to say what, to whom?'). Also filming the artisanal activities, informal political discussions with friends over tea, and quasi-philosophical reflections of the young drum-maker Jules César (who also walks the St Léon streets playing his djembe to announce Bouba's screenings), and the abstruse philosophical rambling of the self-appointed public writer Abbo, who daily chalks up his impregnably mystical phrases on a metal gate, Teno draws an analogy with both. Jules César, for example, is filmed in one particularly long sequence as he finishes tightening the skin on a djembe drum, the mainly close-up shots emphasizing both the physicality of the labour and precision of his craftsmanship, an effort accentuated by the nerve-jangling wrenching sound of the rope pulling taut against the wooden rim of the drum, and the shots of Jules César wiping the sweat from his brow. His craftsmanship and his description of his pleasure in working well to satisfy his clients become an analogy for Teno to question filmmakers' relationship to their audiences, their craft and their role.

Finally, exile, belonging, filiation and transmission are central themes in *Hommage*, *Clando*, *Vacances au pays*, *Une Feuille dans le vent* and *Chosen*, as shall be seen later in the last section of this chapter, *Spanning Borders*, and the themes of resistance and survival traverse all of Teno's works in different forms, as shall also be developed later.

Photos 6a-b *Lieux saints*: Abbo the public scribe writes his daily cryptic missives on a neighbourhood gate; a typical screening inside Bouba's ciné-club.

> *Chaque génération doit dans une relative opacité découvrir sa mission, la remplir ou la trahir.*
>
> Frantz Fanon[26]

Whatever their themes, all of these works display Teno's own deep commitment to, and concern for, his country and compatriots and to the issues that affect their daily lives and well-being. Fiercely critical of the abuses, failings and incompetence of Cameroon's postcolonial leaders and elites, Teno in different guises repeatedly contextualizes the complex colonial history of his country, from it having being a German colony, to being put under British and French mandates after the First World War, to the 1955-71 'Hidden War' of independence that pitted the UPC (Union of the Peoples of Cameroon) rebels against the French colonial authorities,[27] to the first independent presidency of Ahmadou Ahidjo in 1960, to the current rule, since 1982, of President Paul Biya, who, then aged 85, officially won his seventh presidential mandate in the October 2018 elections.

Teno systematically relates this history to the contemporary political situation in which his films are both set and embedded, a context from which they cannot be separated. His is an analytical, questioning cinema, then; it does not just depict, but also seeks to understand the complex state, predicament and conditions of postcolonial Cameroon and often more broadly of Africa. Here – as Teno's films so often reveal – the 'post' of postcolonial is not an ending, the closing of the colonial chapter, nor 'the movement of linear transcendence of two mutually exclusive states', to quote Stuart Hall, but rather 'a shift or transition conceptualised as the reconfiguration of the field'.[28] Indeed, as Teno's filmic analyses repeatedly demonstrate, we are in the realm of the on-going 'coloniality of power' that has survived the moment of political independence,

---

[26] Fanon, *Les Damnés de la terre (The Wretched of the Earth)*, 252 ('Each generation must out of relative obscurity discover its mission, fulfill it, or betray it'), 206.
[27] The term is a reference to the groundbreaking 2011 book by Thomas Deltombe, Manuel Domergue and Jacob Tatsitsa, *Kamerun! Une guerre cachée aux origines de la Françafrique, 1948-1971*, which, for the first time, traced the history of this civil war absent from history books, and still unrecognized today by both the French and Cameroonian authorities. See, for example: Clarisse Juompan-Yakan, 'Hollande reconnaît la repression française au Cameroon', *Jeune Afrique*, 9 July 2015, following President François Hollande's 2015 statement on a visit to Cameroon acknowledging France's 'repression' of Cameroon's independence movement in the 1950s and 1960s, but carefully avoiding the term 'war'. Earlier, in 2009 at a press conference in Yaoundé, then Prime Minister François Fillon denied all French involvement in the assassination of UPC militants: www.dailymotion.com/video/xjpo4l. At 1 minute 24, Fillon states: 'I categorically deny that French forces participated in any way in assassinations in Cameroon. All this is pure fabrication.'
[28] Hall, 'When Was "the Post-Colonial"? Thinking at the Limit', in Chambers and Curti, *The Post-Colonial Question*, 254.

as described by South American decolonial thinkers, such as Anibal Quijano, Walter Mignolo or Ramón Grosfoguel.[29] Teno's films repeatedly seek to analyse and understand this colonial continuum and the ways in which it affects contemporary Cameroonian political systems, their often lopsided co-existence with endogenous political systems and social structures, the country's social, political, economic and cultural dysfunctions, and above all its violence. Violence is indeed a theme at the core of all of Teno's films, be it colonial violence (political repression, assassinations, repression of protests, forced labour, the predation of resources, ideological violence, the repression of culture and language, and so forth); postcolonial violence (dictatorship, 'democrature', the repression of contestation, psychological violence, imprisonment, torture); the violence that ordinary citizens can inflict on one another (popular justice, marital violence, gender violence); or the violence of impoverished living conditions and lack of basic infrastructures – a violence that can easily become self-destructive.

This is particularly eloquently portrayed in *Chef!*, which starts out, as previously described, with Teno's spur-of-the-moment visit to his hometown of Bandjoun for a weekend of celebrations during the inauguration of a statue to former *Fô 'A-Djo* Kamga Joseph III. As Teno's irreverently mocking introductory voice-over comments, this turns out to be less a cultural event and a rare opportunity to see ritual dances and masquerades unperformed since the *Fô*'s death in 1975, than a political meeting sponsored, as the lingering shots on the event's banners reveal, by beer companies.

Teno's initial sketching of a reflection on the awkward balance between ancestral power – its rituals increasingly emptied of their signification – and the colonially imposed capitalist political system embodied by the besuited ministers and business men present at the ceremony, veers, again unplanned, into a broader reflection on authority, authoritarianism, power and violence when the next morning, the filmmaker stumbles across a scene of popular justice. The fluidity of the camera, which pans around the circle of gathered villagers

---

[29] The concepts of the 'coloniality of power' and the 'colonial matrix of power' first used by Anibal Quijano in 1992 to refer to the hegemonic global power structures that emerged in the modern era of colonialism, have since been expanded upon by Quijano and other South American decolonial theorists. Quijano describes the concept as follows: 'What is termed globalization is the culmination of a process that began with the constitution of America and colonial/modern Eurocentered capitalism as a new global power. One of the fundamental axes of this model of power is the social classification of the world's population around the idea of race, a mental construction that expresses the basic experience of colonial domination and pervades the more important dimensions of global power, including its specific rationality: Eurocentrism. The racial axis has a colonial origin and character, but it has proven to be more durable and stable than the colonialism in whose matrix it was established. Therefore, the model of power that is globally hegemonic today presupposes an element of coloniality.' *Coloniality of Power, Eurocentrism and Latin America*, 533.

Photo 7 *Chef!* The tension and violence rapidly escalate as the crowd determines whether to punish the terrified accused youth.

ready to punish the young thief, Kuate, reinforces the sense of the youth's entrapment. Cutting from protagonist to protagonist as the camera follows the admonishments of the angry men, the pacifying reasonings of one elder, the terrified Kuate's face and his cowering body as he is ordered to strip, or filming the watching crowd as the action continues off-camera, Teno captures the palpably rising tension and imminent danger during this almost unbearably long sequence. Things suddenly accelerate as men in the crowd appear to lose patience with the talking and move in to kick and slap Kuate – Teno's voice-over has already warned of the violent, at times fatal turn such instances can take – the camera's now jerky movement amidst the scuffle translating the sudden escalation of the tension. As we just about make out one man taking Kuate's head in his hands, the action half-masked as he steps in front of the camera, his sudden blur of movement and the heavy thudding sound off indicate that he has just head-butted the lad, the camera cuts abruptly to black, Teno's voice-over us informing that he stopped filming at this point to intervene. Yet seconds later, the scene resumes in an ellipse, the teen now ominously wearing a cord around his neck; the smoother camera movements indicate, however, that the immediate danger to Kuate has at least temporarily abated, the camera moving again with the crowd as the youth is taken off to the neighbourhood chief's, who advises that he be taken to the police. As the film returns to images of dancers, the festivities almost surreally continuing meanwhile back at the chiefdom, Teno muses in voice-over, drawing a parallel between the authority of the mob and the mob-like behaviour of the authorities, and the paradoxical near killing of a petty thief when 'le sport national bien avant le football est le pillage en toute impunité du patrimoine nationale par les chefs, petits et grands' ('the national sport, far more popular than football, is the plundering of our resources by our leaders, our chiefs, big and small'), the final words spoken most certainly not innocently to coincide with shots of the current *Fô* as he leaves the ceremony.

Teno's films repeatedly examine not only the violence of Cameroonian history, then, but how the as yet unbroken cycle of past violence repeats in the present. A powerful metaphor for the repercussions of such violence, and indeed for what Teno repeatedly portrays as the chaos of contemporary Cameroon, repeats in several works: that of the disarticulated, broken body. In *La Tête dans les nuages*, for example, to conjure the 'chaos' of the country where, the film has shown, ordinary Cameroonians are forced at every level to come up with informal solutions to make up for the state's chronic failings, Teno's final voice-over evokes the image of an uncontrolled and uncontrollable body: 'Imaginez un être ... les pieds dans une énorme poubelle, la tête enfouie dans les nuages, totalement incapable de contrôler le reste des mouvements de son corps' ('Imagine a person ... their feet in a huge bin, their head stuck in the clouds, totally incapable of controlling the rest of the movements of their body'). In *Une Feuille dans le vent* Ernestine similarly describes her broken family, deserted by her father: 'The head was no longer there, the tail was left to itself, and the intestines were left anyhow', before describing herself as being 'in bits and pieces', her own body and family clearly a metaphor for a country torn asunder. Repeatedly too, Teno captures the marks and scars of political violence on bodies, whether symbolic – the decapitated statue of Kwame Nkrumah filmed in *Une Feuille dans le vent* – or real, such as the body of assassinated independence leader Félix Moumié that his ageing father can only dream of bringing home from Guinea to bury in Cameroon in *Afrique, je te plumerai*; Kuate's stripped naked torso on the verge of being lynched in *Chef!*; Sobgui's trussed and tortured body and his bloody feet in *Clando*; or Ernestine Ouandié's long, detailed verbal accounts of the devastating physical and psychological abuse inflicted on her as a child by her aunt, then by her mother, and of course the fact that Ernestine ultimately took her own life. In Teno's films, these are 'palimpsest bodies', to borrow Anny Curtius' term, that bear the fissures of 'wounded memories'.[30] They literally embody 'the site of suffering' on the other side of 'the abyssal line' that, as Boaventura de Sousa Santos describes, traverses the modern Western world and thinking,[31] creating a 'zone of non-being' where the bodies of the 'ontologically degraded' are no longer treated as bodies, but as sub-human objects that can be abused and assaulted.[32]

Despite the gravity of his subjects and themes, and despite some very rare instances of Teno's own audible despair – for example, in his final voice-over commentary at the end of *Vacances au pays*, which describes Cameroon's 'long journey to arrive at a dead end' ('un longue voyage pour entre dans une impasse') and the country's 'sombre tomorrows' ('sombre lendemains') – he is no nihilist. In spite of everything, his films always ultimately contain and/or end on the optimistic belief in the possibility of improved lives for the majority, of the recognition of all the unsung heroes' struggles and sacrificed lives so that 'all our dead rest in peace' ('tous nos morts … réponsent en paix', *Vacances au pays*), a notion later powerfully echoed in *Une Feuille dans le vent*. Concomitantly, Teno's films always focus too on the remarkable resilience and resistance of his fellow citizens, never victimizing them, but rather highlighting their agency and actions (as opposed to reactions), their survival.[33] Or, as Patrice Nganang writes: 'Teno's films … go a long way in the impotent closure of the autocratic society to look for small and disturbing moments of renewal. Such moments of renewal are moments of resistance.'[34] These moments of resistance may be small and daily, such as the man in *Afrique, je te plumerai*

---

[30] Curtius used the term in her fascinating paper, 'Zabou la pacotilleuse fissurée : diaspora, folie, catastrophe climatique et civilisationnelle dans *Timbuktu* d'Abderrahmane Sissako', given at the *Congrès 2018 du CIÉF*, discussing Sissako's character Zabou, who says in the film: 'Les fissures c'est moi. Je suis fissurée de partout', translated by the film's English subtitles as: 'The cracks, it's me. Cracked open from head to toe.'

[31] de Sousa Santos, 'Epistémologies du Sud', a paper given at the *Colonial Abyssal* conference in Paris, 5 April 2018.

[32] See de Sousa Santos, *Beyond Abyssal Thinking*, 52. The violence inflicted on, and borne in, Black bodies of course has contemporary resonances, from the Black Lives Matter movements that have spread from the USA to Brazil and to Europe, to the inhumane treatment of those risking their lives to reach and cross the Mediterranean Sea.

[33] I borrow this important distinction from Gloria Anzaldúa, who argues in *Borderlands/La Frontera: The New Mestiza* that while counterstances are a vital 'step towards liberation', they are ultimately not 'a way of life'. Anzaldúa argues, rather, that the oppressed must develop new consciousnesses unlimited by and not dependent on what they are reacting against, concluding: 'The possibilities are numerous once we decide to act and not react', 100-101. I take the opportunity here to thank Paola Bachetta and the organizers of the inspirational *Gloria Anzaldúa: Translating B/borders* conference in Paris, 16-17 May 2019 (Université Paris 8, Université Diderot Paris 7, University of California, Berkeley, the Society for the Study of Gloria Anzaldúa, University of Texas, San Antonio, and Universidad de Guadalajara) for prompting me to return to the writings of Anzaldúa.

[34] Nganang, 'Deconstructing Authority in Cinema: Jean-Marie Teno', 147.

filmed teaching his two children to read and write by the roadside when he is unable to pay their school fees, or the stand-up comedian Essindi Mindja who lampoons the dictatorial Paul Biya. Or again, the mutual support *tontines* that communities organize; or Sobgui becoming an officious taxi driver in Teno's fiction film *Clando*. Or, finally, all the people working in the informal sector on whom the camera repeatedly and respectfully focuses from film to film, from the civil servant who makes and sells *accra* fritters outside the ministry where she works in order to supplement her paltry salary in *Tête dans les nuages*, to the mechanics who recycle old car parts in *Vacances au pays*, to the many shots of roadside hawkers, or the multiple lengthy and lovingly filmed scenes of craftsmen at work, capturing their skilful gestures. For indeed, as Nganang continues: 'In postcolonial African countries where the state does not fulfil its main duties, the so-called informal sector of the economy becomes one of the places where the energy of the native can be productive.'[35]

These moments of resistance may also occur in the private, family space. They may take the form of talking back, or, at other times, of silence, like that which the senior wife Elise opposes, refusing to speak before Teno's camera in *Le Marriage d'Alex*. They may at times too be brutal, urgent, a form of survival, for instance the play of power between senior and junior wife as both women vie for their status and rights in this polygamous marriage. Or, for example, the slap that Ernestine recounts finally giving her abusive aunt in *Une Feuille dans le vent*. They may too be historical, political, at times heroic moments of resistance, such as the first Cameroonian trade unionists' violently repressed demands for their rights from the French colonial regime, and the creation and struggle of the pro-independence UPC party narrated in *Afrique, je te plumerai* and *Une Feuille dans le vent*; or the account in the former of Célestin Monga's open letter denouncing President Paul Biya's 'fake democracy' in 1991, published by the independent, opposition newspaper *Le Messager* – whose very existence, despite repeated censorship and closure over the years, was a form of resistance itself – and which led to Monga and newspaper editor-in-chief Pius Njawe's arrest and trial. Or, again, the political opposition movement in *Clando*; the female activists and women's rights groups given voice in *Chef !*; the liberation theology of the Namibian Lutheran Church described in *Le Malentendu colonial*, which took the Gospel spread by the European missionaries and colonialists to subjugate African people and turned it into an inspiration for liberation, this church also becoming a vanguard in the anti-Apartheid struggle. By focusing with relentless commitment on these ordinary/extraordinary characters and their minor/major actions, Teno highlights their agency, engagement, resistance, whatever the many hardships they face; by bringing

---

[35] Nganang, 'Deconstructing Authority in Cinema', 148.

forth their stories, he thus, like the griot figure who conveys collective memory, highlights, celebrates and keeps alive the memories of their struggles.

Yet, for all their serious commitment, Teno's films are never short of humour, which courses through his oeuvre, one not excluding the other. Like in other earlier serious committed works, such as Sembene's searingly satirical *Mandabi* (1968) and *Xala* (1974), Teno's humour is satirical too, wry, the juxtapositions of his montage ever-ready to pick out the ironic contradictions in situations, just as his ubiquitous voice-over commentaries are full of irony, their tone often audibly mocking. This humour is a form of resistance too; like the court jester, or the 'mad person' archetype that populates African literature and cinema incarnating the voice of resistance, humour liberates speech, making it possible to say things that would otherwise be controlled and censored, like, for example, when the stand-up comedian Essindi Mindja openly ridicules the autocratic President Biya in his sketch at the end of *Afrique, je te plumerai*.[36] This humour also prevents us, as spectators, from being overwhelmed by a comprehensible sense of pessimism in the face of the chaos or violence that Teno so often portrays; it keeps in sight the notes of hope, of utopia, offering the 'energy, the force to contest, an invitation to emancipatory dreams', and representing 'an act of rupture', that breathes 'creative force back into dreams of indocility and resistance, justice and freedom'.[37]

Both in its forms and in its themes, then, Teno's work is assuredly marked by its force of contestation and challenge: its challenge to authoritarian falsehoods, erasures and denials; a challenge to colonial myths and their contemporary off-shoots; to all forms of injustice and domination. It is a challenge, too, to silencing, objectification, and assignations of all kinds: a kind of affirmative response to Gayatri Spivak's famous question, can the subaltern speak? Not only can this 'subaltern' speak, as shall be developed in the next chapter; he does so as and when he likes, on his own terms, out of turn, refractorily, refusing formats and formatting, in ways that challenge rather than comfort. Teno's cinema ultimately reflects and incarnates his own resistance, too, in relentlessly making documentary at a time in the 1980s and 1990s when, as seen in the previous chapter, fiction was by far the favoured form in African film. It also embodies his resistance both to the dominant forms and codes of documentary cinema, and to the pressures, trends and fads over the decades from funders, programmers and sometimes academics, which, often subtly, demand that African cinema be 'more this' or 'more that', documentaries more

---

[36] For a more detailed analysis of the role and representations of the marginal figure of *le fou* (mad person), see Sawadogo, *Les cinémas francophones ouest-africains (1990-2005)*.

[37] From the collective *Manifeste de l'Atelier IV*, drawn up at the Atelier IV, 10-12 June, 2017, Collège d'études mondiales, Cité internationale des arts & ~~La Colonie~~, Paris. Curated by Françoise Vergès.

observational, voice-overs less present, less emphatic, works more aestheticized, more polished, more 'perfect' (who remembers Julio García Espinosa's warning: 'perfect cinema – technically and artistically masterful – is almost always reactionary cinema'?[38]); in short, less challenging, less political. The price Teno has often had to pay for this intractable resistance and freedom has often, in funding terms – or rather, lack thereof – been brutally punishing. Continuing to make films in such conditions in itself constitutes an unwavering commitment and a form of resistance.

---

[38] Espinosa, 'For an Imperfect Cinema', 24.

The Cinematic 'I': Subjectivity, Voice

> *Coming to voice is an act of resistance. Speaking becomes both a way to engage in active self-transformation and a rite of passage where one moves from being object to being subject. Only as subjects can we speak. As objects, we remain voiceless – our beings defined and interpreted by others.*
>
> bell hooks[1]

Another enduringly salient characteristic of Jean-Marie Teno's work is its narrative voice. Since *Afrique, je te plumerai*, Teno has assumed a first-person *je* ('I') in his prominent voice-over commentaries; prominent, that is, in the central role they play in structuring and unifying each film's overall narrative. Since reaching a kind of apogee in Teno's most narrated (and most autobiographical) *Vacances au pays*, they have in recent works nonetheless become more intermittent in their frequency; less a direct commentary on a given situation or moment, and more an often poetic personal reflection. Back in the early 1990s when documentary still either predominantly favoured the voice-of-God commentaries already seen in Chapter 1 (notably in the information or current-affairs-type documentaries seen on television), or, alternatively, the voicelessness of observational documentary in which, particularly since the 1970s, commentary had become increasingly viewed as suspect, controlling, curtailing the spectator's space to see or to hear the reality before them on the screen, Teno's embracing of an outspoken first-person narrative was clearly atypical and against both grains. On the one hand, by speaking in the first person, it challenged the still-common acceptation that documentary was primarily an objective vehicle of knowledge, or 'some sort of discourse on reality rather than a form of personal expression'.[2] It also challenged the unspoken authority that omniscient voice-overs infer, raising *en creux* questions of the situated nature of discourse and of subjectivity, placing them at the heart of Teno's work. On the other, both in the wake of colonialism's silencing of the colonized, and before the continued silencing and side-lining of the voices of the still-marginalized – a highly specific context, then, that differed considerably to that of the predominantly Western observational filmmakers (or filmmakers following the Western tradition) – speaking out in this way was a radical, political and situated act that had little to do with the Western context and its trends.

---

[1] hooks, '"When I Was a Young Soldier for the Revolution": Coming to Voice', in *Talking Back*, 12.
[2] de Bromhead, *Looking Two Ways*, 1.

Before looking at Teno's voice-overs themselves, it is important to briefly contextualize the filmmaker's choice of a subjective, first-person commentary in this specifically postcolonial moment, which, as has already been discussed, remains marked by what decolonial thinkers aptly describe as the on-going coloniality of power. Colonization, as Achille Mbembe points out, constructed the colonized not simply as 'an alter ego (another self)', but as Other, as outside the circle of humanity, incapable of manifesting subjectivity and consciousness.[3] Invalidating 'all expressions of the colonized's existence (their forms of knowledge, their culture, their very being)', to cite Nadia Yala Kisukidi,[4] this practice of power, which claimed to 'know' the colonized, assigned them a fixed and necessarily subordinate identity and place. Considered 'devoid of subjectivity' and 'lacking interiority', the colonized, Seloua Luste Boulbina adds, were 'conjugated in the third person, without them really being considered subjects'.[5] Marked by 'a colonially perturbed relationship', Luste Boulbina continues, this altered 'the way in which individuals and communities experienced and perceived themselves'.[6] It is in this context of ontological negation that Teno's claiming of a first-person voice, of subjectivity, right back in 1992, was not only boldly radical but also necessary. It was part of what Ethiopian filmmaker Haile Gerima described as Africans' effort to reconstruct their 'disfigured selves'.[7] It was, to cite Stuart Hall too, part of a process of becoming the subject, rather than being 'positioned and subject-ed'.[8] Judging by the fact that it took Teno two films to feel legitimate enough to speak in his own name, this is manifestly not a self-evident process. Indeed, in *Hommage*, then in *Bikutsi Water Blues*, Teno adopted forms of subterfuge to speak of his own experiences without seeming to, firstly using his two fictional characters' dialogue to voice his own conflicting and conflicted perspectives, secondly by creating a journalist figure as his onscreen avatar. But I would also argue too that, some thirty years on, in a still 'colonially perturbed' world that often continues to assign Black people to a status of non-being, excluding them from 'social, political and cultural belonging' and criminalizing them 'as the carriers of terror, terror's embodiment and not the primary object of terror's multiple enactments', to

---

[3] Mbembe, 'African Modes of Self-Writing', 6-7.
[4] Kisukidi, 'Laetitia Africana – philosphie, décolonisation et mélancolie', 56 ['toutes les expressions de l'existence des colonisés (leurs savoirs, leurs cultures, leur être même)'].
[5] Luste Boulbina, *L'Afrique et ses fantômes*, 35. ['sans subjectivité', 'qu'extériorité', 'Leur identité se décline à la troisième personne, sans qu'ils soient réellement des sujets.'].
[6] Luste Boulbina, *L'Afrique et ses fantômes*, 15. ['marqués par un rapport à soi colonialement perturbé … tant la colonialité des rapports a pu modifier la façon dont ces individus et ces collectivités se vivent et se perçoivent.'].
[7] Gerima, speaking at the British Film Institute Screen Griots Conference, London, 9-10 September 1995.
[8] Hall, 'Cultural Identity and Cinematic Representation', 70-71.

Photo 8 *Bikutsi Water Blues.* The journalist character, or the filmmaker's avatar, before Teno later moved on to overtly embrace his hallmark subjective voice.

cite Christina Sharpe,[9] claiming this voice, asserting this subjectivity as Teno has since continued to do remains the act of political self-affirmation and of resistance that bell hooks described in the opening citation back in 1989.

Flowing, then, through each film since *Afrique, je te plumerai* and through the oeuvre as an ensemble, working with the other elements of the soundtrack as a kind of musical pacing, a caesura, Teno's voice-over commentaries take on a variety of registers and fulfil different functions at different moments of each film as they guide, question, and at times provoke the spectator. Intervening in the opening sequences, they habitually set the scene of the film, stating the director's initial point of departure, his initial intention, laying down a sort of filmic roadmap. Some films rapidly depart from this initial intention as, Teno informs us, some hitherto unforeseen event erupts, such, for example, as the violent repression of the 1990s pro-democracy demonstrations that occurred just as he began filming material for a work originally destined to be about the state of Cameroon's publishing sector in *Afrique, je te plumerai*. In others,

---

[9] Sharpe, *In the Wake*, 14-15.

Teno describes his lack of specific intention, for example in *Chef!*, where, after contextualizing the film's opening festivity scenes in Teno's hometown to celebrate the former *Fô 'A-Djo* and after establishing his own questioning of figures of authority, Teno describes how, having been convinced by a friend to come ('Toi! Toi qui fais des images, ne manque pas ce weekend à la chefferie, ça va chauffer!' ['You! You're a filmmaker, don't miss this weekend at the village. It will be great!']), he simply began to film 'sans projet de depart' ('with nothing specific in mind'). The film's actual theme of authority and power only took form, we learn, after Teno the next day witnesses a triggering instance of popular justice. The voice-over thus clearly bares the mechanisms of Teno's creative process and the way in which he first films, then pieces together his material into a narrative. Written during the montage – that is, after the events that appear to us, the spectator, to unfold before our eyes – the different temporalities of the voice and the images remind us that this is a filmic construction, not a real-time event, which the filmmaker steps back to comment and interpret. This after-the-event commentary thus adds a layer to the film's complexity, injecting a reflexive critical distance from the immediacy of the filmed material.

Continuing to intervene at regular intervals throughout each film, the voice-overs confer a structure, functioning as a thread that collates, links and gives overall coherence and meaning to the often polyphonic, layered, and often non-linear and fragmented narratives. At times, the voice adopts a classic narrator role, providing contextualizing information to facilitate our comprehension of a situation, propelling the narrative development. Yet, as it is openly subjective, this voice repeatedly reminds us that everything we are going to see is being mediated through Teno's 'I'/eye; it is, quite literally, his point of view. At times intervening in counterpoint to the images, commenting on, subjectively interpreting, and – in the case of the colonial archive footage that Teno incorporates (see later) – challenging them, what they show, and what their omniscient, un-situated narratives recount, the voice-overs challenge the ideological discourses and subvert the message of this footage and give Teno's own outspoken (in both senses of the word), subversive, at times mocking readings. This overtly embraced subjectivity is reinforced by the frequent word-play and the poetic, and sometimes lyrical style of Teno's carefully worded texts that depart from a more habitually neutral journalistic or factual documentary style – a departure that is again further reinforced by their at times audibly impassioned, at times scathing, at times musing, at times amusing, and often ironic multi-tonal deliveries.

Teno's voice, then, is what Michel Chion calls an 'I-voice', engaging directly with the screen space and the subject matter, so that 'the voice and image dance in a dynamic relationship'.[10] Distance is thwarted; proximity with the spectator and a point of identification are created, 'such that we sense no distance between [the voice] and our ear', as Chion describes.[11] A familiarity develops, drawing us into an empathetic communion, as is reinforced by the filmmaker's choice to always record his voice-over texts himself – a decision taken *in extremis* when making *Afrique, je te plumerai*, despite his conviction that he did not have a fittingly radiophonic voice.[12] From film to film, we recognize Teno's unmistakable melodically flowing tone, creating a growing rapport between us, as if hearing again from an old acquaintance. 'No longer just a witness, but an interlocuter', to cite Olivier Barlet,[13] Teno speaks to us directly, then, informing, guiding, questioning, and at times needling us in a way that acknowledges and addresses us as an embodied spectator, actively engaging both our intellect and emotion.

While this voice undeniably assumes its own form of authority – that of the auteur filmmaker, whose subjective reflection and line of reasoning we are asked, as Laura Rascaroli comments, 'to take ... to connect with, to share or reject'[14] – by speaking in the first person, by positing what Rascaroli calls a 'well-defined, extra-textual authorial figure as the point of origin and constant reference'[15], by stating his positionality and partiality – Teno's voice is not a balanced, objective, or neutral one – the filmmaker rescinds the officialized, normalized authority – the 'truth' – of the unidentified documentary 'voice of God' that habitually positions the spectator in a passive state of contemplation. In *Afrique, je te plumerai*, for instance, Teno introduces the film as 'a reading of history' ('une lecture de l'histoire'). The choice of the words is by no means inconsequential: the film is just that – a reading, his, an interpretation that in no way purports to be definitive. Teno does not claim to convey *the* truth; he does not speak about his subject matter authoritatively, with detachment, or from the outside; he comments and reflects from within. He offers us *his* interpretation, then, one with which – however compelling and emphatic his arguments are – we are ultimately free to disagree. He does not so much tell it *as it is*, then, but rather how *he* sees it.[16] Or, as Teno states himself:

---

[10] Chion, *The Voice in Cinema*, 50.
[11] Ibid.
[12] See Part II of this book, *In Conversation*.
[13] Barlet, *Contemporary African Cinema*, 305.
[14] Rascaroli, *The Personal Camera*, 14.
[15] Ibid., 3.
[16] Teno is at times accused either of intervening too much in voice-over, or of being too controlling. In his introduction to *Cinema and Social Discourse in Cameroon*, Alexie Tcheuyap, for example, claims that Teno's role as producer, director, distributor and narrator of his works is due not just to financial constraints, 'but also [to] the need to *control* the production and thought', bringing to mind 'the image of autocrats who ...

I adopt multiple positions. Sometimes I reflect, sometimes I joke, because telling stories is also to invite the viewer on a journey, during which we can exchange, communicate. Viewers can follow my thoughts and, if they feel at any point that it does not work for then, that is fine. They know where I am starting from and I never conceal where I am going. By doing so, I simply offer people a different vision, and also remind them that there can be multiple versions of the story.[17]

Teno's authority as a filmmaker is, then, as Anjali Prabhu aptly describes, 'both the site of his commitment and the nodal point for dialogue',[18] a dialogue both with the other voices that are heard in his works, and with the interpellated spectator. It is indeed a voice that does not exclude others; on the contrary, the filmmaker weaves multiple voices into his narratives – those of an array of people directly involved in the events related, and/or specialists (historians, activists, trade unionists, journalists, and so forth) – who add their readings and layers of interpretation to create a composite, polyphonic form that perhaps reached its apotheosis in *Une Feuille dans le vent*. Here, Ernestine Ouandié's incredibly powerful voice and testimony essentially is the film, its core, its body and soul. Described by Teno as 'a dual first-person narrative' in which Ernestine Ouandié and he together 'build a memory of the events in Cameroon',[19] Teno's own voice is very much secondary. Superposed together, then, these independent voices harmonize together like melody lines, giving what Edward Said described as a 'plurality of vision [that] gives rise to an awareness of simultaneous dimensions'.[20]

Interestingly, while speaking in the first-person singular, it is often plurality that is suggested in Teno's 'I'. Coming in the 1990s at a time when first-person documentary was developing across the world to the point – at least in North America – of becoming a genre, Pat Aufderheide argues, Teno's embracing of the first person nonetheless differs notably from the subjective documentaries that Aufderheide describes: namely films rooted in often very intimate personal experiences and stories (testimonial films, filmic diaries, personal

---

are everywhere at the same time' (13, 14). In *Documentary Film: A Very Short Introduction*, Patrica Aufderheide reminds us, however, that while the late-1960s move to un-narrated observation 'allowed viewers to believe they are being allowed to decide for themselves the meaning of what they saw', in reality this is of course actually controlled through directors' editing choices (12).

[17] Speaking during our public conversation/joint presentation at the *Digital Media and New Cinema from the Global South* Symposium, Michigan State University/University Michigan Ann Arbor, 3-5 April 2014.
[18] Prabhu, *Contemporary Cinema of Africa and the Diaspora*, 203.
[19] Speaking during our public conversation/joint presentation at the *Digital Media and New Cinema from the Global South* Symposium.
[20] Said, *Reflections on Exile*, 148.

essays) that bring the viewer into the filmmaker's own world, and, usually, into contact with broader social issues and alternative points of view too; films giving disenfranchised people a voice on their behalf, bearing witness or giving visibility to under-represented groups; or, finally, films that were often though not exclusively autobiographical.[21] While one can certainly detect elements of Aufderheide's description in Teno's works, the most salient difference boils down to the question of individualism. Speaking in the first person is indeed habitually associated with some form of autobiography and, as a genre, Western autobiography is usually associated with the individual. While the idea of self-narration is an important one in the decolonization process,[22] Teno's 'I' is rarely an exclusively individual one, even in its most autobiographic moments, such as, for example, when he narrates personal childhood memories in *Afrique, je te plumerai* and *Vacances au pays*. His 'I', rather, is a collective one, his own personal experience always set in resonance with, and amplified by, broader Cameroonian – or even African – experiences.

Vacances au pays, Teno's most autobiographical film to date, for example, starts in a classically autobiographical way: thirty-three years after being a secondary school pupil in Yaoundé, the filmmaker tells us he is about to make the same journey home to the family village that he used to make in the school holidays. Already striking in its sheer length, the introductory sequence lasting a total of nine minutes, Teno repeatedly fluctuates between speaking in the first-person 'I' to the collective 'we' and back in this opening voice-over. Mediated through his camera/eye, this personal journey home is not so much that of an individual – Teno – nor simply a quest to find or question his own roots – although it is of course that too. It is not a performance of the self, then, but rather a journey into, and a critical questioning of, the situation of contemporary Cameroon and its quest for modernity,[23] a situation symbolized by the

---

[21] See Aufderheide, 'Public Intimacy'.
[22] For more on this process, see, for example: Achille Mbembe, 'African Modes of Self-Writing'.
[23] The concept of 'modernity' and the well-documented issues it raises in African contexts needs unpacking. Many scholars, such as Ali Mazrui in *World Culture and the Black Experience*, have long pointed to the need to decolonize the term modernism, so it no longer be simply equated with Euro-modernism. Mazrui points out that Euro-modernism was a logocentric phenomenon born out of the converging forces of rationalism, 18th-century Enlightenment, the development of the sciences, industrialization and democracy, all of which encouraged societal changes in Europe understood as liberating, freeing societies from feudalism and theocracy. Yet, as Clyde Taylor argues in 'Searching for the Postmodern in African Cinema', the same modern period saw the introduction of the transatlantic slave trade, colonization and other exploitation of the non-Western world. South American decolonial thinkers rightly argue that slavery and colonialism are constitutive, even, of Western modernity. Taylor continues, adding that, while Africa's 'modern' period is defined by its experience of, and transition through, colonialism, it is

famous Lycée Lerclerc, once the pride of the country and the place where the post-independence ruling elites were schooled, today a derelict abandoned ruin, shamefully hidden away from public view. Teno's own experience is not about him, as such; it serves as an example, or even a metaphor, for broader issues. It is not an introspective 'I', then, but an 'extrospective' one; not one that asks 'Who am I?' as Fanon described, but rather who the filmmaker and his fellow compatriots and Africans are.[24] This brings to mind Achille Mbembe's observation: 'Whether social forms, institutions or logic and rationality, everything here is always conjugated in the plural. The principle of One is unknown to us', an outlook that favours relationality, interactions and potentiality.[25] While this is not necessarily exclusive to an African context (in her discussion of the concept of *ubuntu*, translatable as 'I am because we are', Séverine Kodjo-Grandvaux indeed insists that the principle of a 'cogito social' can also be found in Plato, Aristotle, Epicure or Spinoza too), in colonial Africa, 'the question of the primacy of the social over the individual for many ethno-/anthropologists resulted in the idea according to which the individual did not exist.'[26] In a postcolonial context, then, Teno's 'I' reclaims the possibility of 'conceiving of the individual *in* society, and not counter to it.'[27] Rather than articulating a Cartesian *ergo sum*, 'I am' – of which, interestingly, there is linguistically no equivalent in Ghomala', the Bamileke language of Bandjoun – the self of Teno's 'I', is, in the Ricoeurian sense, a selfhood, or an identity in the making. For, as Stuart Hall reminds us, identity is as much 'a matter of "becoming" as well as "being". It belongs to the future as much as to the past.'[28] It is in this sense, then, that Teno's 'I' is very much part of a decolonial quest for identity.

After an explosively turbulent three-minute pre-credits sequence that captures and situates the 1990 pro-democracy protests and their violent repression that took place just as Teno began shooting what would become

---

also defined by the birth of its anti-colonial liberation movements: 'If there is an African modernity ... then, it is a counter-modernity, a movement in opposition to the debilitating effects of Euro-modernism', suggesting a plurality of paradigms and experiences (136).

[24] In *The Wretched of the Earth*, Fanon states that colonialism forces those it dominates to ask themselves constantly: 'In reality, who am I?' (250).

[25] Mbembe, 'L'Afrique qui vient', 30 ['Qu'il s'agisse des formes sociales, des institutions ou des logiques et rationalités, tout ici s'est toujours conjugé au pluriel. Le principe de l'Un nous est inconnu'].

[26] Kodjo-Grandvaux, *Effets de mirroir: penser l'Afrique, penser le monde*, 61 ['la question de la primauté du social sur l'individu s'est soldée chez nombre d'ethno-/anthropologues par l'idée selon laquelle l'individu n'existerait pas'].

[27] Ibid, 62 ['penser l'individu *dans* la société et non contre elle'], emphasis added.

[28] Hall, 'Cultural Identity and Cinematic Representation', 70. My acknowledgements to Laura Rascaroli too for her discussion of Descartes and Ricoeur in *The Personal Camera*, 8-9, from which I have drawn here.

Photo 9 *Afrique, je te plumerai*. Teno for the first time embraces his now-characteristic first-person voice, clearly stating his position of enunciation.

Afrique, je te plumerai, and over early-morning shots of a now calm Yaoundé waking, Teno's commentary shifts to the first person as he informs us that he is about to offer a reading of Cameroonian history 'du point de vue de l'indigène que je suis', ('from the point of view of the native I am.').

The words are significant. Not only does Teno in his first-ever subjective voice-over acknowledge the situated nature of both documentary discourse and historiography by clearly stating his own 'position of enunciation';[29] he, as 'a native', claims the privilege and legitimacy to think and speak. Considering, as Michel Foucault argues in *The Order of Things*, that societies posit rules and classifications to control discourse and delimit disciplines, designating specialists who alone are 'qualified' to enter the discursive space and speak, Teno-the-native's self-attribution of this right is both radically political and (pun intended) undisciplined. The appropriation and embracing of the term *indigène* ('native') is eminently political too, referencing as it does, Patrice Nganang

---

[29] Hall, 'Cultural Identity and Cinematic Representation', 68. Not by chance, Teno returns to the question of enunciation in his 2009 film *Lieux saints*, in which, reflecting on the place and role of African cinema today, he asked: 'Who speaks?', but now adding: 'to say what to whom?'

observes, the *Régime de l'indigénat*, or the exceptional, extra-Republican repressive legislative powers and punishments first introduced in Algeria after French conquest in 1830, and later extended to France's other colonies, creating the status of *indigène*, the lowest echelon of colonial society.[30] Just as Subaltern Studies scholars, such as Ranajit Guha, embraced the Gramscian term 'from below' to describe their formulation of new narratives of Indian and South Asian history in the 1980s, Teno too thus clearly situates himself 'below', with his fellow powerless and ontologically denied subalterns, and states that this is a point of view that has value. For Teno, this is a deliberately political gesture:

> It was asking people to do what no one ever did: to identify with a Black person looking at the world. I thought to myself that the utmost political gesture was to bring people to see through the eyes of someone they did not want to identify with ... a nobody.[31]

It is, ultimately, a form of self-defence,[32] an assertion of one's worth, of one's existence for, as Fabiana De Souza writes: 'Asserting this place we speak from is to exist there where we think; it is to think there where we form a body.'[33] It is indeed a recognition and valorization of that place, in the same way that in *L'odeur du père*, V.Y. Mudimbe describes his thinking as 'being from a place, a space; and I do not see how nor why my word ... should be, more than anything else, a cry and a witness to that singular place.'[34] African filmmakers are often

---

[30] Nganang, 'Deconstructing Authority in Cinema: Jean-Marie Teno', 147. In vigour until the Brazzaville Conference in 1944, the *Régime de l'indigénat* did not respect the general principles of French Republican law, allowing notably for collective sanctions for any resistance to the colonial order (striking, refusing to execute forced labour, forced conscription, or to pay taxes levied in the colonies alone), deportations, and restrictions on circulation.

[31] From the interview in Part II of this volume, 'In Conversation'.

[32] I refer here to Elsa Dorlin's understanding of self-defence in her fascinating book, *Se défendre. Une philosophie de la violence*. From France's 1685 Code noir, which forbade slaves from bearing any form of weapon, even sticks, to the colonial regime in Algeria's ban on arms for *indigènes*, while authorizing colonial settlers to carry them, Dorlin examines how 'the technology of power' and its systems of domination historically oppose bodies 'worth defending' and those disarmed and left 'defenceless' or 'undefendable' (14), between subjects who have the legitimacy to defend themselves (legal, free subjects) and those who, dispossessed of themselves, have none (slaves, the colonized, women, criminals, etc.) (91). This organized disarming of subalterns, which turned the right to self-defence into an 'exclusive privilege of a dominant minority' (14), Dorlin argues, situates the notion of self-defence at the heart of all struggles of liberation, from the clandestine practices and mechanisms of self-defence practised by slaves (song, dance, music, martial arts, etc.), to the later recourse to arms of independence struggles.

[33] De Souza, 'Réactualiser l'archive, réécrire l'histoire: des pratiques artistiques décoloniales', *Revue Asylon(s)* 15, February 2018 ['Revendiquer ce lieu d'où l'on parle, c'est exister là où l'on pense, c'est réfléchir là où nous faisons corps'].

[34] Mudimbe, *L'odeur du père*, 14 ['Je pars du fait que ma conscience et mon effort son d'un

questioned about who they make their films for; Teno, then, perhaps hereby shifts the importance to the place they are making them from.

Speaking from this place, Teno also situates himself within and as a part of the worlds he films, or states his relationship to them (like, for example, when filming his non-native Ghana in *Chosen*), thereby constantly recalling his extra-diegetic presence. At times, Teno even actually becomes a filmic persona, even if his presence is more suggested than visible. In *Afrique, je te plumerai*, for example, he on several occasions adopts a subjective camera point of view, creating the illusion that he is filming when in reality, he worked here with the cameraman Robert Diannoux. This initially playfully tricks us into thinking that Teno is behind the camera to reinforce the illusion that certain scenes unfold in real-time when they are in fact enactments, like, for example, when Teno pretends to propose his film to the director of the Cameroonian national television, in reality played by an actor. Yet the hammed-up clownish acting, the preposterous dialogue and actions, and clear lampooning – just like Marie, the faux journalist's later complicit winks and nods to the camera – all of course gradually call our attention to the staging. Laughing at our own being 'had', the joke is ultimately not on us, however, but on documentary and its claims to show reality, reinforcing our complicity with the filmmaker.

This complicity, or camaraderie, is also reinforced, finally, by another recurrent feature of Teno's voice: its irony. Teno indeed frequently pokes fun at pompous or delusional elites or officials, for example when the faux journalist Marie mockingly imitates General De Gaulle's famous 'Je vous ai compris' before his portrait in *Afrique, je te plumerai*, for example,[35] or the film's mocking enactment of Teno's above-mentioned visit to the Pacman-playing national television director. Irreverent irony is audible too in Teno's voice-over at the

---

lieu, d'un espace … et je ne vois ni comment ni pourquoi ma parole … ne devrait pas, avant toute autre chose, être le cri et le témoin de ce lieu singulier'].

[35] Pronounced before a huge crowd in Algiers on 4 June 1958, fifteen days after General de Gaulle had come out of retirement to restore order. The unstable Fourth Republic was indeed teetering on the brink of collapse after riots by French Algerians and the military in furious protest at the French government's desire to negotiate with the Algerian National Liberation Front (FLN) – considered *the* ultimate betrayal – and as paratroopers from Algiers were thought to be about to land in mainland France. De Gaulle's words 'I have understood you. I know what has happened here. I see what you were trying to do. I see that the road that you have opened in Algeria is that of renewal and fraternity' were famously elusive, with no one really certain whether this was a declaration of support to French Algeria, a recognition of equal rights for all, or support for Algerian independence. They perfectly symbolize the political manoeuvring and cynicism of a De Gaulle who, for pragmatic reasons, would overtly accept Independence in the French colonies, while at the same time covertly intervening to ensure that only leaders who would protect French political and economic interests took over power. This on-going de facto dependency and neocolonial imbrication is known as 'la Françafrique'.

start of *Chef!*, describing Bandjoun's former *Fô*'s attempts to develop his village by imposing European culture while also trying to preserve ancestral practices as 'le grand écart sans échauffement et sans entraînement' ('the splits, without limbering-up and with no training'). It is present too in the lampooning of the bumptious sub-prefect in the hamlet of Ebebda in *Vacances au pays*, an 'important and very busy' man, as Teno ironically informs us in voice-over on paying a visit to his office as the official is filmed imperturbably reading his newspaper, the chirpy brass-band circus music further reinforcing the irony. It is hard not to delight in this mischievous tone as we, the spectator, along with the filmmaker (the people from below), get a rare opportunity to ridicule these figures of authority. Not only a refreshing interlude in films that portray often gruelling realities, this irony also injects a certain critical distance from the subject that Teno is addressing, encouraging us too to step back and laugh. It thereby creates what Trinh T. Minh-Ha calls an 'interval', or a space 'between the meaning of something and its truth ... a break without which meaning would be fixed and truth congealed', there, then, where the viewer is engaged in thought.[36]

Teno is quite capable of turning the irony on himself, too, using it as a powerful, cruel alienation effect. In *Afrique, je te plumerai*, for example, shots of a contemporary second-hand book market in Yaoundé selling comic books trigger childhood memories. The images segue into a black-and-white sequence of children reading, playing, dancing, of a class in school, to a staged enactment of three schoolboys (one imagines the young Teno) going to see a Bollywood film at the cinema. The film's images fill the screen that the boys watch, and fill our screen too, the dancing women's melodious 'nightingale voices' continuing over the following shots that return to children playing outdoors as Teno's voice-over wistfully recalls the star-induced dreams of the Bollywood heroes. But, as the sequence draws to a close, and the filmmaker mock-wistfully sighs, 'ah, l'enfance, l'indépendance ... et sa cohorte de violence' ('ah, my childhood, independence ... and its companion violence'), off what sounds like tyres screeching to a halt appear to cause a girl in the shot to start, as we cut jarringly to archive images of police beating a man, the archives' cut sound even more chilling as the silence is broken only by the added sound effects of the amplified dull thuds of the police blows.[37] The shock of the

---

[36] Trinh T. Minh-Ha, 'Documentary Is/Not a Name', 76.
[37] Jarring juxtapositions are a common distancing technique in Teno's montage in general, and particularly powerful throughout *Afrique, je te plumerai*. Right from its opening images, the film indeed begins with a slow, smooth 180-degree panning shot of the city of Yaoundé filmed from a hilltop, the soft light and calm of the early morning contrasting dissonantly with the harshness of words, which contrast again with Teno's beguilingly lulling voice – 'Yaoundé, ville cruelle. Tu as bourré nos têtes de tes mensonges officielles'

Photos 10 a-b-c-d-e-f *Afrique, je te plumerai*. As the nostalgic childhood sequence draws to a close, Teno's wistful voice-over becomes self-mocking, the harsh turn of the words jarring with the images of the children playing. The shock transition from the children to the violent archive images, with sound cut, further accentuates the brutality of the latter.

d

e

f

transition jerks us brutally back to the reality of the violence of this period, to critical consciousness, Teno refusing to allow himself, or us, to revel in even a fleeting nostalgic lull of tender childhood memory, as if to reprimandingly say, 'Wake up!, there can be no nostalgia for the colonial era'.

('Yaoundé, cruel city. You stuffed our heads with your official lies') – before the sequence cuts even more jarringly to the jerky, hand-held shots now down in the chaotic city streets, in the fray, as angry youth protest to demand democracy and the armed forces fire live ammunition at the crowds.

(Hi)stories, Memory: Decolonial Readings of the Past

> *You dare say History, but I say histories, stories.*
> *The one you take for the master stem of our manioc is but one stem among many others.*
> Patrick Chamoiseau[1]
>
> *The present still carries the spectres of the past hiding inside it.*
> Stuart Hall[2]

Postcolonial African cinema has explored the questions of history and memory with striking consistency as filmmakers have looked to re-examine their continent's colonially maligned, erased and silenced pasts. This question of course poses questions of epistemology, of objectivity, of who is telling whose history, and how. What, even, is history? 'A legend', 'a memory', V.Y. Mudimbe answers, 'an invention … and a reflection of our present.'[3] These questions are central to several of Jean-Marie Teno's works in which he turns his camera to the past. But before looking specifically at the ways in which Teno's films repeatedly address the past, and in order to understand the centrality of this question, it is worth briefly considering the concurrent and complementary processes that in the West led to the dismissing and erasure of Africa's epistemologies and ways of telling and understanding its past, and even of the very idea of African history.

With 17th to 18th-century European rationalism and Enlightenment, History with a capital 'H' became considered a scientific discipline. Seen as impartial, chronologically linear, as distinct and separate from both (unscientific) memory and from the present, it was also a hierarchical history, as Seloua Luste Boulbina reminds us: 'Historiography as we know it names the "big men" and leaves human beings in their anonymity. It transcends the blood and tears to deliver a rational discourse on what took place. Everything is done as if the earth must be seen from the skies above to be properly apprehended.'[4] Invisibilizing its own Eurocentrism and partiality, and taking itself to be universally valid, this rationalist understanding and narrative of history was imposed as official, as

---

[1] Chamoiseau, *Texaco*, 88.
[2] Hall & Schwarz. *Familiar Stranger*, 24.
[3] Mudimbe, *The Invention of Africa*, 195.
[4] Luste Boulbina, *L'Afrique et ses fantômes*, 37 ['L'historiographie telle que nous la connaissons nomme les "grands hommes" et laisse les êtres humains dans l'anonymat. Elle prend de la hauteur sur le sang et les larmes pour délivrer un discours rationnel sur ce qui a eu lieu. Tout se passe comme si la terre devait être vue du ciel pour être correctement appréhendée'].

authoritative, to the exclusion of other epistemologies and methodologies of studying and interpreting the past.[5] Oral transmission of history, in particular – the most common form in Africa – was written off as unscientific and unreliable.[6]

Concurrently, in the effort first to justify and legitimize the slave trade and later the imposition of European colonial rule in Africa, in the 1880s, racial theories, such as those developed in Gobineau's 1853 *Essai sur l'inégalité des races humaines*, established a hierarchy of races.[7] In keeping with this logic, Africa, placed at the bottom of the ladder, was necessarily also cast as a continent without what were deemed to be the ultimate markers of civilization – writing and history – a vision that is clearly articulated in Hegel's introduction to *Lectures on the Philosophy of World History*, 1837:

---

[5] For a thorough and fascinating analysis and deconstruction of the Western philosophical concept of universality from Descartes to the present, see Grosfoguel, 'Decolonizing Western Uni-versalisms: Decolonial Pluri-versalism from Aimé Césaire to the Zapatistas'. Arguing that the most 'permanent influence of Cartesianism ... is the faceless, zero-point philosophy that would be taken up by the human sciences from the 19th century onward as the epistemology of axiological neutrality and empirical objectivity of the subject, which produces scientific knowledge'. Grosfoguel suggests that many thinkers have continued 'to produce knowledge from the zero-point, that is, without questioning the place from which they speak and produce this knowledge'. (89) He adds that the concept of universality that has remained stamped on Western philosophy since Descartes is 'an abstract universalism. Abstract in two senses: 1) Universalism Type 1: The first, in the sense of utterances, a knowledge which is detached from all spatio-temporal determination and claims to be eternal. 2) Universalism Type 2: The second, in the epistemic sense of a subject of enunciation that is detached, emptied of body and content, and of its location within the cartography of global power from which it produces knowledge. As a result, the split of the subject from body and space allows Descartes to produce knowledge with claims to truth, universally valid for everyone on earth ... the second sense of abstract universalism, the epistemic sense of a subject of enunciation that is faceless and placeless in spatio-temporal terms, that of the ego-politics of knowledge, has persisted in our own times through the zero-point of Western science – even among those who have criticized Descartes –, and this represents one of the most pernicious legacies of Cartesianism', 89-90.

[6] The French historian Yves Person (1925-1982) was among those who, in the late 1960s and 1970s, began rehabilitating oral sources as valid historical material. See Fauvelle & Perrot, *Yves Person : Historien de l'Afrique, explorateur de l'oralité*.

[7] So-called racial superiority was indeed used as an argument to justify Europe's colonial 'civilizing mission'. Defending France's policy of colonial conquest before Parliament on 28 July 1885, for example, Jules Ferry declared: 'It must openly be stated that, indeed, the superior races have a right over the inferior races. I repeat that the superior races have a right, because they have a duty. It is their duty to civilize the inferior races.' ['Il faut dire ouvertement qu'en effet les races supérieurs ont un droit vis-à-vis des races inférieures. Je répète qu'il y a pour les races supérieurs un droit, parce qu'il y a un devoir pour elles. Elles ont le devoir de civiliser les races inférieures.']. Assemblée Nationale, 'Jules Ferry (28 juillet 1885)'.

Africa proper, as far as History goes back, has remained – for all purposes of connection with the rest of the World – shut up; … it is no historical part of the World; it has no movement or development to exhibit. Historical movements in it – that is in its northern part – belong to the Asiatic or European World … What we properly understand as Africa, is the Unhistorical, Undeveloped Spirit, still involved in the conditions of mere nature and which had to be presented here only as on the threshold of World's History.[8]

More shocking still than these 19th-century discourses, however, is their enduring vision today, as witnessed in the then French President Sarkozy's extraordinarily Hegelian *Discours de Dakar* delivered – ironically – at the Cheick Anta Diop University in 2007:[9] 'Africa's tragedy is that African man has not sufficiently entered history. The African villager, who, since time immemorial, lives with the seasons, whose life ideal is to be in harmony with nature, knows only the eternal repetition of time.'[10]

For thinkers such as Frantz Fanon, Amilcar Cabral, and Kwame Nkrumah, such delegitimization of African cultures and pasts was indeed central to the process of colonial domination. As Fanon wrote, for example: 'Colonialism is not satisfied merely with holding a people in its grip and emptying the native's brain of all form and content. By a kind of perverted logic, it turns to the past of the oppressed people, and distorts, disfigures, and destroys it.'[11] In this context, then, and in the ongoing effort to 'delink' from epistemological coloniality, filmmakers such as Teno, like the earlier liberation thinkers, position questions of history and memory at the heart of the processes of decolonial reconstruction.[12]

---

[8] Hegel, *The Philosophy of History*, 91 & 99
[9] Named, of course, after one of Africa's most eminent – and, in France, the most contested – historians.
[10] For a transcription of the complete speech in French, see 'Allocution de Nicolas Sarkozy, prononcée à l'Université de Dakar', *Le Nouvel Afrik.com*, 29 July, 2007, www.afrik.com/allocution-de-nicolas-sarkozy-prononcee-a-l-universite-de-dakar, accessed 11 July 2019. The speech was met with widespread furore, and was deconstructed by a number of African scholars. See, for example, Mbembe, 'Nicolas Sarkozy's Africa'; Gassama, *L'Afrique répond à Sarkozy : Contre le discours de Dakar*.
[11] Fanon, *The Wretched of the Earth*, 210.
[12] Walter Mignolo draws on the work of Quijano to define delinking as 'a de-colonial epistemic shift leading to other-universality, that is, to pluri-versality as a universal project', bringing 'to the foreground other epistemologies, other principles of knowledge and understanding'. Mignolo, 'Delinking', 453.

Reconstructing Archaeologies of Memory

To bear the burden of memory one must willingly journey to places long uninhabited, searching the debris of history for traces of the unforgettable, all knowledge of which has been suppressed ... Travelling, moving into the past ... [one] pieces together fragments ... For black folks, reconstructing an archaeology of memory makes return possible.

bell hooks[13]

After a first wave in the 1970s and 1980s of what Manthia Diawara fittingly called 'colonial confrontation films'[14] – that is, classic historical reconstitution fiction films, such as Ousmane Sembène's *Emitai* (1971), *Ceddo* (1977) and later *Camp de Thiaroye* (1988), or Med Hondo's *Sarraounia* (1986), which, from an African point of view, recount violent and dehumanizing episodes of colonial history hitherto erased from, or silenced, in Western historiography and restore memories of African struggle and resistance[15] – Teno's mid-1980s to early 1990s films *Hommage* and particularly *Afrique, je te plumerai* mark a shift to what I shall call decolonial history-memory films.[16] Teno's approach to the past in his works is indeed not simply – although it is that too – one of an important unearthing and restoring the 'missing chapters' of history hidden and buried by colonialism, countering what Françoise Vergès describes as the political and structural 'process of forgetting' that produces 'a *mutilated history*', and ignores 'the interactions and intersections' – a process 'that erases or ignores entire moments, and defines spaces in which time is believed to pass immutably, where tradition is thought to reign and communities live apart in isolation, their inhabitants waiting for modernity'.[17] Nor is it simply an again-important inclusion of

---

[13] hooks, *Black Looks: Race and Representation*, 172-3.

[14] Diawara, *African Cinema*, 152.

[15] While adding alternative viewpoints to, rather than challenging, dominant historiography, the militancy of such works at the time, their political weight, should not be underestimated, as can be measured from these films' reception, notably in France. *Emitai* was not distributed in France for six years, and, under pressure from the French, was banned in a number of Francophone African countries; President Senghor, known for his proximity to France, banned *Ceddo* in Senegal; *Camp de Thiaroye* was given a single screening in Paris ten years after its release in 1998, and only then distributed by Med Hondo; and *Sarraounia* was only given very limited distribution in France after being slated by the critics for being exaggeratedly anti-French.

[16] Other such works include David Achkar's *Allah Tantou* (1991) and Raoul Peck's *Lumumba, la mort d'un prophète* (1990).

[17] Vergès, *Le ventre des femmes*, 13, 15, 15-16 ['un processus de l'oubli' / 'une *histoire mutilée*' / 'des interactions et des croisements' / 'qui efface ou ignore des moments entiers et dessine des espaces où le temps semble s'écouler de manière immutable, où régnerait la tradition et vivraient des communautés refermées sur elles-mêmes et dont les habitants seraient en attente de la modernité'].

hitherto excluded groups and perspectives in order to rewrite history 'from below' – a retelling that challenges the hegemony of the narratives of the victorious and dominant, as described by historian Dipesh Chakrabarty,[18] although again, it is that too. More than a redressing of an absence, an invisibilization, it is the need, to cite Françoise Vergès, 'to find the words' – the images, I would add here – 'that could bring back to life that which had been condemned to inexistence, worlds that had been ejected from humanity'.[19] Both 'an act of resistance' to the 'violently imposed narratives of colonization', in the words of Bettina Escauriza, and a creative act, for, 'to remember is not simply an individual, internal process, but a way for people to return to a place of being, of having been, and to become again'[20], Teno's approach is perhaps above all a challenge to the very epistemes, methodology and structures of history as a Western discipline, recognizing this as 'only one among other ways of remembering the past', to cite Chakrabarty again.[21] Embracing subjectivity and memory and taking filmic inspiration from orature, its structures and modes of transmitting history and collective memory, Teno indeed recreates and questions the past conducted from a viewpoint situated firmly in the present and with an eye to the future, blending and oscillating between different temporalities and adopting non-linear chronologies.[22]

---

[18] In his key work *Provincializing Europe*, Dipesh Chakrabarty indeed writes: 'As the writing of history has increasingly become entangled with the so-called "politics and production of identity" ... the question has arisen in all democracies of whether to include in the history of the nation histories of previously excluded groups. In the 1960s, this list usually contained names of subaltern social groups and classes, such as, former slaves, working classes, convicts, and women. This mode of writing history came to be known in the seventies as history from below. Under pressure from growing demands for democratizing further the discipline of history, this list was expanded in the seventies and eighties to include the so-called ethnic groups, the indigenous peoples, children and the old, and gays, lesbians, and other minorities. The expression "minority histories" has come to refer to all those pasts on whose behalf democratically minded historians have fought the exclusions and omissions of mainstream narratives of the nation. Official or officially blessed accounts of the nation's past have been challenged in many countries by the champions of minority histories. Postmodern critiques of "grand narratives" have been used to question single narratives of the nation. Minority histories, one may say, in part express the struggle for inclusion and representation that are characteristic of liberal and representative democracies', 97.

[19] Vergès, *Un féminisme décolonial*, 126 ['il fallait ... trouver les mots qui redonneraient vie à ce qui avait été condamné à l'inexistence, des mondes qui avaient été jetés hors humanité'].

[20] Escauriza, 'That which will become the earth: anarcho-indigenous speculative geographies', 92.

[21] Chakrabarty, *Provincializing Europe*, 106.

[22] Interestingly, a number of film works in the 1990s saw the (re)emergence and/or inclusion in their diegeses of the griot figure, either as a narrator who draws contemporary lessons from the past, or, more obliquely, in certain filmmakers' identification with the griot's role in linking past, present and future. At the start of Adama Drabo's fiction *Taafe*

As already discussed, in *Afrique, je te plumerai* Teno proposes a reading of Cameroonian history from his point of view as a native. It has already been demonstrated that by thus situating his position of enunciation, Teno effectively points, in relief, to official History's failure to address or state where it is speaking from, and rejects its omniscient position of authority, its single narrative and its claims to rational impartiality. Moreover, if the filmmaker turns to his country's past, it is above all to better understand the political violence that flared up in Cameroon as he started shooting in 1991 and the general climate of repression and cultural alienation. In the process, through colonial archive footage that I shall come back to, and through interviews with Cameroonian historians, trade unionists and the families of the assassinated Union of the Peoples of Cameroon (UPC) leaders, Teno gives an alternative reading to both the official French and Cameroonian state's versions. This again throws into relief, and repairs, the absences and damaging falsehoods, namely the then rarely recounted colonial practices of violent repression, forced labour, predation of natural resources, suppression of local cultures (the example of the little-known Sho-mon alphabet and schools developed by the Sultan Njoya circa 1895 and later banned by the French colonial authorities), the repression of Cameroon's nascent trade union movement, the repression of the UPC, the country's leading independence, and later opposition, party, first by the French, then under autocratic Presidents Ahijo and Biya. In the process, the film insists too on instances of both Cameroonian collaboration and resistance.[23] Identifying writers as the

---

Fanga (Mali, 1997), for example, the griot narrator character tells both the audience gathered in the Bamako compound, and by extension the spectator: 'My duty is to capture the past to prepare the present and the future.' This echoes Senegalese filmmaker Djibril Diop Mambéty's earlier cited comment: 'griot ... is the word for what I do and the role the filmmaker has in society ... the griot is a messenger of one's time, a visionary and the creator of the future' (in Givanni, 'African Conversations: Interview with Djibril Diop Mambety', 31-2).

[23] Scholars including Françoise Vergès, Simon Gikandi, Nadia Yala Kisukidi and Achille Mbembe all point to the imbrications and joint – although necessarily asymmetric – roles played by both Europeans and Africans in establishing colonial power structures, thereby deconstructing the binary dualism of dominant Europeans versus passive and victimized Africans. In *Le ventre des femmes*, Vergès writes, for instance, that: 'Colonial and postcolonial powers are always exerted with the accord and backing of part of the colonized society', that citizens 'are never passive actors, whether they back coloniality or fight it'. Vergès calls for further reflection on 'how active or passive consent to policies of dependency is obtained', often through 'a policy of fragmentation and hegemony' which causes 'the oppressed to adopt and defend the very condition that oppresses them' ['Le pouvoir colonial et postcolonial s'exerce toujours avec l'accord et le soutien d'une partie de la société colonisée. ... Les citoyens ... ne sont jamais des acteurs passifs, qu'ils soutiennent la colonialité ou qu'ils la combattent', (14) / 'comment le consentement actif ou passif à des politiques de dépendances s'obtient' (14) / '[une] politique de fragmentation et d'hégémonie [qui fait] adopter et défendre par les opprimés la condition même qui les opprime' (15)].

witnesses of their times – a role also attributed to griots – Teno rhizomatically weaves what turns out to be a completely staged, fictionalized and at times tongue-in-cheek journalistic investigation of the French-dominated contemporary Cameroonian publishing sector into an unchronological analysis of Cameroonian history from the colonial era to present. While characteristic of oral transmission, the non-linearity here is completely at odds with the conventions of Western historiography. This reference to orature's modes of transmission of the past are all the clearer, of course, in the third strand of this weave: namely the black-and-white fictionalized reconstructions of Teno's own childhood memories, which themselves introduce the subjective alongside official, depersonalized history. Here too, recounting his grandfather's allegorical *alouette* (skylark) tale, told to explain the process of colonization and decolonization to his grandson, restores a different mode of narrativization of the past, while also retrospectively giving meaning to the film's title and to Teno's ironic singing of the French nursery rhyme *Alouette, gentille alouette*, the melody of which twangs repeatedly throughout the film.

In the 2000s, Teno has twice returned to history and memory in *Le Malentendu colonial* (2004) and *Une Feuille dans le vent* (2013). Wishing to return to and further develop his exploration of the question of colonialism and the on-going coloniality of North-South relations first broached in *Afrique, je te plumerai*, yet struggling to find funding for this in France where he was repeatedly told that colonialism was over, a finished chapter of history, a page that it was time to turn,[24] Teno responded to an invitation from the German television channel ZDF to make a film to mark the centenary of the Herero genocide perpetrated by the Germans in German South West Africa (Namibia) in 1904.[25] Left frustrated too by *Afrique, je te plumerai*'s often negative reception in France, which, in focusing critique on the film's unorthodox, experimental form, tended to evacuate any real discussion of the colonial history that the film radically exposed at the time, Teno decided this time to let the content take precedent over the form, favouring a simpler, linear narrative and a clearly pedagogical approach that would be 'unattackable'.

Starting in Wuppertal, Germany, the home of the Rhenish Mission Society, the film transitions rapidly to Wuppertal, South Africa, where the Reformed and Lutheran missionaries set up their first station in 1829. The film soon returns again to Germany in a toing-and-froing that suggests an imbrication

---

[24] This is a commonly held opinion in French political circles, as exemplified by President Emmanuel Macron's tweet on 4 July 2018 during a visit to Lagos: '60% of the Nigerian population is aged under 25. That's 60% of the population which, like me, did not witness colonization. We are the new generation. We are going to dispel prejudice by rebuilding a new future through culture.'

[25] Teno responding to my questions about the genesis of the film, August 2017.

of the spaces, enhanced, as Teno's voice-over informs us, by the fact that the mission station was thus named after the missionaries' hometown river, the Wupper, a hundred years before two fusing towns in Germany took the name of Wuppertal: 'Pour une fois la colonie précède la metropole. L'Afrique devance l'Europe' ('For once, the colony preceded the metropole. Africa was ahead of Europe'). Yet it also symbolizes the essential link between Africa and Europe that the missionaries embodied. The film indeed unfolds to shed light on the complex role that the European missionaries played in Africa, unveiling the contradictions and hypocrisies of their relationship with the colonizing powers. Christian evangelization is thus shown in the film to be a forerunner of European colonialism in Africa, and an ideological model for the on-going coloniality of the asymmetrical relations between North and South today.

Invited by the current missionaries to dig into their archives, and surprised by their call on the German government to recognize and apologize for the country's at the time little-known implication in colonial crimes, Teno interviews present-day missionaries who lucidly unveil the contradictions, short-sightedness and Eurocentric supremacy of the mission mentality, its prejudices about those they sought to evangelize, their actions and the connections between the missionary and colonial projects. Characteristically, one thread of this complex narrative leads unexpectedly to another as, in a digression while questioning a German ethnographer about the Wuppertal missionaries, Teno learns that Joseph Merrick, a freed slave, had already being working as a missionary in Bimbia on the Cameroonian coast two years before the first German missionaries arrived in Cameroon. The film follows this unexpected tack, journeying to Cameroon on Merrick's trail, in the process restoring the memory and historical trace of this erased figure, and throwing new light on his work to adapt his religious message to the local community, turning the Gospel from a tool for 'subjugation and servitude' to one of liberation – an approach that is later echoed at the end of the film when Teno interviews Bishop Kameta of the Namibian Lutheran Church. But first returning again to Germany, the film traces how the head of the Rhenish Mission Society became an ardent advocate of German colonization in the early 1870s and how missionaries – many of whom had learned the local languages to better spread the Gospel – acted as translators when Europeans negotiated land concessions with African rulers to legitimate their territorial claims when dividing up the continent at the Berlin Conference in 1884-85 – the 'colonial misunderstanding', as historian Paulin Oloukpona-Yinnon explains in the film, being the Europeans and Africans' radically divergent concepts of land ownership.

Following the history chronologically, the Berlin episodes of the film lead logically back to Namibia, and to accounts of the Herero people's resistance to the Germans right from 1885, and the events leading up to 1904, which are

Photo 11 *Le Malentendu colonial*. Bishop Kameta of the Namibian Lutheran Church describing its liberation theology and the instrumental role it played in the anti-Apartheid struggle.

pieced together through interviews with historians and illustrated with archive photos and old illustrations. The film thus again uncovers the little-recorded history of this war, described by historian Joachim Zeller as 'a void, a black hole in Germany's collective memory' – the war which, we learn, culminated in the German authorities' order to exterminate the Herero men, women and children. They were thus shot on site, driven into the desert and left to die, or rounded up in concentration camps that prefigured the Nazi concentration camps. Revealing, too, that one leading Rhenish missionary in German South West Africa, Heinrich Vedder, was a National Socialist in 1933, the film clearly traces the roots of the Holocaust back to the African colonial context, countering the long-held acceptation that the Holocaust was an isolated moment in the history of Europe; a connection that Aimé Césaire (*Discourse on Colonialism*, 1950) and Hannah Arendt (*The Origins of Totalitarianism*, 1951) both highlighted, both referring to the 'boomerang effect' of colonization.[26] The film also reveals how the racial legislation that the Germans introduced in Namibia was

---

[26] Césaire wrote that: 'no one colonizes innocently, that no one colonizes with impunity either; that a nation which colonizes, that a civilization which justifies colonization – and therefore force – is already a sick civilization, a civilization that is morally diseased, that irresistibly, progressing from one consequence to another, one repudiation to another, calls for its Hitler, I mean its punishment', *Discourse on Colonialism*, 33.

precursory to South Africa's racial legislation and apartheid regime, Heinrich Vedder also having become a National Party senator in South Africa in 1951.

Despite its more classically chronological narrative mode and its more typical repairing of 'mutilated history' – which was still clearly necessary at the time given the then lack of knowledge/acknowledgement of the content depicted – Teno's weaving together here of such a complex and incredibly dense mass of material, from the Rhenish Mission Society's photographic archives to the testimonies of both African and German church people and historians, taking us from Germany, to Cameroon, to Namibia, adopted what was still then in Europe a relatively new connected, global, transversal reading of the past that moves away from national histories to connect localities, phenomena and temporalities.[27] Toing-and-froing from the past to the present too, the film also points to the lasting consequences of this history, calling on European countries to critically examine their colonial past, rather than burying themselves in charity and humanitarian work framed by Europeans from the missionary days to the present as an 'altruistic gift', which simply maintains a white saviour 'colonial logic' in a new form.

Remembering, finally, is also at the heart of *Une Feuille dans le vent*, a poignant testimony to both the late UPC leader and independence hero Ernest Ouandié, executed by the Cameroonian authorities in 1971 for his on-going role in the independence struggle and war, and the daughter he never knew, Ernestine Ouandié. Here, private and public history intertwine as Ernestine's personal story is set against, and resonates with, the wider fate and history of Cameroon already explored by Teno in previous works. But also – or rather – here, the filmmaker foregrounds what the rationalist approach to history has largely evacuated: namely the devastating psychological impact that historical events can leave in their wake, impacting individuals and their trajectories, and a country's collective psyche.[28]

In an incredibly lucid account delivered spontaneously, with no artifice or pathos to the camera, and with a composure and clarity that belie the harshness and pain of her story, Ernestine Ouandié relates her childhood growing up in Ghana in her father's absence, resented and mentally and physically abused

---

[27] Earlier in the United States, various overlapping schools of 'world', 'global' or 'connected' history – advocated, for example, by historian Sanjay Subrahmanyam – truly took off in the 2000s. Their approaches to historiography consider the past through the pluri-focal, non-Eurocentric, decentred lens of the circulations, interactions, exchanges and connections between different geographic/cultural areas. Valorizing non-European sources and perspectives, they foreground relationality, rather than compartmented national histories.

[28] For a further fascinating reflection on history and subjectivity, see the chapter 'L'histoire, une architecture intérieure' in Seloua Luste Boulbina's *Afrique et ses fantômes*, 37-65.

by her aunt, then her mother, who blamed her for her father's abandonment.[29] Teno's unobtrusive camera very gently and progressively frames Ernestine more closely as the film progresses (yet never actually in close-up), maintaining a respectful distance that avoids sensationalism. Shot predominantly from low-angles that further magnify this remarkable woman, her demeanour and composure, the minimalism of the filming set-up, the un-stagedness of the setting, the un-aestheticized banality of the veranda wall backdrop, all focus our undivided attention on Ernestine's raw and entirely captivating situated testimony, the content taking precedent over any formalism. Ernestine speaks, and Teno allows her words to invade the screen as he takes an entirely secondary place. Her words command that we listen, and we listen long: delivered in unbroken passages that the montage at times allows to run for up to ten minutes, this unconventional length and the immediacy of the direct-camera address are at times almost unbearable, as we are literally put face-to-face with Ernestine's pain. Any pretence to objectivity or rationalism is evacuated as emotion and the personal are fully embraced. Yet, as suggested by the off-screen ambient quotidian sounds that from time to time invade the diegesis as Ernestine talks, this extraordinary account is nonetheless totally inscribed in Cameroon's ordinary daily life. Mixing her direct testimony with the rare archive images of the UPC, the political repression of the period in Cameroon, Ouandié and his arrest – oscillating, then, between past and present – and filling the blanks with stark black-and-white ink illustrations that re-imagine the scenes that have no visual archives, Teno weaves together both Ernest and Ernestine's stories, his own voice only intervening sporadically to contextualize and occasionally to ponder the lessons that might be drawn.

Ernestine, who, we learn from one of Teno's first voice-overs in the film, took her own life in 2009, describes the pain and frustration of the continuing silence that in Cameroon still surrounds the fate of her father and his comrades

---

[29] During our joint presentation at the *Digital Media and New Cinema from the Global South* Symposium, (Michigan State University/University Michigan Ann Arbor, 3-5 April 2014), Teno recounted how filming Ernestine's testimony was unplanned. He had gone to meet Ernestine at her home in 2004 to carry out research for a possible film on her father when Ernestine spontaneously began to deliver her own account. Realizing the intensity and importance of her story, Teno went to fetch a camera and, with her agreement, began what ended up being a three-hour impromptu recording on the veranda, without a tripod, the camera balanced on his knees. Master of both her own image and her words, it was for the first time in Teno's career that the filmed subject commanded the filmmaker, forcing his hand, as he described it. Initially uncertain what to do with this powerful and painful testimony, it was only when Teno learned of Ernestine's death five years later that he returned to the rushes and, haunted by her words that retrospectively took on new meaning, decided to make a film in her honour, against the backdrop of Ernest Ouandié's story, bringing 'the two stories parallel with one another', both to write this (hi)story and, by addressing it, to break the cycle of trauma.

Photo 12 *Une Feuille dans le vent*. Ernestine Ouandié delivers her powerfully raw testimony, the mise-en-scène's lack of formalism and the unembellished setting leaving the spectator literally face to face with her words.

– their 'second death' as she describes it. Lamenting the dearth of books on this chapter of Cameroonian history, she evokes how this breakdown in transmission affects not only her and her family – she recounts being unable to properly answer her son's question on seeing the only photo she has of Ernest Ouandié of why his grandfather was handcuffed – but also the rest of the population, left not knowing 'where we belong'. The film not only recounts a chapter of the past, then, it addresses the importance of historical transmission. Calling for the country, as does the film, to at last address its painful, unspoken past, Ernestine states emphatically: 'Silence over all this will bring us nowhere. It is time we break the chain, that look back before we could see forward. When history is written, the roaming souls will come to rest.'

These restless 'roaming souls' echo with Ernestine's final question in the film concerning the impossibility of finding peace and rooting without knowing one's past: 'How do you expect a leaf without a stalk to live?' Spoken too off-screen over shots of leaves as the film opens, we this time, at the end of the film's journey, understand the relevance of these opening words. A loop is looped, again belying the linearity of historicity. As Ernestine continues, likening herself to that leaf, we, with the foreknowledge of her suicide given earlier in the film by Teno's voice-over, also realize that she is presciently describing her own later fate: 'the leaf will die out of starvation. It will fall, it will dry off, and the wind will do what with it? Blow it left, right, up and down, and it will disappear, one day'.

The 'roaming souls' that Ernestine refers to, the leaf in the wind (the film's English title), evoke the transgenerational transmission of trauma; they are, in Alice Cherki's words, 'the subjective impacts of politics and history on the subconscious dimension of what is passed from one generation to the next', raising the issue, as does the film, of whether people 'inherit this violence, or rather its non-elaboration?'[30] In *Une Feuille dans le vent*, this trauma is indeed both personal/familial, and collective: that of Cameroon and the trauma of its unacknowledged war of independence, mass killings and assassination of the UPC leaders, but also that of the continent and its still unaddressed and undigested history of colonization. Interestingly, ghostly 'roaming souls' traverse and haunt many of Teno's films – they are Stuart Hall's spectres of the past that hide in the present – from the famous chilling footage of Patrice Lumumba's arrest in both *Afrique, je te plumerai* and *Clando*,[31] to the photos of the assassinated Cameroonian independence heroes Ruben Um Nyobè, Félix Moumié and Ernest Ouandié in *Afrique, je te plumerai* and, in *Une Feuille dans le vent*, to images of Kwame Nkrumah's headless statue, destroyed when Nkrumah was ousted by a coup in 1966. If ghosts are the departed, the absent, these ghostly figures also symbolize the absences of official historiographies, both European and African, and what Mbembe calls these figures' 'exile into the night of the unnamed'.[32] Often refused a sepulchre in their own countries, as seen in the

---

[30] Cherki, 'Fanon au temps présent. L'assignation au regard', 152. Psychiatrist, psychoanalyst and biographer of Frantz Fanon, Alice Cherki was Fanon's student at the Blida-Joinville psychiatric hospital in Algeria from 1955-1956, then one of his assistants at the Charles Nicolle hospital psychiatric day centre in Tunis. Both participated in the Algerian National Liberation Front. ['les incidences subjectives du politique et de l'Histoire sur la dimension inconscient de ce qui se passe d'une génération à l'autre' / 'Héritent-ils de ces violences ou plutôt de leur non-élaboration ?'].

[31] Assassinated in 1961, Patrice Lumumba, the first Prime Minister of Congo, is a constant figure and reference in African cinema. Souleymane Cissé recounts that it was seeing the newsreels of Lumumba's arrest that inspired him to make films; the ghost of Lumumba haunts the streets of Brussels in Balufu Bakupa Kanyinda's *Juju Factory* (2007), which, like Raoul Peck's *Lumumba, la mort d'un prophète* (1990), is also laced with extracts of Lumumba's speeches; and the arrest images and extracts of Lumumba's speeches also pepper Alain Gomis' *L'Afrance* (2001).

[32] Mbembe, speaking of Um Nyobè, whom he describes as a leading martyr of African independence. See Paul Yange, 'Achille Mbembe'. ['exilé dans la nuit de l'innommé'].

testimony of Félix Moumié's elderly father in *Afrique, je te plumerai*, who dreams only of bringing his assassinated son's body back to rest in Cameroon, these ghostly figures, it would seem, need injustice to be addressed/redressed to find rest; they need the records set straight, for, as Salman Rushdie writes in *The Satanic Verses*: 'What's a ghost? Unfinished business, is what.'[33] Identifying the ghost to be 'the colonial spectre', too, Olivier J. Tchouaffe insists on the importance, for Cameroonians, to embrace this spectre 'as part of the national psyche', for, 'Running away from the ghost is running away from oneself, from a promise, from a response, from taking responsibility for tomorrow.'[34] This is the history then, the ghostly trace, that Teno seeks to face, not just to recount, but to make peace with it, in a vital stage of making sense of and decolonizing history.

Decolonizing the archive

The image wanders ghostlike through the present.
Siegfried Kracauer[35]

Finally, I would like to focus on Jean-Marie Teno's repeated use of historical colonial archives in his films in ways that not only pose questions of the archives themselves, of their authority, revealing their ideological constructions, but which also work as a decolonizing gesture. From his very first film, *Hommage* to his recent *Une Feuille dans le vent*, and of course including their most extensive use in *Afrique, je te plumerai*, Teno has incorporated black-and-white colonial archive footage as a way to address the asymmetry of power and representations of Africans in official Western historiography. Archives themselves are, of course, intrinsically related to notions of power, authority and legitimacy. As Jacques Derrida points out in *Archive Fever*, the word 'archive' is derived from the Greek *arkheion*, the house or residence of the commanding magistrates, or *archons*. On account of their publicly recognized authority, it was in their homes that official legal documents were filed, giving the *archons* the power both to safeguard and to interpret them. Being put in this place marked these documents' passage from private to public; or, in other words, their institutionalization. As Derrida notes: 'There is no political power without control of the archive … Effective democratization can always be measured by this essential criterion: the participation in and the access to the archive, its constitution, and

---

[33] Rushdie, *The Satanic Verses*, 129.
[34] Tchouaffe, 'Colonial Visual Archives and the Anti-Documentary Perspective in Africa', 86.
[35] Kracauer, 'Photography', 430.

its interpretation.'[36] Describing in Part II how, as 'just a young African guy who nobody knew or cared about, a nobody', he completely officiously first gained access to the French army archive footage that he uses, Teno's arrogation of the privilege and the authority to interpret the colonial archive was thus itself a veritable act of insurgency. Furthermore, in his films, he does not just simply incorporate this archive material to contextualize, illustrate, or to historicize a past event or period as is usually the case in documentary practice; the material itself is deconstructed as Teno works to challenge its propaganda message and disinformation. In so doing, this material is reworked into new writings and readings of that past, 'retrieving and displaying lost memories, but also adding new ones', as Olivier J. Tchouaffe writes, thereby bringing forth 'the tension between knowledge and memory'.[37]

Revisiting these archive images of Africans filmed by the European colonial powers with the intention of conveying a specific discourse and serving to construct a body of categorizing knowledge of the continent that justified colonial subjugation – what Mudimbe famously called 'the colonial library'[38] – Teno's 'native' readings work against the grain to operate a political *detournement*.[39] Taking and subverting these images to make them say something radically different to their original message, he creates a counter-discourse that re-situates Africans at the heart of the very (hi)stories that negated, objectified, and reduced them to silence. By displacing these images from their original context, by subverting their intent, by juxtaposing these images of the past with contemporary images of Cameroon, Teno introduces a critical distance that unveils the ideological constructions at play in them. Countering their abstract omniscience, too, contesting, as the filmmaker comments, 'the very notion of this "voice of God" which claimed to speak the truth to us Africans without us ever knowing who this voice belonged to, nor where it was speaking from',[40] Teno gives new meaning to these images. Escaping the rule, the authority, and no less the coloniality of that library, or archive, he performs, then, what Stuart Hall describes as 'an engagement, *an interruption*', which seeks 'to enter critically into existing configurations to re-open the closed structures into which they have ossified'.[41]

---

[36] Derrida, *Archive Fever*, 4.
[37] Tchouaffe, 'Colonial Visual Archives', 85.
[38] See Mudimbe, *The Invention of Africa*.
[39] I borrow Michael Witt's use of the term to describe Jean-Luc Godard and the Dziga Vertov group's political cinema of the 1970s and their reworking and rewiring of mainstream television and film images to make them say things they were not originally destined to, thereby unveiling their reproduction of dominant ideology. Introducing the BFI Southbank Centre's Jean-Luc Godard season, London, 27 February 2016.
[40] See Part II of this volume, 'In Conversation'.
[41] Hall, 'Constituting an Archive', 92, original emphasis. Here, Hall draws on and reworks a

Produced in the past, these images are re-read in the light of the present, in the desire to reconfigure the future. This, as Fabiana De Souza writes, injects 'an interpretive political dimension to history', which represents both a 'transgression' on the part of those speaking, thinking, creating from and via the margins, the border, and 'an emancipatory gesture'.[42] This brings to mind bell hooks' positioning of marginality as 'a site of radical possibility, a space of resistance', one of refusal, of power, that 'offers the possibility of radical perspectives from which to see and create, to imagine alternative, new worlds'.[43]

At two moments in *Afrique, je te plumerai*, then, Teno edits together these archive images that he obtained almost fortuitously from the French Army's Communications and Audiovisual Production Unit (the ECPA), and newsreel footage produced by the Ministry of the Colonies' Press and Information Service for what, as already seen, were openly described at the time as propaganda purposes: in other words, to support and promote the colonial enterprise through the construction of the French national myth of its so-called 'civilizing mission', insisting on the loyalty, devotion and gratitude of the 'contented' colonial subjects, erasing any notion of challenge or revolt, of colonial violence, and, of course, silencing any form of African voice or viewpoint.

On the first occasion that Teno incorporates these images, fourteen minutes into the film, the relatively short 1-minute 20-second sequence and its voice-over narration of the European 'Scramble for Africa' and the German conquest, then loss, of Cameroon after the First World War, serve typically to historicize the period. Yet already, their booming original voice-of-God commentaries jar anachronistically with the film's preceding sequences of political unrest, violent repression and censorship in contemporary Cameroon, the juxtaposition revealing the irony of the voice's evocation of France's 'pacification' mission, its teaching the Cameroonians the notions of 'discipline', and announcing the beginning of a 'French creation'. The second approximately 12.5-minute archive

---

citation already mentioned earlier in his text from *The Material World: Some Theories of Language and Its Limits* by David Silverman and Brian Torode (London: Routledge, 1980), 5.

[42] De Souza, 'Réactualiser l'archive, réécrire l'histoire des pratiques artistiques décoloniales', *Revue Asylon(s)* 15, February 2018, www.reseau-terra.eu/article1406.html, accessed 9 February 2018 ['une dimension politique interprétative de l'Histoire' / 'un geste émancipateur']. De Souza's reference to the border draws on Gloria Anzaldúa's concept of 'borderlands' and 'border culture', a place 'in a constant state of transition' inhabited by the 'prohibited and the forbidden … *Los atravesados* … those who cross over, pass over, or go through the confines of the 'normal' (see Anzaldúa, *Borderlands/La Frontera: The New Mestiza*, 25). Anzaldua's concept was later further developed notably by Walter Mignolo in his writing on 'border thinking', at the border of, or outside, the colonial matrix of power, and drawing on non-imperialistic knowledges, epistemologies and languages (see Mignolo, 'Geopolitics of Sensing and Knowing. On (De)Coloniality, Border Thinking, and Epistemic Disobedience').

[43] hooks, 'Marginality as a Site of Resistance', 341, 343.

sequence comes much later, over half-way through the film. Divided into smaller segments, Teno deploys a variety of deconstruction techniques. At moments, his montage juxtaposes the archive images with contemporary footage that counters and contradicts what the archives recount. Archive images of children being schooled, the voice-over boasting France's 'civilizing'/educational mission, follow on directly from the contemporary sequence describing the French colonizer's closing of the Sultan Njoya's schools.

Elsewhere, archive images of Cameroonian workers loading Europe-bound ships with export produce, boasting the construction of Douala's modern port, and scenes showing the distribution of 'prizes' (storm lamps, pots, clothing) for good harvests are intercut with the present-day interview of 90-year-old Nji Fifen, who describes the terrible forced labour conditions and exploitation he experienced at the time. His testimony, and those of historian Jean-Pierre Essomba and trade unionist Leopold Moume-Etia, intersperse with and contradict the previous or following archive images. Moreover, Essomba and Moume-Etia's testimonies are initially added in voice-over to the archive images, replacing the original commentaries so that their descriptions of colonial violence work in stark counterpoint to the original discourse. Here, too, Teno also replaces the archives' original histrionic Western music with drumming, both further Africanizing the archives and literally drumming home with each repeated beat the arduous repetitious manual gestures of the labourers. Finally, Teno replaces the original un-situated archive voice with his own situated first-person commentary, at times ironically mimicking the tone and tenure of the original commentaries, at times impassionedly denouncing the conditions and treatment of Africans from the days of the slave trade to the postcolonial present. The music is cut too, then finally replaced with amplified sound effects that create a sinister, oppressive ambiance that most evocatively reframes and gives other interpretations to these same visual images. By contesting, then cutting the archives' omniscient voice of authority and thus their hegemony, by stopping them from repeating their ideology and distortions, Teno 'de-propagandizes' the archives, to borrow Samia Henni's expression.[44] The official French archives of the past are thus re-visited and re-actualized, creating new, contemporary Africanized meanings. Henceforth, the African bodies in the archives are no longer simply anonymous, subjected and silenced; they are re-signified as Teno and his interviewees assert their

---

[44] Presenting her *Discreet Violence: L'architecture et la guerre française en Algérie* exhibition at La Colonie in Paris, architect and researcher Samia Henni described her choice to include commentary-free, rough footage shot by the French authorities in colonial Algeria, rather than the edited, commented official colonial films, as an attempt to 'de-propagandize' the archive. Paris, 19 June 2018.

Photos 13a-b-c-d-e-f *Afrique, je te plumerai*. Subverting the authority of the colonial archives. Cameroonian voices gradually replace the original colonial voice-over commentary, whose discourse is also challenged by local testimonies (here of Nji Fifen), Teno's film in the process creating a new decolonial archive.

Critical Insights | (Hi)stories, Memory: Decolonial Readings of the Past

d

e

f

agency, speaking as named subjects, inscribing their voices over these images to create their own discourses and, ultimately, new archives.

In 2013, Teno revisited this same archive material again, this time weaving it into *Une Feuille dans le vent*, which, through the figure of Ernestine Ouandié, also revisits the painful, repressed history of Cameroon's war of independence, and the repression and elimination of the leading members of the independentist UPC party. This return in itself sets up an echo, a resonance with the earlier *Afrique, je te plumerai*, a resonance that is both thematic (both works addressing the still-silenced history of Cameroon's troubled independence era, albeit the second from a far more personal perspective) and stylistic, *Une Feuille dans le vent* marking a return to the formal inventiveness, mixing of media, and narrative experimentation of Teno's earlier films. In the same way that thematic and stylistic leitmotif punctuate and structure the individual films, which themselves are often marked by the circular narrative structures commonly found in oral literature, the re-used archives thus become a leitmotif too here, setting up a circularity in Teno's oeuvre as an ensemble.

Like in *Afrique, je te plumerai*, in *Une Feuille dans le vent* Teno's voice-over replaces the original archive commentaries to create a counterpoint to the images. His looping of the original voice-over commentaries to produce a cacophonous stuck record effect that derisively undermines their message and authority, or his complete cutting of the original soundtrack to replace it with unnaturally amplified or looped sound effects – such as the dull thuds of beatings and of marching feet over archive images of independence-era repression by the Cameroonian army, always seconded by anonymous white armed mercenaries – accentuate the chillingly sinister nature of these images, soliciting our emotive response, the aim clearly not being 'documentary' realism or verisimilitude. In the same archive sequence, Teno ironically juxtaposes the upbeat Cameroonian national anthem, whose original words – changed only in 1978 – themselves jar with the chirpy melody 'ô Cameroun berceau de nos ancêtres, autrefois tu vécus dans la barbarie', ('O Cameroon, birthplace of our ancestors, in the past you lived in barbarity'), so that its following line 'Comme un soleil tu commences à apparaître' ('Like a sun you start to shine'), coincides with the images of a soldier's boot stamping on the head of a prisoner, thereby producing a brutal dichotomy that creates a critical distancing effect and a glaring contrast that further accentuates the violence of the images. Moreover, the final line heard, 'Peu à peu tu sors de ta sauvagerie' ('Little by little throwing off your savageness'), not only suggests the degree of alienation of Cameroon's leaders (the images show President Ahidjo shaking hands with a number of anonymous white besuited officials), but also echoes painfully with Ernestine Ouandié's immediately preceding words describing her aunt's castigation of her as a 'bastard', 'with a father supposedly coming from a country where human flesh was eaten regularly'. Shortly afterwards in the sequence, the camera zooms in on a newspaper page so we read: 'Les colonies c'est finie' ('Colonization is over') as we hear General De Gaulle's famous 'Je vous ai compris', yet our position in the present affords us the hindsight of knowing how fallacious this statement would turn out to be. Also, by juxtaposing this with footage of Ruben Um Nyobè and the UPC members – who, as Teno's voice-over comments, 'ont refusé de courber l'échine, de baisser la tête' ('refused to yield, to bow their heads') and fought for 'une vraie indépendence économique et politique' ('true economic and political independence') – with archive images of the independence war destruction and violence, Teno points to the glaring divide between the French political discourse and the reality on the ground.

Finally, *Une Feuille dans le vent* also indirectly poses the question of what is missing from the archives: the images *en creux*, the latent images, the dearth of material that was never institutionalized, the private images of ordinary folks, of the vanquished, the subaltern, the colonized. To compensate for the lack of visual material available to filmically reconstruct both Ernestine Ouandié's family history – the meeting of her parents, her childhood life story – and Ernest Ouandié's execution – images deliberately eradicated by the Cameroonian authorities – Teno commissioned artist Kemo Samba to illustrate these passages-without-archives, the missing images. Accompanied either by Ernestine's testimony, by 1960s Ghanaian highlife music that conjures the era, by Ben's Bellinga's poignantly haunting saxophone theme music, or finally by the gunshot sounds of Ernest Ouandié's firing squad followed by the sound of a falling tree, Samba's beautifully stark black-and-white line-drawings that Teno sometimes films fixed, sometimes zooms in on or tracks over to create the impression of moving images, solicit our imaginations in a way that is ultimately perhaps all the more evocative and poignant than actual film footage.

Through their often experimental approaches, then, Teno's history-memory films thus open up and multiply readings of the past, creating new spaces for voices hitherto denied and countering official silences and un-remembering. This focus on history is never a nostalgic celebration or reification of some mythicized past to which, the work recognizes, there can be no simple return, no recovery; indeed, the past is always re-experienced via the present and 'completely mediated and transformed by memory, fantasy and desire', as Stuart Hall reminds us.[45] Teno's efforts to challenge and rectify the distortions and erasures of hegemonic Eurocentric historical accounts, to re-write African and diasporic populations back into the heart of necessarily connected local and global histories are, then, always a part of an effort to understand the

---

[45] Hall, 'New Ethnicities', 30.

Photo 14 *Une Feuille dans le vent*, imaging the execution of Ernest Ouandié. Kemo Samba's specially commissioned ink drawings both draw attention to, and compensate for, the absences of the official archive.

current complexities and future perspectives of Africa's postcolonial societies, translating the lessons of the past in terms of the present, to cite Christopher Miller.[46] Drawing on the (colonial) past, these films not only excavate hidden experiences and histories but, in a dynamic process, create other memories as they reflect on the (postcolonial) present, for a (decolonial) *devenir*, or becoming.

---

[46] See Christopher Miller, *Theories of Africans: Francophone Literature and Anthropology in Africa*, 98.

Spanning Borders in One Stride: Transnationality, Circulations and Exile[1]

La première chose que l'indigène apprend, c'est de rester à sa place, à ne pas dépasser les limites. C'est pourquoi les rêves de l'indigène sont ... des rêves d'action ... Je rêve que je saute, que je nage, que je cours ... que je franchis le fleuve d'une enjambée
Frantz Fanon[2]

It is not walking on water that is the miracle, it is walking on land
Asian Proverb[3]

A final constant, or leitmotif, that I wish to look at in Jean-Marie Teno's work is its transnationality.[4] This transpires both in his films' themes and aesthetics, and in Teno's own positionality, adding complexity to his representations and eschewing simplistic binary categorization. From *Hommage* to *Clando*, *Vacances*

---

[1] Several elements of this section are drawn and expanded from my chapter 'Crossing Lines: Frontiers, Circulations and Identity in Contemporary African and Diaspora Film', first commissioned for and published in *A Companion to African Cinema*, ed. Kenneth W. Harrow & Carmela Garritano, 444-63.

[2] *The Wretched of the Earth*, 51 ['The first thing which the native learns is to stay in his place, and not to go beyond certain limits. This is why the dreams of the native are always ... of action ... I dream I am jumping, swimming, running ... that I span a river in one stride'].

[3] Cited by filmmaker-writer-scholar Trihn T Minh-ha, speaking at the conference/retrospective of her work organized by the Collège d'études mondiales/Fondation Maison des Sciences de l'Homme, at the Fondation Gulbenkian, Paris, 8 March 2017. In a world of closing borders, Minh-ha embraced the figure of the walker and walking as a form of resistance and a creative gesture open to the world.

[4] While early theorizing of cinematic transnationality focused predominantly on issues of transnational production, distribution and screening, by the mid-2000s, as William Higbee and Song Hwee Lim point out in 'Concepts of transnational cinema: towards a critical transnationalism in film studies', scholarship turned to 'the individual and collective narratives of migration, exile and displacement that are a central component of transnational cinemas' (11). By 'transnational', I am referring not only to Teno and his works' transnational funding, production and distribution, then, but also, in keeping with Higbee and Lim, to the fact that Teno's work emerges 'from within a specifically diasporic configuration that, implicitly or explicitly, articulates the relationship between the host and home cultures, and is aware, at same time, of the interconnectedness between the local and the global within diasporic communities ... [bringing] into question the fixity of national cultural discourses' (11). As Higbee and Lim recall, 'all border-crossing activities are necessarily fraught with issues of power' (18), which requires a critical awareness of the political asymmetry and shifting identifications, and, attentiveness 'to questions of postcoloniality, politics and power' (18).

au pays, *Une Feuille dans le vent*, and *Chosen*, these works indeed explore, and are characterized by, their fluidity, circulations, and border crossings, be these geographic, aesthetic, generic, visible or invisible. Teno himself is a transnational filmmaker, of course. Having lived between the African, European and American continents since 1978, his work offers striking representations of itinerancy, migrations, circulations, frontiers, transculturality, and both de- and re-territorialization. This is indeed characteristic of much postcolonial African cinema, reflecting the transnationality of many of Africa's filmmakers, and the circulations and exilic or diasporic experiences of many of their characters.[5] These protagonists throughout the history of African cinema have indeed with striking consistency crossed, re-crossed, or their movement been hindered by national borders and their controls, or by the unspoken, invisible, yet no less real lines that compartmentalized the colonial, and later the postcolonial city, creating spaces of inclusion and exclusion, of power, control, brutality, but also interstices and liminal spaces; the 'borderlands' of Gloria Anzaldúa, or the 'third spaces' of H.K. Bhabha.[6]

Cinema too, of course, is inherently a medium of movement, of moving images, of space, of *mise en espace* (framing, shot composition). Given colonialism's violent appropriation and confiscation of Africa's territories and spaces, and given what Simon Gikandi calls the resultant, irreversible 'mutual imbrication and contamination' of Europe and Africa,[7] it is unsurprising that explorations of territories, shifting and multiple spaces and places, whether political, psychological or symbolic – 'the unstable zones and contested boundaries that conjoin and divide metropolitan cultures and colonial spaces', to cite Gikandi again[8] – are at the heart of both Teno and other filmmakers' work as a reflection of the postcolonial condition.

In Western political and cinematic landscapes that continue to convey stereotypical and often stigmatizing visions of the African presence in their midst when they do not simply invizibilize it, transnational films centre the lives and experiences of exiles, migrants and Black communities. Embodying

---

[5] Daniela Ricci's *Cinémas des diasporas noires : esthétiques de la resconstruction* indeed focuses on this theme through her detailed socio-aesthetic analysis of five contemporary diasporic films: *Rage* by Newton Aduaka (Nigeria/UK, 1999), *L'Afrance* by Alain Gomis (Senegal/France, 2001), *Juju Factory* by Balufu Bakupa-Kanyinda (RDC/Belgium/France, 2005), *Teza* by Haile Gerima (Ethiopia/Germany/USA, 2008), and *Notre étrangère* by Sarah Bouyain (Burkina Faso/France, 2010).

[6] In *The Location of Culture*, Bhabha defines the processes of hybridity that occur when cultures collide and converge not as constituted by two traceable original moments from which a third emerges, but rather as the 'third space', which gives rise to something new and unrecognizable, a liminal space in which new cultural identities are formed and reformed.

[7] Gikandi, *Maps of Englishness*, xviii, 15.

[8] Ibid., 2.

and reflecting an African/diasporic presence in the world, portraying experiences of displacement and cultural hybridity, of the tensions and fragility associated with in-betweenness, with simultaneously being 'a part of' and 'apart', with living in a dominant culture in which Black people are permanently confronted with continuing prejudices and preconceptions concerning their identity, transnational films such as Teno's help to break out of the reductive and constricting ethnic absolutism of Others' visions born out of a colonizing process which, as Fanon stated, assigned the colonized to a fixed identity and place. Questions of belonging and circulation are, of course, eminently political in a world seeing a new upsurge in unbridled expressions of xenophobia and racism, of tightening borders and building of walls; in short, a world in which not everyone is equal in their freedom of movement. It is interesting, for that matter, that movement – equated with civilization and humanity, or supposed lack thereof – has long been at the heart of European preconceptions concerning Africa since its 18th- and 19th-century racializing discourse positioned the African continent as 'immobile' and 'unconnected' from the rest of the world. Returning again to his posthumously published *Lectures on the Philosophy of History*, Hegel, for example, declared:

> Africa proper, as far as History goes back, has remained – for all purposes of connection with the rest of the World – shut up … enveloped in the dark mantle of Night …
>
> At this point we leave Africa, not to mention it again. For it has no movement or development to exhibit. (91, 99)

Strikingly, the need to challenge and redress this misconstrued vision of a historically immobile Africa remains in the 21st century – a challenge that has come notably with the relatively recent advent of connected, or global approaches to history, as described earlier. Historian Patrick Boucheron, a leading advocate of a *histoire-monde* in France, indeed recently reminded that the African continent was already part of 'a world system' that revolved around the Indian Ocean in the 15th century.[9] Achille Mbembe, too, has pointed out

---

[9] Speaking at *La Nuit des idées*, Quai d'Orsay Paris, 27 January 2016. Twentieth-century archaeological discoveries also confirm Africa's ancient commercial exchanges with China via the Silk Route as early as 500 years BCE, its religious exchanges with the Christianization of Ethiopia in the 1st century and the Islamization of sub-Saharan Africa as of the 8th century; and its cultural and intellectual exchanges, Timbuktu being a renowned international centre of Islamic scholarship in the 14th and 15th centuries, to mention but a few examples. Likewise, we also have confirmation today of African presence in Medieval Europe, prior to the trans-Atlantic slave trade. See, notably, Miranda Kaufmann's *Black Tudors: The Untold Story*, or the knowledge today that 10% of Lisbon's population was Black in the 15th century (Patrick Boucheron, *La Nuit des idées*).

that it was in fact Europe's colonizing forces that sought to restrict and control the movement that characterized Africa's predominantly open societies:

> the precolonial history of African societies was a history of people in perpetual movement throughout the continent ... The cultural history of the continent can hardly be understood outside the paradigm or itinerancy, mobility and displacement. It is this very history of mobility that colonisation once endeavoured to freeze through the modern institution of borders.[10]

In the contemporary context, emancipatory movements like Pan-Africanism, or recent calls by thinkers such as Achille Mbembe or Nadia Yala Kisukidi to do away with borders on the continent indeed seek to restore freedom of movement for Africans.[11] The recurrence of the theme of movement in transnational works such as Teno's can be understood not only as a reflection of contemporary intra- and extra-African migratory realities, then, but also as an eschewing of the fetters of an enduring colonial imagination.

Addressing the question of movement, of one's place in the world, these films also address the social and political implications of both postcolonial exilic circulations and their corollaries: permanence, attachment, belonging, 'imagined communities', (im)possible return, and home.[12] Integral to his own filmic gaze, Teno's transnationality is not simply a source of inspiration, but also affords him a pluralistic vantage point that, in Edward Said's words, 'gives rise to an awareness of simultaneous dimensions, an awareness that – to borrow a phrase from music – is *contrapuntal*.'[13] Asserting this critical distance and plurality of vision, embracing this complexity and eschewing the binary, Teno focuses on the multiplicity of experiences of characters and figures who experience migration as a rupture, a separation, an absence, a source of loneliness and suffering, or, on the contrary, as a form of freedom, adventure, and sometimes contestation, or again most frequently, as all of these in differing degrees and at different times. From his very first film *Hommage*, Teno has addressed, and embraced, the often-conflicting duality of transnationality. Through the oppositional viewpoints of his (semi)fictional returnee character, Boniface, and that of his childhood friend Dieunedort who has never left his village, Teno stages these conflicting perspectives. There where Boniface sees beauty in the poor

---

[10] Mbembe, 'Afropolitanism', 27.
[11] See, for example, the 2nd session of the *Ateliers de la Pensée* organized by Achille Mbembe and Felwine Sarr in Dakar (1-4 November 2017): Matteo Maillard, 'Ateliers de la pensée #2', *Le Monde Afrique*, 14 November 2017.
[12] I refer, of course, to Benedict Anderson's concept of the socially constructed community, imagined by those who consider themselves as belonging to it in *Imagined Communities: Reflections of the Origin and Spread of Nationalism*.
[13] Said, 'Reflections on Exile', 148.

neighbourhoods and local artisanal activities – his impeccable, lyrical French indicating his worldly-wise higher social status – Dieunedort, his French heavily accented, sees poverty and hard, poorly retributed toil. As the film progresses, however, we come to realize that the cosmopolitan versus village voices and inflections are in reality the two faces of the same coin, the fictional characters' dialogue allowing Teno, himself a returnee (first from the city to the village, then from Europe to Cameroon), to express his own duality and contrasting/conflicting insider-outsider perspective and vantage point, a theme that he has later returned to in several films (*Vacances au pays*; *Chosen*).

Like Teno himself, whose own belongings are multiple, or in the words of Stuart Hall, belonging 'at one and the same time to several homes (and to no particular 'home')',[14] the filmmaker's cinematic aesthetics also cross genre boundaries and resist easy categorization. Their frequently fragmented portrayal of itinerancy and hybridity brings to mind Teshome Gabriel's concept of a 'nomadic cinema'.[15] And, as is the case for the nomad wandering from place to place, Séverine Kodjo-Grandville reminds us:

> To wander, to stray is not necessarily to go astray or off-track. It is also the possibility of traversing different realities, of inhabiting them, of accepting the unforeseeable and the not-yet, precisely because one refuses to walk an already traced path and to be confined to it.[16]

Exploring circulations, Teno's films also explore their corollary: rooting. Several works, notably *Vacances au pays*, *Une Feuille dans le vent*, and *Chosen*, indeed examine filiations and family histories, often reconstructing genealogies. Rooted in personal, biographical and autobiographical experiences, travelling backwards and forwards in time, they incarnate a range of journeys, departures and returns filmed with few ellipses, in cars, on trains, on foot. These, like the real and symbolic journeys in oral tales, are always a quest for the self too, for complex and fluid identities that eschew assignations and claim a shifting, polymorphous African presence in the world. At the same time concrete, reflexive and symbolic, they are as much about 'becoming' as they are 'returning'.

Vacances au pays, to take one example, begins with Jean-Marie Teno's return to Yaoundé, thirty-three years after attending school there. After visiting his now

---

[14] Hall, 'The Question of Cultural Identity', 308
[15] See Teshome Gabriel, 'Thoughts on Nomadic Aesthetics and Black Independent Cinema: Traces of a Journey'.
[16] Kodjo-Grandvaux, Séverine. 'Effets de miroir', 70 ['Errer, ce n'est pas nécessairement se tromper et divaguer. C'est aussi la possibilité de traverser des réalités différentes, de les habiter, d'accepter l'imprévisible et le non-encore, parce que justement l'on refuse de marcher sur un chemin tracé d'avance et d'y être entravé'].

abandoned and derelict Lycée General Leclerc, once Cameroon's most prestigious secondary school, Teno retraces the route back to his old neighbourhood, then embarks on the trip back to his grandparents' village, Bandjoun, which he used to visit once a year as a child. Given the failed promises of an exogenous, imposed modernity that he points to in the city, the filmmaker announces that this is a journey to see what has become of his home village, once the symbol of 'l'archaïsme que nous devions rejeter pour espérer un jour devenir modernes' ('the archaism we had to reject if we hoped to become modern one day'). Teno thus embarks us on this road trip back, the journey home mediated through his eyes. The trip becomes ours too, then, as the camera, filming from inside a moving car for long sequences of the journey, sutures the spectator into the vehicle.

On the way, the camera captures day-to-day scenes that one by one fall into place like a puzzle as the journey advances. Collectively, and juxtaposed with Teno's incisive voice-over comments, questions and ironic remarks, they paint a picture of the complexities, contradictions, and absurdities of contemporary Cameroonian life. During the long sequences of the actual road trip, the voice-over also weaves personal childhood recollections into the present-day footage. The film thus also becomes a journey into memory, a kind of *Notebook of a Return to the Native Land*, to cite Césaire. Returning, Teno is an 'insider-outsider', both intimately connected to his subject matter, a member of the community that he films with such attention, yet at the same time with the critical distance of all those who have gone afar and continued to grow elsewhere. His experience in the film brings to mind Assia Djebar's description of writing about Algeria from exile, of her 'proche éloignement' ('near distance'), of 'roaming in a territory where past and present respond to one another'.[17] In making this 'trip to the country', to cite the English title of the film, Teno indeed (re)connects past and present, urban and rural spaces, hopes and realities, illusions and disillusions, seeking, as he often does in his films, to make a return that will shed new light in order to help to analyse and better understand the country's present predicament.[18] The journey is a quest for understanding, then; it is, again, a becoming.

The film's journey also allows Teno to address the questions of filiation and transmission as it examines the rupture in the flow of endogenous knowledge systems and inter-generational transmission resulting from the colonial

---

[17] Djebar, *Idiome de l'exil et langue de l'irréductibilité* ['Déambuler dans un territoire où passé et présent se répondent'].

[18] This brings to mind the words of the character Sobgui in Teno's fiction feature *Clando*, which also focuses on exiles and returns: 'If you reach the point where you don't know where to go anymore, retrace your steps and start again. Come back to the source and grow.'

encounter, its imposition of Western modernity, and its acculturation. The Western-style education that Teno received in Yaoundé in the 1960s and 1970s (bringing us back full circle to the opening sequence of the Lycée General Leclerc) taught him and his generation, he tells us, to scorn their elders and their 'archaic' values. Yet, he asks: 'Le respect des aînés est une des valeurs fondamentales de notre culture ... Comment se respecter en méprisant ses grands-parents?' ('The respect of our elders is one of our fundamental values ... Can you respect yourself if you despise your grandparents?'). Visiting a village elder on arrival, the camera down low at the sitting man's level, the latter directly addresses Teno/the camera to insist on the importance of filiation: 'Si quelqu'un laisse des enfants derrière lui, on ne dira pas qu'il est mort, mais qu'il s'est seulement absenté' ('If a person leaves children behind, people won't say he's dead, only absent'), before admonishing the younger generations for no longer knowing their genealogy, and by extension, their culture.

Teno continues in the following sequence to address his own acculturation in what is his most personal autobiographical voice of all his films. As the camera pans around his own family compound in slow motion, giving the shot an ethereal quality that is accentuated by the mysterious mood and sense of anticipation of the music's sparse cello and xylophone notes, Teno states:

> It was here that I first saw my grandfather talk to a tree, thanking it for guiding me to the family home. A few years later, I remember my own embarrassment when I was left alone in a room where in a corner stood a calabash filled with palm oil, food for my grandfather who had recently died. His skull was buried there. I was supposed to ask for his blessing before going to Europe. For a moment I stood silently, then finally murmuring, I asked his permission to go around the world. I imagine, wherever he was, my grandfather smiled, for he also loved to travel. Outside the rain began to fall.[19]

The discomfort that Teno describes before a belief system that considers the invisible spirit world to be omnipresent, and the worlds of the living and dead to be connected and interpenetrating clearly demonstrates how the binary duality and opposition of the 'modern' Cartesian education that Teno and his

---

[19] Originally in French: 'C'est dans cette cour que j'ai vu pour la première fois mon grand-père parler à un arbre, pour le remercier d'avoir guidé mes pas vers la maison familiale. Quelques années plus tard, je me souviens de ma gêne quand on me laissa seul dans une pièce avec dans un coin une calebasse percée dans laquelle on avait mis de l'huile de palme, pour nourrir mon grand-père décédé quelques années auparavant et dont la crâne était enterrée là. Je devais lui parler, lui demander sa bénédiction avant le voyage vers l'Europe. J'étais resté là sans voix pendant un moment, et finalement, dans un murmure, je lui avais demandé de me permettre de faire le tour du monde. J'imagine que là où il était, mon grand-père en avait souri, car lui aussi aimait voyager. Dehors, la pluie s'est mise à tomber.'

generation received left them at odds with their local systems of knowledge – the damaging destruction of dominated people's cultural markers to which Fanon referred.[20] Teno's 'trip to the country' can also, then, be understood as a quest to reconnect the broken ties with his ancestors and their values, to re-establish the continuities and communal similarities that help frame identity. This personal experience of acculturation of course mirrors the broader Cameroonian situation, Teno's 'I' resonating with the collective 'we'. This is particularly clear in the subsequent long sequence of Bandjoun's annual 'Development Congress' set up in the 1970s to maintain ties between the population that has left and those who remain, bridging the divides created by the rural and overseas migrations; in the past a dynamic moment of exchange, collective collaboration and local democracy, the filmmaker reveals how the event – now sponsored by a local drinks company – has been rid of its substance and turned into a consumerist extravaganza.

At the end of the film, Teno delivers the final words of his commentary over images of his family compound. The camera pans and comes to rest on an adjacent path leading into the distance. The fencing along both sides of the path draws our gaze to the vanishing point, as if inviting us to set out too into the distance as we imagine the young Teno setting off on his journey to Europe. Strikingly, this shot echoes the very same shot in Teno's first short film, *Hommage*, evoking the fictional protagonist's departure from Bandjoun to the city and abroad; a reference, too, to both the filmmaker and his father's departures. These departures also resonate with Teno's mention of his grandfather's love of travel, creating a kind of filial transmission, or a thread, like the threads that run through his oeuvre in a cinematic filiation or circulation. In travelling back to the village to try to understand where Cameroon's sham modernity went wrong – its 'long voyage pour rentrer dans une impasse' (its 'long journey to arrive at a dead end') – and how endogenous modernity can really be put to the service of the people, Teno's journey is an attempt to find a way out of the blockages and dead-ends to surpass the barriers of acculturation and, in reclaiming broken memory and filiation, to restore the flows and circulations.

An actual journey symbolizing a personal journey of healing and finding oneself and one's direction is also the thematic and structuring core of Teno's only fiction feature to date: *Clando*. The film broaches a number of themes relating to issues of migration and circulations: the complex ties between Africa and Europe; their embedded spaces and cultures; migrant experiences; and the corollary question of return. In a non-linear construction that weaves together multiple temporalities, the plot is gradually pieced together to tell the story of Sobgui, a Douala-based computer scientist who is arrested, tortured

---

[20] See Fanon, *Les Damnés de la terre / The Wretched of the Earth*.

and imprisoned for letting student activists photocopy political opposition material in his office. On his release, jobless and left impotent by the trauma of his experience, Sobgui struggles to make ends meet by working as an unlicensed taxi driver – or 'clando', short for 'clandestine' – a precarious and vulnerable situation that leaves him prone to police harassment and bribes. Psychologically scarred, professionally unstable, his relationship with his wife suffering, he seizes the opportunity to leave for Germany when he realizes he is also at threat from political henchmen.

As a taxi driver, Sobgui already journeys through the city of Douala, which, right from the opening images, is seen from his moving car, initially shot from his subjective point of view as he navigates the different districts and negotiates the city's literal and metaphorical blockages and hurdles (traffic, police stops, run-ins with angry official taxi drivers); these are Fanon's 'lines of force' that compartmentalize the colonial and postcolonial city, and bring to mind earlier African film classics, such as Ousmane Sembène's *Borom Sarret* (1962).[21] Sobgui's subsequent arrival in Germany is also marked by the barriers of border and customs controls as he is twice questioned by suspicious German authorities in the long airport arrivals sequence. These hurdles contrast with sense of movement of the sequence that immediately follows. Shot from inside a moving train, and again from Sobgui's point of view, the German countryside flashes by as, off, we hear the character's interior monologue: 'Partir, c'est réussir un peu ta vie. Déjà tout petit, quand tu portais un beau costume, tes camarades te regardaient avec envie et disaient: "Il est parti"'. ('To leave is to have made it. When we were kids, if you had a nice outfit, your friends would look at you with envy and say, "He's gone!"'). Freedom of movement is then exactly that – a freedom – and a sign of privilege and status.

A physical journey, a business trip, and a quest to find a lost compatriot, Sobgui's travel abroad is also of course a quest to find his lost self, and – partly through the meeting with activist Irene – a (re)discovery of his direction in life and in his country's political struggle. This quest is symbolized and mirrored by the journey in Sobgui's recurrent nightmare sequences, the metaphor accentuated by the juxtaposition of the shots of Sobgui looking out of the German train window and of the passing landscape, to those of him handcuffed in the moving truck of his nightmare and the shots of the passing Cameroonian bush, the bush insect sounds linking the two spaces. Likewise, Sobgui's dilemma of whether 'to shoot or not shoot' mirrors his quandary in Germany whether to act or not act; we irresistibly hear Hamlet's existential 'to be or not to be' too. Sobgui's journey and his encounters in Germany provide him with inner understanding, then; with new resolve and knowledge, he can take his own

---

[21] Fanon, *Les damnés de la terre*, 68 / *The Wretched of the Earth*, 38.

Photos 15a-b-c On location shooting *Clando*, Douala, 1994. Filming the prison scenes; in the cell, with cameraman Bonaventure Takoukam; director of photography Nurith Aviv.

d

e

f

Photos 15d-e-f Sobgui's clandestine taxi; shooting in exteriors; Teno directing lead actor Paulin Fodouop.

advice to 'return to the source and grow'. This quest for self-knowledge is characteristic of oral literature. Adopting a typical mirror structure in which two characters' trajectories compare and contrast, offering two different possible paths, Sobgui's positive initiatory experience of Germany is contrasted with the downward spiral of his childhood friend, Rigobert Chamba, whom he is asked to try to locate during his trip after Chamba breaks off all contact with his family back home. While Chamba's story at first appears to be a classic tale of disillusionment, hostility and racism in Europe, Teno in fact complexifies the portrait: once well-established, wealthy and married with children, we learn from other members of the Cameroonian community that it was his own behaviour that destroyed his family and triggered his decline into his current precarity and embitterment. And yet, despite his current situation, Chamba is insistent that he prefers to remain in Germany where, he says, 'personne ne me juge' ('no one judges me'). This raises the very real dilemma of the pressure that many African immigrants feel to succeed in Europe, to support their families, and not to lose face. Yet, interestingly, the film does not just portray, but also challenges this burden. Chamba's predicament echoes the allegoric hunter tale – allegory again being a frequent narrative characteristic of orature. A hunter refuses to return home until he has caught something to feed his starving village, loses his way and nearly starves himself before unwittingly stumbling home only to find that the village's fortunes have improved in his absence. Narrated in voice-over in three fragmented instalments, it is only when the final episode of the tale is narrated as Chamba is reunited with his estranged father on the telephone that the symbolic meaning of the first two parts becomes clear. The end of the tale echoes too with Sobgui's arguments to convince his friend to return to Cameroon, re-qualifying this return as a new departure rather than a defeat.

Throughout the film, the German and Cameroonian spaces are rarely distinct and separate; mutually imbricated and contaminated, as Gikandi comments, they overlap and interpenetrate, both transformed by the colonial and postcolonial encounters. This is particularly clear, for example, in the mirroring of the *tontine* (mutual support fund) sequences filmed in both Douala and Cologne in almost identical ways. The perpetuation of this typical Cameroonian practice in Germany not only serves to bring together and lend cohesion to the Cameroonian community, reinforcing its unity and ties, of course; it also Africanizes this European space, as do the Cameroonian food, clothing and music in the later party scene, or the phone call there between Chamba and his father. As mentioned above, the soundscape also frequently overlaps in continuity from one space to another, like, for instance, at the end of the film when Sobgui is seen in bed next to the sleeping Irene in her Cologne flat; off, the increasingly loud sound of insects foreshadows the coming transition as the scene cuts directly to Douala, the city again seen, just as in film's opening shots, from inside a moving car. Back in this Cameroonian space, Irene and Sobgui's off-screen conversation continues in voice-over, again the soundtrack linking the European and African spaces.

Finally, journeys are also central in Jean-Marie Teno's 2017 film, *Chosen*, a film set in both the USA and Ghana. In March 2010, as Teno's voice-over recounts seven minutes into the film, Teno met the US-based Ghanaian university professor Naana Banyiwa Horne at an African Literature Association conference in Arizona. In line to become a Queen Mother (a female chief) back in Ghana, the wayward, unconventional professor who had been living and teaching in the United States for some thirty years, half-jokingly invited the filmmaker to her royal enstoolment ceremony that July. Intrigued, and enticed by the thought of visiting the country of one of his childhood heroes, the legendary Kwame Nkrumah, Teno sets out on her trail, 'like a hunter tracking the unknown'. In the Pan-Africanist spirit of Nkrumah, Teno journeys, then, into a different culture to his own – though, interestingly, one already evoked in his previous film, *Une Feuille dans le vent* through the account Ernestine Ouandié narrates of her Ghanaian childhood.[22] Thus commences *Chosen*'s filmic journey into Teno's first journey to Ghana and Naana's journey to chieftaincy, a journey that gradually reveals itself to be a broader, metaphorical one, echoing that of both the filmmaker and the character – and of a generation of Africans – all of whom having 'left one day', Teno comments, 'are now struggling to find the way back home'.

Starting in the film's present tense, circa 2016, in Gainesville, Florida, its fragmented narrative progressively weaves together what turns out to be Naana's complex life journey, embracing this complexity. The film thus tos-and-fros between spaces (Naana's two homes, and two families, in Gainesville and in Accra, Apam and Akwamufie in Ghana), between times (Gainesville in 2010 before the trip back to Ghana; July 2010 on arrival in Accra, then in Apam, and during the enstoolment ceremony in Akwamufie; then some time on, back again in Gainesville), and also between the worlds of the living, the dead, the ancestors, the past and the present.

Teno, a foreigner in Ghana and unable to speak Akan, lets his intuition guide him as he films the unfolding ritual enstoolment ceremony. But, as he tells us, his observation of faces and intonations soon tells him that beneath the surface, all is not what it seems. Garnering the elements of Naana's incredible

---

[22] Similarly, Teno raises the question of sacrifice at the end of *Une Feuille dans le vent*, a theme that becomes a central thread of *Chosen*, just as both films address the question of trauma. Several other of Teno's works, for that matter, also start or end with epitaphs and dedications to the famous or anonymous figures who have sacrificed their lives to freedom (*Afrique, je te plumerai, Chef !, Vacances au pays*), as his films seek consistently to restore these unsung heroes to their rightful place in Cameroon's and Africa's pantheons.

Photos 16a-b Naana Banyiwa Horne is led to her enstoolment ceremony in Akwamufie, Ghana and, later during the ceremony, now enstooled Nana Ansomaa III, Twidan Abusua Hemmaa of Akwamufie, Apaa and Surrounding Areas (*Chosen*).

backstory over time in a piecemeal fashion, Teno chooses to recreate his own gradual fragmented understanding by delivering the story non-linearly, the pieces of the puzzle only falling into place progressively, but ultimately creating a rich and fascinating cyclical journey that echoes the African cyclical world view that Naana exposes in *Chosen*. The path to understanding is indeed rarely a straight one, and Teno captures and reconstitutes the meanders, dead-ends and back-tracking requisite in the journey of learning. He warns us that Naana, 'a gifted storyteller', leads him here and there, just as she tells us that, when she first went back to Ghana trying to trace her family heritage as a research scholar, locals told her 'all kinds of fabrications'; in numerous African cultures, knowledge comes with initiation, it must be earned, and the journey itself is as important as reaching the final destination.

Taking us from Naana's enstoolment in 2010 backwards and forwards in time, crossing geographical places, and creating intimate spaces in which Naana and the constellation of characters around her speak (her father, sisters, daughters, and close friends), what at first seems like a focus on the Akan matrilineal power system becomes an exploration of a complex web of interrelated themes that resonate and echo throughout the film to collectively form a journey: motherhood, fatherhood, sisterhood, filiation, death, trauma, loss, relationships to the past, to the ancestors, rooting, cyclical world views, responsibility (sacrifice?), conformity and non-conformity (freedom?), exile, (im)possible return, belonging, and hybrid cultures and lifestyles. Running throughout the film is the question of belonging; Baldwin's famous quote from *Giovanni's Room* irrepressibly comes to mind: 'You don't have a home until you leave it and then, when you have left it, you never can go back.'

Here as in other films, the Ghanaian and American spaces of *Chosen* contrast sharply, and yet overlap and intertwine. Naana's two families – her Ghanaian father and sisters; her American husband and children – mirror and contrast, their lifestyles, cultural behaviour and visions at the same time radically different, and yet in other respects alike, as is acutely witnessed in the lengthy sequences of Naana's elderly father's 90th birthday celebration in Accra, which contrasts in both age and ambiance with Naana's daughter's baby-shower in Gainesville, the late-life/soon-to-born celebrations also capturing the circularity of the life-death-life cycle so present in the film. Moreover, in the USA, Naana holds onto her culture and heritage, giving her children Akan names in honour of their ancestors, pouring libations to the ancestors, wearing African cloths, teaching Ghanaian dance; indeed her sister Ewurama back in Ghana points out that she herself is more Westernized in her clothing than Naana.

Visual, musical and thematic leitmotifs quickly emerge throughout the film and in the different spaces, creating repetitions that – like in oral narratives – structure the intricately unfurling narrative threads and emphasize the connections and intersections between the different worlds. Libations, for example, are poured by Naana in the opening 2016 scene of the film, surrounded by her husband, daughter and son at the family home in Gainesville, but also repeatedly in Akwamufie in 2010, during the different ceremonies that mark Naana's ritual cleansing, enstoolment, and integration into the royal court. Sacrifices too punctuate the different rituals, the symbolic meaning of which is explained as a purification, or a cleansing, opening up paths of communication with the ancestors. Indeed, as the filmic journey unfolds, we soon come to realize that Naana's journey to her enstoolment is a journey to make peace with her own traumatic losses of her mother, when Naana was just aged 14, and later of her baby daughter. As advised by the US-based *Ifá*[23] priest charged with naming the baby, Naana feels the need to retie bonds and reconnect with her lineage; accepting the stool of her female ancestor is part of that process. For her sisters back in Ghana, we sense, putting Naana forward to occupy the empty royal stool was perhaps also a way to bring her back home. But as the film illustrates, filming Naana's grown children in Gainseville and the quintessentially American baby-shower of her granddaughter, Naana's roots are now also in the USA. She is in a sense 'homeless', as she says poignantly to the camera, there being 'no one place where I can feel completely at home.'

The uncertainties of transnational experiences in *Chosen* and the complexity of its identities undoubtedly mirror the uncertainties of Africa's contemporary socio-political situations, and Teno's works capture these tensions. Questioning filiations and roots, yet, at the same time, in an almost antinomic movement, crossing borders, going forth, Teno claims what Assia Djebar described as 'the utmost freedom, that of movement, of journeying, the remarkable possibility of disposing of oneself to come and go.'[24] Claiming the freedom to journey, to explore, to define oneself beyond all essentialism is also a form of resilience and resistance.

---

[23] A Yoruba religion and divination system.
[24] Djeba, *Idiome de l'exil et langue de l'irréductibilité* ['la première des libertés, celle du mouvement, du déplacement, la surprenante possibilité de disposer de soi pour aller et venir'].

Conclusion: For a Decolonial Aesthetics?[1]

> *Déchirons le rideau qui masque le possible*
> Manifeste de l'Atelier IV[2]

By approaching and examining Teno's collective oeuvre, or repertoire, from these different angles and perspectives, by pointing to the threads running throughout, I hope to have both brought some of his films' principal stylistic and thematic traits to the fore, and contextualized them within the broader theoretical and socio-political contexts which both frame them, and which they frame. These, of course, are not exhaustive: they are insights, exploratory pointers and tracks, opening up other paths and further explorations – other *possibles* that aim to trigger further dialogues.

These different threads and aspects do all though, I believe, exemplify the many ways in which Teno and his cinema refuse, as Fanon put it, to 'stay in [their] place', refusing others' definitions and assignations. In the image of Teno himself, as shall hopefully transpire from our following Part II conversation, Teno's works are indeed unruly, resisting the dominant conventions of cinema, the pressures to conform to changing fashions, and the demands and expectations of cinema's various gatekeepers. Shifting out of the normative, the convergent, to paraphrase Gloria Anzaldúa, they embrace and trace a divergent thinking and aesthetics.[3] I indeed often joke with Teno, whose path and relations with institutions – and on occasions with other filmmakers – has at times been a conflictual one, that he is not so much a filmmaker as a troublemaker, a *trublion*, in the sense of: 'an outspoken person who provokes disorder and disturbs order and tranquility'. This, to me, is a compliment, of course, for the order that his work troubles is a colonial one, past and present; it is patriarchal order, an authoritarian political order, and an unjust, dysfunctional social order. And in troubling these, Teno's work challenges quietude, certitudes, and invites the spectator to reflect.

---

[1] A nod here to cultural theorist George Shire, who, in using this qualification in a personal exchange about Teno's work a couple of years back, triggered in my mind this particular questioning.

[2] 'Let us rip down the curtain that masks the possible'. Opening words of the *Atelier IV Manifesto* signed by the participants of the *Atelier IV*, 10-12 June 2017, curated by Françoise Vergès for the Collège d'études mondiales, Cité internationale des arts & La Colonie, Paris.

[3] Anzaldúa, *Borderlands / La Frontera: The New Mestiza*, 101.

Defending freedom and resolutely free, Teno's is a cinema of resonances and circulations, a cinema that embraces complexity and refuses categorizations, limits, and limitations. A cinema of resistance, a cinema of hope, it is a cinema that on all levels eschews coloniality. In so doing, it unquestionably incarnates a decolonial aesthetics.

Photo 17 Jean-Marie Teno, c. 1993.

Part II
In Conversation

In the Beginning…

When and where did everything start? And what are your earliest memories?

I was born in 1954 in southern Cameroon, in other words not in my parents' home region. One of my earliest memories is the school at the Catholic Mission right by where we lived, and the colonial administrator, whom we used to see at Mass. On the one side there were the Whites, and on the other the Blacks. Everything was divided, separate. It was the colonial era.

I also remember on 1 January 1960 when we went to parade, our chests puffed out, singing that national anthem with its terrible words: 'O Cameroon, birthplace of our ancestors, before you lived in barbarity. Like a sun you start to shine, little by little emerging from your savagery…' I remember thinking that the barbarity was the colonial period, but no! What's more, coming via my parents from the West of Cameroon where the war of liberation was still raging at the time, there were a whole load of things that were said at the time about the struggle, about the repression of the UPC [Union of the Peoples of Cameroon], there were the underground fighters' decapitated heads that the authorities exhibited at the entrance to villages to create a state of terror. Villages that the French army dropped Napalm on … All this was taking place during my childhood.

I remember travelling to my parents' home region in Western Cameroon. It was awful: every time we reached a police or military barrage, we all had to get out of the bus. All the adults were made to sit on the ground while the police searched completely brutally, treating our parents with contempt. It was the same contempt that we met with in our local districts. At times, the police and/or the army would decide to lock down a district. They called it 'the curfew'. They would encircle the neighbourhood, force all the men out and sit them at the crossroads while they searched all the houses. So, there was constantly this terrible sense of humiliation in our parents' eyes, and I can say in all honesty today a feeling of submission that was passed on to us children. The adults were afraid to speak about it. Moreover, coming as I did from a family from the West, but living in southern Cameroon, we had to be far more careful than anyone else, because people from the West were very easily assimilated with the underground fighters, who would be labelled terrorists today.

In the 1960s, we were surrounded with violence, then, and yet it was also a time of so much hope. We had just gained Independence and we thought things were going to be alright. Later we realized that the state used the UPC freedom fighters, who were still fighting in the bush – there weren't that many of them, maybe 300 to 400 – as a way to create a politics of fear in the country, establishing a dictatorial state that is Cameroon today. My childhood memories are a conflicting moment of joy, hope, and at the same time of acute violence that continues today.

Did the advent of Independence change things in your life as a child?
I couldn't really tell; I was only six years old. We would hear the word 'Independence', see the parades, it was a time of celebration, of singing songs. The adults were happy. But at the same time, you couldn't really see much difference from what went before. The violence continued … We also continued – this I remember – to learn 'Our ancestors the Gauls' in school in spite of everything.[1] The same school programmes stayed in place.

It was a pretty exceptional period. Were you at all aware so at the time?
I was aware of the injustices. But I wasn't the most affected. I saw that the injustice was systemic, as it was the police who brutalized and oppressed everyone. But in 1965, at the age of eleven, I left the South with my father, whom I had lived with separate from my mother since I was five, and moved to Yaoundé for my secondary studies. I went to the Lycée Leclerc, the most prestigious secondary school in the country, where the country's intellectual and administrative elite was educated. It was a paradoxical situation: I was living in Nvog Ada, a poor peripheral working-class neighbourhood of Yaoundé, where I was the only child to go to secondary school. At thirteen or fourteen, my friends were all apprentice tailors, apprentice mechanics, etc. I had to cross the entire neighbourhood on foot, as I used to walk to school, and I'd eventually reach this place where I'd see all these rich kids arriving by car, being dropped off, all spruced up, well-fed, clean, smart, and with that self-importance typical of those we used to call at the time 'the well-housed, well-fed'. It was my first awakening to injustice. I used to say to myself: 'what did they do to be able to come to school in these conditions?' And: 'why not me?'

At the same time, I could see Europe, its standard of living, and I wondered why some were born with everything in Europe while not us in Africa. I discovered these things in stages. Yet I didn't dream of going to Europe; it wasn't something that attracted me. My neighbourhood was great, there were really wonderful things there. As I was one of the only ones to go to secondary school,

---

[1] An officially sanctioned national narrative developed by 19th-century French historians established the myth that the French descended culturally and genetically from the Gauls. Under the Third Republic in particular (1870-1940), French school children – and school children in the French colonies, using the same textbooks – were thus taught that their ancestors were Gauls. Even after Independence, numerous Francophone African countries continued teaching predominantly French history.

I was a kind of star. When people said *le lycéen* [the secondary school kid], it was me. Some of the neighbourhood folk were really proud of me. Thanks to my tailor friend, Fiom – may he rest in peace – whose model I was, when I was fifteen or sixteen, I was one of the most elegant guys in the school; I was 'hot' as we used to say! Our school uniform was simply grey; we could wear the style we liked. So, I was always at the cutting edge of fashion! My friend Fiom would measure me up and try all the latest styles on me, his boss then adding the finishing touches. Yet I had no shoes! I had flares, tight-fitting shirts, but I needed shoes to finish it off. It's there that my friend Ben's Belinga came in – the same person who did the music for *La Tête dans les nuages*, *Clando*, *Vacances au pays* – a friend from the neighbourhood who used to skip school until the day his older brother gave him a saxophone. Then one fine day we saw him proudly wearing the outfit of the *Tulipes Noires*, the band of the big neighbourhood bar called *Le Philanthrope*. We were so impressed! One day we were talking, and he said: 'Hum! I see you going to that school there. You need shoes. I'm going to sort you out.' And he took me to the room of his brother, aka 'President', the lead musician of the *Tulipes Noires*, who had an amazing collection of shoes. Ben's said: 'Go in. Look. Choose a pair!' I chose a beautiful pair of woven leather shoes – really expensive – the most fashionable at the time! I didn't realize they were brand-new, that he'd only just got them. For six months at school, I was in seventh heaven. But, of course, as I used to walk to school and back in the morning, at lunchtime, and then again after school, they soon wore out! And one day, I bumped into the President, Ben's brother, and he finally realized where his woven leather shoes had gone! He laughed about it; he was a true gentleman!

What was your path after that?

From 1965 to 1973, I lived in Yaoundé. My father worked there until 1970. After that, he left, leaving me behind in Yaoundé. I lived on my own, fending for myself. I attended school as well as I could; in short, I was a teen left to my own devices in an old abandoned house, where all my older friends would come with their girlfriends. It was the time I saw the most films because they would give me money to go to the cinema, leaving them the house!

What memories do you have of the cinema as a child?

The very first film I saw as a child was *Robin Hood*. It was an outdoor public screening; I think it must have been in about 1959. I was about five and we went to the crossroads, to the Mission, where they'd strung up a canvas screen. The first screening was put on at the Mission, but the missionaries weren't very happy because the film wasn't religious enough. So, the second screening was in the town, on the public square. When the horses galloped towards us, some people were afraid! At the same time, it was such a fantastic moment. Later, there was a cinema in our neighbourhood that screened a lot of Indian films, in Hindi, what's known as Bollywood. When we were about seven, eight or nine years old, it was the place we spent most of our time; that and playing football in the street in Sangmelima, a small town in southern Cameroon where there were very few cars. Whenever we wanted to play football, we'd set up our goalposts in the middle of the street and play. When cars came along, either they hooted or, seeing us, would simply take a different street! At the cinema at the time, we used to watch Hindi Bollywood films, westerns, Italian sword-and-sandal films (*Hercules Against the Moonmen*, *The Titans*); we'd re-tell each other the plots all day long during the pauses of our endless football matches.

Later, as a teen, I continued going to the cinema as often as I could, and before the feature, they used to show newsreels, sometimes with pretty long reports of up to forty or so minutes, which people found dull. But I liked them, not for what they said, but because you'd see people in them, their everyday lives, and I liked that, in spite of the often strange commentaries. But, one of the major deeply marking moments for me was later seeing my first Cameroonian film, *Pousse-Pousse* by Daniel Kamwa in 1974, a film about a concrete social issue: the dowry practice. It's the story of a poor young man's struggle to marry the woman he loves, as his future in-laws keep raising the dowry price. It's a comedy that addresses a reality, a real social issue that affects a lot of people in Cameroon, posing the question of whether poor people have the right to love too. Can they get married like everyone else, without having to face the harshest of situations? For me, this film illustrated the situation in which the majority of Cameroonians found themselves at the time. They were faced with such financial precariousness that it was a hurdle, preventing them from making themselves a life, from getting married even. This situation where money was taking on an increasingly great place in society was a hangover from the colonial era. For me, this was the proof that cinema could really be in touch with society. Another milestone for me was Jean-Pierre Dikongue-Pipa's *Muna Moto* in 1975.

Did you ever imagine you'd make films one day, when you were a child?

No, it never crossed my mind. Not even when I was in secondary school. For a long time, I wanted to write in order to speak about what I was living, but at the same time, censorship was rife. At that time life was very difficult for journalists. Whenever they said something that the state didn't like, they were locked up and beaten. There was a cruel and violent censorship against anyone who didn't toe the government line. What's more, as I was pretty good at maths, I was someone naturally destined to become something like an engineer.

Photos 18 a-b The Wouri and Capitole cinemas in Douala and Yaoundé on the release of *Bikutsi Water Blues*, its posters displayed on the facades, 1988-89.

You said that after a while, you were no longer able to live on your own in Yaoundé…

Yes. So, from 1973 to 1974, I went to live in Bafoussam, near my village in the West, where my mother had moved back, to finish my final year of high school. It was my first year living with my mother since she'd left my father when I was five. It wasn't easy. I think she still thought that she was dealing with a three- or four-year-old child. My sister who's younger than me had more freedom than I did, and I, who was used to fending for myself, found myself with no freedom at all. As soon as I could, then, in 1974 or 1975, I went back to Yaoundé, where I enrolled at the university for a year. But I won a scholarship from the British Council to study in England, at Portsmouth Polytechnic.

How did you get your scholarship to study in Britain?

They used to play ads on the radio all the time saying that the British Council was offering scholarships. I was enrolled at university in Yaoundé, but I hardly ever went. As I had specialized in Sciences at high school, I enrolled in Maths and Physics, like everyone else. But I wasn't interested! That year, I met a guy who got me to sell collections of Mao's *Little Red Book*. I used to go door-to-door trying to earn money. But I didn't earn a penny; I didn't manage to sell a single copy! I spent my time trying to sell, going everywhere with the *Little Red Book* collection, looking for openings. The chance to apply for this scholarship came along and I found myself among those who got a grant to go to England.

What did going to Europe represent to you?

Nothing. It wasn't something I dreamed of. I applied for the scholarship because everyone else was applying. Going to Europe never even crossed my mind. I filled in all the applications there were, just like everyone else, and it happened that this time round I was selected. And to be honest, I had already missed one opportunity at the time because, when I passed the exams to enter the final year of high school, I had a friend who was terrible at maths whose older brother got me to help him. This brother worked in a ministry and there were scholarships going at the time to study cinema in China and he thought I should apply! I remember him saying: 'There's nothing here, apply, I'm the one in charge', but I didn't do it at the time because the idea of going abroad didn't appeal to me. I regretted it later! It was ever since then that my path seemed by chance to be taking me towards cinema, which, unconsciously, attracted me, but which I never imagined embarking upon yet. I didn't go in that direction immediately. It was completely by chance that that one happened to have been a film scholarship.

I had no particular desire to leave. So, I found myself with this scholarship to go to study Electronical Engineering in England, but even once I was there, a lot of people on my course, my friends, said to me: 'You shouldn't be studying Electronics. Why don't you study Electronics and Business Management?' Many of my friends that first year, who weren't really into the sciences, had switched to that. That's what I was advised to take the following year. I was willing to, but the British Council had begun to drag their feet over renewing my scholarship because there had been several reports saying that I was giving political speeches at the Students' Union despite us all having had to promise not to get involved in politics. It's true that that year I was more interested in the Socialist International and I used to spend my whole time at the Students' Union giving speeches and handing out the *Socialist Worker*! The British Council were really not happy! As they kept me waiting for a response, I ended up saying, to hell with it, I'm going back to Cameroon. So just as they were finally doing the necessary so I could stay, they saw me show up in Yaoundé. The woman at the British Council was very disappointed.

What year was that?

I returned to Cameroon in 1976, but in November. Classes had already started, so I couldn't enrol at the university. I found myself there, completely at a loose end in the neighbourhood, and so I started to look for work. I wound up working at Radio Cameroun as a sound assistant.

At the same time, I was conscious of all the social inequality and of the fact that there were not very clever people who, because they had a degree, were the bosses. So, I said to myself: 'What's life about, in fact? Is all you need a degree?', and I decided that it was important to study after all. So, while I was working at the radio, I passed an exam to enter the Ecole Polytechnique in Cameroon. I got in and enrolled in a three-year programme to become an engineer. On this course, there were a lot of French lecturers. And these French people spent their time not only teaching us engineering, but also notions of management. They spent their time telling us: 'Tomorrow, you will have to manage personnel. In such and such a situation, you need to act like this or like that', but I didn't want them to turn me into some kind of completely formatted little boss, with colonial attitudes. I started to hate this environment. I started thinking to myself: 'You can also react according to the situation, or according to other parameters', in short, it was my *Socialist Worker* side, my social conscience coming out. And I was deeply annoyed to see my fellow students and even some friends swallow all that and accept being conditioned in a way that barely took local realities into account, always with directives from on high. The thought of spending three years subjected to that was unbearable to me.

At the same time, I passed an entrance exam to go to study at the Institut national de l'audiovisuel (INA) in France, on a two-year senior technician course. So, in 1978, with an INA scholarship, I was able to go to study in France – studies that were less prestigious than at the Yaoundé Ecole Polytechnique. People told me: 'You're mad!', but I didn't care. I already knew at the time that if I left, given the mentality in the country, I wouldn't be coming back. So, I left the Ecole Polytechnique in Cameroon to go to INA. In short, I was always dropping one thing to be able to advance on to the next.

I thus found myself at INA and, at the same time, I enrolled in an IUT [University Institute of Technology] to take a diploma. It was at that time that my father died, in December 1979, shortly before the end of my course. I then decided to do a degree in Audiovisual Techniques at the University of Valenciennes, as video was taking off at the time, then a Master's in Audiovisual Communication. During my studies, I did some internships in television, and ended up finding a job at France 3 in Paris. At the time, the news was still shot on 16 mm. The journalists would go out to film in the morning, the images were developed the same day and edited in-house and the sound mixed ready for broadcast that very same night on the news. It was pretty crazy, but really exciting.

The technology started to change too. Video equipment and its incredible formats progressively replaced celluloid. The role of the video technicians changed too. From adjusting the cameras and the big 1- or 2-inch sound recorders on set, we started to receive images sent from all over the world that had to be inserted into news reports that were maximum 2-minutes long, and that sometimes had to be cut down to news in brief. This was work that the film editors didn't want to do at first, as it wasn't at all creative, so we video technicians started to do it. It was rudimentary, but fun.

Video formats continued to evolve. We went from three-quarter inch to BVU, and there, you really had to edit. But the film editors didn't want anything to do with these machines because they felt that they belittled their editing work. They had all been to the IDHEC film school, studied editing, and were used to celluloid editing tables. This all caused a lot of conflict. We, the video technicians, found ourselves editing more and more as television transitioned from celluloid to video.

In 1986, to avoid social conflicts at France 3 Paris caused by these changes in television, all the video technicians were sent on an almost year-long training course in film. It was great! There were five of us. We used to go to a studio every day to learn the history of cinema, the history of editing. We each had a 16 mm editing table at our disposal to play around with. I took advantage of this year-long 16 mm course paid for by the television to come up to scratch with the film editors trained at the IDHEC, or who had trained by working as assistants on several films until they obtained the status of chief editor. At the same time, the celluloid film editors were sent on a course to learn to use video.

When I started working at the television, they had their own little lab. At that time, I was getting interested in cameras. I bought an ARRI ST 16 mm camera that I shot images with and that I'd take to the TV lab. That's how I started editing these images myself, and gradually getting to know this tool. That's how I started making my first films. It was a most torturous path!

Today, looking back at your childhood, your youth, can you see any seeds, anything that later led you to cinema? And not just cinema, but to the style of cinema you adopted: a committed, questioning one ... You mentioned your secondary school, your awareness of injustice. From early on, one can detect a certain non-conformism in you...

In truth, the first thing that most marked me was this awareness of injustice and my choice not to conform. In the early 1990s, I chose to no longer cut my hair because I didn't want to resemble all those people whom I considered corrupt.

But, regarding my cinema, I don't think the seeds of what you want to do later can necessarily be found in your childhood. I above all have the feeling that, for me, the idea of having a camera was always an idea of having a wonderful toy to play with. I loved the idea of filming, of photographing. But, honestly, I never took it seriously to the point of wanting to go to film school.

I used to look at other people's photos, the way they were framed. I'd find them nice, but it was as if it wasn't enough for me. I think that what always attracted me to cinema was the possibility it offered of taking ordinary things, everyday life, and reconstructing them into a narrative – one that was the closest to what I wanted to recount, a narrative that said something other than the things that were constantly before our eyes. Was there anything in my childhood that encouraged that? I really don't know.

Where, then, did this desire to recount things come from? Not to be in the group, not to cut your hair?

It perhaps comes from the fact that I often evolved in groups of people who had very different lives to mine, whose form of normality was different, and who thus had dreams that I refused to identify with. Was it because in secondary school I was always the smallest in my class, because I was always the one who had nothing? Is it all that which meant that at some point I wanted to assert that singularity? To accept this situation and perhaps unfortunately no longer fight my way out of it, but on the contrary, in an almost suicidal way, to always return to this state of deprivation?

When did this non-conformism turn into political engagement? Perhaps not in the sense of being an activist, but…

I've often been an activist! When I was at university, I was one of the few Africans here in France who was constantly involved in the anti-Apartheid movement. I met the President of Namibia at one point. It was funny because, when he was still in the opposition, he came and met with everyone in the anti-Apartheid movement and I was the only Black person. As soon as he saw me, he immediately spoke to me in his language and I said: 'But, I'm from Cameroon'. He answered: 'Oh? And you're an activist?' I was about 25 years old, and he said: 'You should come and see us in Namibia'. That same year, I also often met Dulcie September, an incredible woman.

I had been an activist since the UK, where I was part of the International Socialist movement and used to canvas, handing out tracts on Sundays at the Students' Union. I found myself surrounded by fascinating people, full of ideas, vocations, and that gave my life meaning. Even though my English was still rudimentary, I even gave a speech at the Students' Union during the election campaign. Later, I took part in all the combats in France: immigrant solidarity, all that. I have lots of slides of the first marches in France in the 1980s, in which immigrants and the French marched together. I've got lots of photos because I took part in those demonstrations.

I can still remember one of those demos: I went along and was practicing filming with my ARRI ST but it was so cold! My hands were completely frozen! This big guy from the CGT [the left-wing General Confederation of Labour union] saw my hands trembling, despite my thin little gloves, which barely protected them. He came over, his hands outstretched and rubbed mine, and my hands were suddenly warm! He gave me a big grin and went off saying 'Courage comrade!' It was really touching!

So, my activism has always been present. But, paradoxically, when I started making films, when I turned to cinema, I wanted to make comedies. I've always loved funny films. When I was younger, I was often the smallest, the cheekiest, I loved to tease. I spent all my time bugging people bigger than me and when they tried to give me a wallop, I'd dart off fast!

This playful humour is present in your films, even if they can hardly be described as comedies!

That's true! I always wanted to make funny films, even romances. My films are often about things that are lacking. Having grown up without maternal love, I thought at one point that romances were what would enable me to fill this emotional void that I have always felt, that I know I'm going to carry on struggling with until the end.

First Encounters, First Steps

Coming back to your first steps in cinema, to when you started filming and experimenting while also working at the television, what sort of things did you first film?

I used to film Paris, the city, the streets. That's how I practised framing, filming, with my little camera.

Were you intending by then to make films?

Oh yes! Even when I was at Valenciennes University, every time I was meant to create a slide show, I gave them little scenarios, even if they were made out of still images. I'd try to tell stories with still images set to music. I'd already been wanting to make films for some time; it was actually doing so that was hard. It's perhaps a trait of my character, but the moment between when I want to film and actually filming, taking action, it's as if there was always a fear, not necessarily a justified one, but one which means that I always tend to put things off.

I remember that making my very first film, *Hommage*, took a very long time. I filmed it the first year that I went to Cameroon with my girlfriend of the time, the late Madeleine Beauséjour, who was an excellent film editor, originally from Mauritius. She kept pushing me, saying: 'so, that film, when are we going to edit it?' I met her at a time when I was involved in independent radio. I used to do interviews, which I'd try to edit. She encouraged me to construct the film. She was a film connoisseur and was also very politically committed, a left-winger. She'd taken part in May '68. She encouraged me to experiment. The desire to do things had always been there, but putting them into action ... So, we ended up editing *Hommage* at a time when I had no money. Madeleine said to me: 'Look, I've got one week'. She gave me the number of someone to ring to find an editing suite and for seven days we shut ourselves in. In seven days, I recorded my text, worked out what I wanted, and in my sitting room with a Nagra that I'd borrowed from the television, I recorded the dialogue with two actors, Abossolo Mbo and Tadie Tuene, who were my friends. We then went into the editing room with the dialogue and cut the film.

What year was that?

1984. I'd never made a film at the time, so I didn't know what the stages were. It was Madeleine who explained to me what you had to do, what had to be done with the sound. At the time, I knew how the news was made, but the things like the mixing, for example, were things we used to do almost intuitively. There was no mixing desk at the television, for example. It was the news, so they used to send a team of one person for the image, another for the sound, and would maybe have a second soundtrack for the music. But here, with a film, you had to edit four tracks, with a voice-over, so it was really with Madeleine's help that I learned what you had to do to put together a film.

Before that, you'd been to your first FESPACO (Ouagadougou Pan-African Film Festival) in Burkina Faso?

Yes, in 1983, after I had finished university and before I made my first film. I came back to Paris in 1981, or 1982, and was working at the television where they had a lab and I was playing around with my camera. One of my experiments at the time was filming Paris, my friends, a group of Africans including Mal-Njam, his little brother Simon Ndjami, Blaise Njoya, Michel Lobe Ewane, and my friend Vianney Ombe Ndzana. There we all were wanting to put the world to rights, and I filmed all of this, making a first short film – *Schubbah* ('Bravo'), about the *Bwana Magazine* experience.

What was *Bwana Magazine*?

It was a news and culture magazine that we launched in the early 1980s, recounting our experiences as young Black people living in France, observing the world around us … It was the time of the Africa Fête music festival, the start of SOS-Racisme after Mitterrand came to power in 1981. It was about young Black people's aspirations in France at the time.

I was responsible for the film section. I wrote a few probably pretty ridiculous articles! I in fact went to the FESPACO to cover the festival for the magazine. And it was there that I interviewed Souleymane Cissé and met Ousmane Sembène. I was one of the rare Black African journalists to go to the FESPACO then; the rest were Europeans.

When you went to the FESPACO for the first time, were you already familiar with Sembène's work? With Cissé's?

I knew Cissé's work, because I had seen *Baara* on French television just a few weeks before. And in the months before the FESPACO, I went to the Cinémathèque de la Coopération and watched practically their entire collection of African films. I knew Sembène's work, of course, but also Gaston Kaboré's, whose *Wend Kuuni* I saw at the Festival des Trois Continents in Nantes. I'd also seen films by Moussa Bathily, Med Hondo, and everything that had been made then. And when I got to the FESPACO in 1983, I tried to see as many films as possible.

What was it that made you go to see those African films at the Cinémathèque de la Coopération in Paris?

I was already aware that the question of representation was important. I wanted to see what others had already done. I wondered where this cinema was at, what films existed, because there weren't many. The question of invisibility was already on my mind at the time, as there were almost no films in France portraying Africans. I remember it was at the time – or perhaps a tiny bit later – when films like *Black MicMac* by Thomas Gilou were huge box office hits. It was the only time you saw Black actors on the screen. At that time too, I used to run into actors like Eric Ebouaney, who was a student still, Alex Descas, Isaac de Bankolé, and Félicité Wouassi. There was no visibility for Black people, for Africans or West Indians.

You were already conscious of the question of representation…

Completely. It was all there, it was obvious, in fact. I was in the midst of it, I observed. There were movements such as Africa Fête putting on concerts, there was Touré Kounda, a great group that I went to film several times; we were all immersed in this Black world. We were aware of these issues.

So, you attended your first FESPACO in 1983, a period when African cinema was still enjoying an overt political effervescence with, for example, the Pan-African Federation of Filmmakers (FEPACI) and their Algiers and Niamey Charters in 1975 and 1981. It was a time of fervent debates about the role of cinema at the FESPACO. What memories do you have of these debates, of this ambiance?

The ambiance was fantastic. It was a space of open debate with the public. You would often stumble across intense discussions on whether we could speak of an 'African cinema', of whether 'African cinema' existed. There was another debate that was very interesting at the time: for a lot of people, African cinema was 'documentary' because our fictions – if you take the first films, such as Ousmane Sembène's *Borom Sarret*, Djibril Diop Mambéty's *Contras' city*, etc. – these films were at the limit between documentary and fiction, often set in real decors, with characters who traverse the city, with people who play their real-life roles. When people needed a carpenter in their film, they went to get a carpenter to play the role, or whatever the trade was, and that helped accredit the notion that African cinema was documentary, which was completely untrue; for me, it was more a cinema rooted in the real. This debate polarized a lot of people, because many directors who wanted to be 'cineastes' decided to distance themselves from all this to make Cinema, with a capital C, so that people would stop shutting them in this box. That's why people like Idrissa Ouedraogo at one point no longer wanted to be considered 'African filmmakers', but simply as filmmakers. It was a fascinating debate.

There was also a debate about the nature of our cinema. Should it just be entertainment, or should it be a means of education? The issues discussed at the time were really worthwhile and were truly worth exploring at that specific moment of the continent's history. Filmmakers really debated, reflected.

Photos 19a-b FESPACO 1983. Jules Takam, Gérard Essomba, Jean-Marie Teno and Sanou Kollo; Screening schedules.

Photos 19c-d FESPACO 1983. Teno shaking hands with the then Prime Minister Thomas Sankara; Gaston Kaboré reading *Bwana* magazine (photo by Teno).

In Ouaga, then, the day after a screening, the director would come to meet the public and answer questions. The public was always present and sometimes asked really disconcerting questions. Many, including the Ouagalese public, got their film education here. Filmmakers had to explain and justify using ellipses; others asked questions about the film's message; often people asked questions relating directly to scenes in the film. But little by little, these debates disappeared from the FESPACO, and it's as if the matter, the film object, interests people less and less – in particular those in charge of the festival because, by no longer providing the framework in which people can discuss cinema, they contributed to the disappearance of this reflection on it. For them, the event, the festivity, became more important than the content. So, I think that, in that respect, the people in charge of the FESPACO became the biggest gravediggers of African cinema at that time. They saw the festival as nothing more than an opportunity to get funding, not as an opportunity to reflect on Africa's societies anymore; it became just an opportunity to hand out a ton of ridiculous prizes to their friends, and they distanced themselves completely from the ideals and objectives of the pioneers of African cinema concerning the place that cinema should occupy in our societies.

By aligning the following editions on themes that were as vacuous as they were insipid, the FESPACO organizers gave themselves a clear conscience while progressively burying any idea of African cinema, accepting the place generously attributed by the European industrial lobbies that control economies and culture.

Does that reflect a general historical evolution? The 1960s and 1970s were committed – utopian even – in many places and on many levels. After Independence, there was still the hope of Pan-Africanism, and all over the world there were liberation movements of all kinds. In French cinema in the 1970s, directors such as Godard, Gorin, Marker or Varda made engagé films; the Groupe Dziga Vertov's slogan about making political films politically comes to mind ... Did the 1980s to 1990s depoliticization you're talking reflect a generalized depoliticization throughout the world?

Yes, but if the world was depoliticising, was that a reason for Africa, which hadn't yet succeeded in its liberation to follow suit? Isn't this policy of mimesis one of the strategies used to maintain a status quo that perpetuates the domination of the continent? Looking back, it's a strategy that continues to function with this blind rush towards an alienating pseudo-modernity that steers us away from the real objectives: a better life for the masses. Depoliticization in Europe has led to the victory of neo-liberalism, which is going to end up bringing the worst xenophobic parties to power in Europe and destroy the last century's social advances. They want Africans, who haven't even managed yet in many countries to put coherent policies in place, to follow such an unjust model and for Africa to open its borders to foreign investors. It's quite simply a mass economic crime, which is resulting in this tragic, constant wave of migration to Europe by any means possible.

Coming back to cinema, the 1980s saw Europe invest a lot of money to professionalize cinema in Africa. This as a result hitched our cinema to European, and particularly French cinema, which indirectly controls our subjects. Setting the creation of a global market as the horizon, African artists are asked to address subjects that are accessible to the rest of the world, to treat subjects in a way that they end up resembling everybody else's, as if that can have any impact whatsoever on the vision we have of ourselves. Africa is becoming the territory of absences, of narratives for others, a bit like is the case for more and more of the best African visual artists, who are making a fortune on the international market without the slightest concern for the impact of their works in their own communities. It's true that, in a land without bread, their economic success imposes them as a model of success. A major mediation effort remains to be put in place to bring these works closer to African publics, and documentary cinema can contribute to that.

At your first FESPACO, you met Souleymane Cissé…

Yes. When I got to the FESPACO, I was delighted to see Cissé because I had seen *Baara* on the television shortly beforehand and I was really, really moved by the film; it had everything that I loved in cinema at the time. The film touched me in the way the relationships between the characters were structured, in the justness of its treatment of social relationships, and above all in terms of the complexity that Cissé introduced in his description of Malian society. The women characters weren't all victims, nor were they all virtuous, and the progressive intellectual who wants to bring changes to the factory was a terrible macho at home. It wasn't just evil African men oppressing women. There weren't goodies on the one hand and baddies on the other. Everything was nuanced and that seemed to me to be closer to reality. The film wasn't at all caricatural. When I got to the FESPACO in 1983, I saw Cissé's *Finyé*, which I liked too, but which, for me, did not have the same force as *Baara*. I asked Cissé if I could interview him and he immediately agreed. I don't think he was used to seeing a Black journalist as I was one of the only ones at the time. I set up my mike and we began the interview. It was most certainly a terrible interview in strictly journalistic terms – it was more of a conversation, a dialogue. We rapidly moved on from *Finyé* because I wasn't as fond of it and because I said to him: 'Let's talk about *Baara*'. I asked him questions about scenes in the film, I told him about things I had seen in *Baara*, until he finally said to me: 'You, young man, you saw things in *Baara* that I didn't know I'd put!' I answered: 'But they were the things I felt'. And he said: 'You know what, instead of playing the journalist, why don't you make films? You have a very cinematographic reading; you should start making your own films, as there aren't many of us. More young people need to make films.' I came away so surprised! This interview lasted the length of one reel; it was a sort of close combat. Unfortunately, I can't find the reel anymore; it's gone missing. I think I may have lent it to someone a long time ago. It's such a shame! But I never forgot this interview and it was this encounter with Cissé that really pushed me to start making films.

I also have to say that when I went to the FESPACO, I was next to a French journalist on the plane. On arrival in Ouaga, I went and asked the great Sembène for an interview. He looked at me and sent me packing because I looked almost like a kid, in sandals, with a heavy Uher reel tape recorder, and an old Nikkormat (the ancestor of Nikons) – I was completely lost behind my equipment! The next day, the journalist from the plane came up to me and proudly said: 'Tomorrow I'm meeting the Maestro for an interview!' I said to her: 'Really? Lucky you!', but I was so annoyed! But when I met Cissé, he immediately said yes. After that, I never asked to interview Sembène again!

That same year, I also met people like Ababacar Samb Makharam, who was really impressive, intellectually speaking. When he spoke, when he talked about his work, his approach, he gave off something majestic. I met nearly all this first generation of filmmakers, who really articulated a discourse about why they made films and that, for me, was essential.

I also met Paulin S. Vieyra. All these filmmakers were practically encyclopaedias, they talked about cinema with such panache, they developed a real discourse … it was such a delight! After the screenings, there was an open space with a tribune in the gardens of the Hôtel Indépendance where people would talk about the films of the day before. These discussions were often retransmitted on the radio, for that matter. Directors like Haile Gerima were present, African-American intellectuals such as Clyde Taylor; in short you had people who came to the FESPACO, who developed a reflection on the cinema and who, when they spoke, were a joy to listen to, because you learned something. It wasn't just grandstanding or hot air!

Without wanting to sound nostalgic or backward-looking, for me, who came to the festival trying to understand the context in which this cinema was being produced, I learned an enormous amount from these conferences, debates, from all these discussions and even from meeting people. I learned. I didn't speak much, I listened, I observed them, and I absorbed it all.

Where did this first generation get their film culture from?
I can't say. But these people took up cameras as if they were arms and tried to organize cinema. When you see how the FESPACO, the FEPACI, and other

bodies were set up in the early days, it was the fruit of a reflection concerning the lack of images of Africa and the lack of an African cinema, but also a reflection on the state of our countries and the place of film and culture at the time. So, I think it was quite normal at a time when people still spoke about education for the masses that all these people thought about how cinema could also help contribute to this key objective: education. And I think that they asked the right questions and that these questions were posed until the time when, little by little, things began to change. And I think that one of the major turning points was at the start of the 1980s; that is, with Idrissa Ouedraogo's film *Yam Dabo* (*The Choice*).

Meaning?

Yam Dabo is the story of a village facing a severe drought. They reach a point where the people are forced to leave. It's a pivotal moment, with the choice of either accepting outside humanitarian aid, or leaving, going away. I really think that at that time, Idrissa clearly posed the essential question of the moment. It was at that time that he imposed himself as a real visionary. *Yam Daabo* was the film that marked a rupture and shows how, when faced with the choice of massively letting humanitarian aid in – and thus relinquishing autonomy – or leaving, people opted for the first and went in the direction of globalization, which has assigned Africa to the place that it continues to occupy today. It was in a way a metaphor for our cinema, a choice that has ended up asphyxiating it. Even Idrissa really struggled to make his films twenty years on. By turning towards the outside world, and by trying to make films that increasingly met the expectations of those abroad, our cinema has ended up losing something essential. How to reconnect with this environment, to find in it the metaphors that can express the things that are truly rooted in our societies, that are in touch with our people's real preoccupations?

After *Yam Daabo*, Idrissa began positioning himself as 'just a filmmaker', not an 'African filmmaker'. Yet at the same time, he could not *not* be that; he was one of the most brilliant. He was a great filmmaker, but he was at the same time an African filmmaker. His stories were fundamentally rooted in the continent; they were universal stories in an African context.

The African cinema born in the 1950s and 1960s Independence era was indeed profoundly rooted in, and marked by, social questions. What did this sense of commitment, this concern for people's conditions and rights stem from?

Our cinema definitely took social rights seriously from its inception and often had our people's concerns in mind, whether seeking to entertain or educate through images. Not only did people need to see stories that concerned them, they needed to be represented on the screen. They needed their issues to be addressed. This was indeed the belief of our first, pioneering filmmakers, who came together in the late 1960s to define the bases of what African filmmaking should be at the time. For them, there were two clear directions: popular education and entertainment. They were the two sides of the coin that they thought cinema should be. Given the high illiteracy rates in the colonial languages, which remained the official language after Independence, many people thought at the time that it would be possible to educate people through images, through films. They believed that cinema had the vocation to entertain – indeed, contrary to what some people suggest today, the notion of entertainment was very much present in early African filmmaking – and, at the same time, to give people elements to find their bearings in the new postcolonial societies. Naturally, then, cinema had both a social and political dimension, addressing people's day-to-day problems and concerns.

While the technology was new, wasn't this function that filmmaking took on in the newly independent African countries simply a continuation of the social role that arts played locally, such as storytelling, or popular theatre? Wasn't filmmaking a new expression of something that already existed, that was socially and culturally rooted?

It was certainly the continuation of both. We mustn't forget that during the colonial era, the colonial authorities used cinema as a way of influencing minds, of assigning people to their place by formulating negative representations of them and their cultures, by valorizing the cultures they introduced and denigrating anything local. So African filmmakers firstly sought to contest that. But at the same time, in order to contest these representations, they turned to modes of narration or to spaces of transmission that existed within families, in social spaces such as *tontines* – community mutual support cooperatives – in the different spaces where people gather and socialize and exchange through stories. The cinema became another such place. And if cinema were to exist amidst all of this, in this new fashionable social space, and if Africans were to make their own cinema, they couldn't completely break away from these existing modes. Just like with music. The major hits of the 1960s and 1970s were songs whose lyrics had meaning for the people. People didn't write songs that spoke only about love; they were always songs that had some kind of moral or message to them. As did stories. So, cinema naturally entered that logic too. Except that film is also destined to travel, to represent the country abroad, to be seen far from its original cultural sphere. How to ensure that local cultural habits would be understood by people who don't necessarily share the same culture? And that's why we later embarked on all these processes of professionalization and universalization, of a dilution, and even a complete destruction of the very idea of narration, of the very idea of a cinema rooted in the space in which people live.

If you think about it, you could say that cinema everywhere in the world in that period shared this dimension. If you think of all the committed films of the late-1960s and 1970s, whether French cinema, Italian cinema, Latin American cinema, independent American cinema … it was a time of great struggle, of social and political struggle. There were movements and struggles for freedom everywhere trying to resist on-going imperialism, hegemony, and later the steamroller of neo-liberal globalization. I think that at that time, everywhere in the world, there was a desire in cinema to participate in what was going on in different societies; in Africa even more so. In societies where people hadn't had a voice, where they hadn't had the means to represent themselves, this political dimension was even greater. Unfortunately, in Africa, we were in countries where there weren't many spaces of mediation. It's not as if in many African countries you could easily descend into the streets to demonstrate or go on strike. It's not as if we had parliaments that functioned, or states that had been created with enough trained figures or leaders who could articulate these struggles. Everyone talked about ending under-development in Africa, as it was called then, about improving peoples' lives, but at the same time, the colonial powers did everything to give the impression that things had changed, without them really changing. Our leaders were up against situations that needed to be changed and yet the former colonial powers controlled the very workings of our economies. They certainly didn't want things to change and spent their time trying to co-opt this new African ruling elite so that their interests would continue to be protected. A new class, a new bourgeoisie thus emerged, while the people continued to suffer. And there were filmmakers who tried to articulate these problems, to ask questions so that citizens could have a better life, so that their problems would be taken into account. They used cinema to that end. When someone like Sembène said, for example, that cinema was an arm to fight against all of this, it was because you could expose a certain number of problems clearly through film, because cinema could help raise people's awareness. This was essential because the education system was not at the service of the people; it was designed to keep them down. In short, in societies where spaces for questioning are limited, this highly seductive popular space called cinema needed to be used to challenge, entertain, and educate the people.

First Films

In the mid-1980s, you were working at France 3 television, you had started going to the FESPACO and meeting other directors, watching other films from Africa and elsewhere, and you started shooting too. Your film *Hommage* was already both a fiction and a documentary. Did you consciously think about the question of film form at that time?

When I started making films, it was a kind of game for me: taking my camera, approaching people, filming them, filming what I saw around me – in other words, the real. But at the same time, I intuitively wanted to tell stories with these images. That's how I started filming the real and trying to give it a form, without necessarily posing the question of film genres. In making films, I wanted to counter the representations that the officials gave of my country, where they said that everything was perfect, magnificent. At the same time, the press was censored, people couldn't say what they were thinking, so I thought to myself that with images, I would be able to show the things that were not okay. Moreover, while I enjoyed watching fiction, when I started making films I wanted to be in the poor areas, to speak about my neighbourhood, to speak about life, to show it. That's how I ended up working in this form called documentary. I must say though, I didn't really know what documentary was at the time. I didn't have much of a documentary culture, but I did want to speak about the life around me. So, I stared filming without really asking myself too many questions.

Were you aware of the existence of other African documentary filmmakers at the time?

Some must have existed, or at least people making film reports. Samba Félix Ndiaye was already making films at the time, there were the works of Moustapha Alassane too. But when I saw the fiction films of Daniel Kamwa, for example, these were films that for me spoke about the world around us. It's true that Kamwa's stories were played by actors, but as he filmed ordinary people in the streets, in their daily lives, they were close to documentary in a way. The first African films were very close to our realities, as the settings were often natural, the actors often non-professionals playing their real-life roles. These films were very close to documentary – docu-fictions – telling everyday stories. When I started making films, the idea of making the sorts of fictions I used to watch at the time – action movies, European and American B-movies, violence, chases – was out of the question. These were not things I was confronted with daily.

When I made *Hommage*, I didn't define it as a 'documentary film', I defined it as the film I wanted to make – a film in which I wanted to talk about the things around me, the real, my environment. I wanted to speak about the society I knew. But at the same time, I had absolutely no desire to respect the 'voice of God' that we used to hear in the news in Cameroon, the newsreels – I didn't know what documentary meant – that were screened in cinemas before the feature, before the action films, the Hindi films; that is, the monochordal authoritarian Pathé voice that was always present, that spoke without us knowing where it was coming from, or from where it spoke, which bothered me. That wasn't what I wanted to do. I thought to myself, how can I show the real without using this monotone voice that reminds me of the news? How to talk about life, how to talk about my contradictions? How to talk about what I deeply felt? How to talk about this in an interesting way and how to contribute something more to what exists already? So, I already started asking myself questions about how to construct a film and for me, it was always obvious that even if I worked with elements of the real, I wanted my narratives to take an almost fictional form. So, when I wanted to make a homage to my father, I knew that it would be a conversation that I strike up with him, he who was no longer there, and that I wouldn't be visible either. At the time, I hadn't yet thought of using a voice-over because I didn't yet know how to say 'I'. Or rather, I wanted to say 'I', but struggled to do so. But I knew that I wanted to be able to construct the narrative with elements of suspense and make it so that it is only at the end that all these elements become clear. So, my approach was a fictional one in which I deliver the information in small brushstrokes and so I introduced this dialogue between two characters. I had two friends – Abossolo Mbo and Tadie Tuene – who were stand-up comedians, who did one-man shows. I also created this dialogue out of necessity. There were two of them, so I thought: 'Okay, a conversation, but between whom?' Between two childhood friends, one who has left, travelled, and returns to the village, and the other who has stayed behind. At the same time, it was also a kind of conversation between me and my father, between the village and elsewhere, in short; I used this mode to be able to play on several levels at once. Ultimately, it is even a conversation between two aspects of the same person.

These two characters are indeed clearly distinguished by their different accents, by their ways of speaking French. There is a clear duality, which you establish in an amusing way and which allows you to tease out the question of these two different visions.

Yes. The question of the duality between so-called 'tradition' and modernity, which was the centre of debates from the 1960s to the 1990s, between the city and the village, has been predominant in African cinema since the colonial era. I had the impression that I had both in me. I used to spend time in the village, loving being with my grandfather, but also in the city with my father. These two characters represent my own contradictions, as it were. Choosing two characters, one in the village, one in the town, and expressing both of their opinions at the same time, was a way of symbolizing the internal conflict that has always inhabited me. People only realize at the end of the film that one of the characters is me, when I acknowledge this in the final shots, referring to my father's death. But both characters are aspects of my own distorted colonized self, an issue that I didn't know how to express at the time in one character. Two characters allowed me to express the dual elements of my personality. So, I constructed a dramaturgy, a thread, a cinematographic narrative in this thirteen-minute short film.

How was the film received at the time?

For me, the aim wasn't simply to show raw reality; it was to take this reality and to try to reconstitute it in an enjoyable way that wouldn't bore people. But when I showed the film in 1984/1985, people said: 'It's neither fish nor fowl! It's not fiction, it's not documentary, it resembles nothing!' But it was what I had wanted to make. And today – though to a lesser degree, no doubt – I continue to make uncharacteristic films. When I'd finished *Hommage*, I didn't even try to enter it into any festivals because, after editing it for seven days with Madeleine Beauséjour, we fell out and I had already started working on *Fièvre jaune taximan*, my next short film. I edited this second short, but it wasn't very good and one day I called Madeleine. We saw each other again, and she helped me re-edit *Fièvre*, which was selected at the Clermont Ferrand Short Film Festival and, as I was sending them the film, I also sent *Hommage* because I knew they were looking for documentaries. I said to them: 'I don't know if it's a documentary, but I've got something'. I then also sent it to the Visions du Réel Festival in Nyon [Switzerland], where it won the Audience Award. As a result, the people from Cinéma du Réel discovered it and called me to show it at the 1986 Cinéma du Réel festival in Paris. There, *Hommage* won the Short Film Award too. And that's where I met Jean Rouch for the first time.

So at the time, my approach was that I wanted to recount things, but to recount them with the elements I had, with my friends, with a form of expression that was as close as possible to that of ordinary people and their habitual way of speaking, and I built the film out of that, with their voices.

Meanwhile, I also made *Fièvre jaune taximan*, a more classically fictional short film recounting the day in the life of a taxi driver in Yaoundé, played by the late Essindi Mindja, and with Jean Bediebe and Félicité Wouassi, whom I bumped into at the airport and asked to play the role of an obnoxious Parisian who takes the taxi; she agreed! There was no written script; Félicité completely improvised. The whole film takes place through the passengers' conversations with the driver, while at the same time showing the city.

In Conversation

Photos 20a-b-c
On location shooting *Le Dernier voyage*, Limbe, 1990. Teno directing actor Narcisse Kouokam.

But, for you, this film was clearly a fiction, unlike *Hommage*...

Yes. For *Hommage*, I simply filmed shots of everyday life in my village. I had gone there with a 16-mm Arri ST camera and four 122-metre reels of film. After four days, the camera broke down. I had a Leica camera, so I carried on taking still pictures. *Hommage* is a mix of film and photos. I believed that with music, dialogue, zooming in or panning over still photos, I could still manage to say things. There are also the double exposures at the end of the film, superimposing the photos of the dance that I took and the photo of my father that I filmed in 16 mm. Perhaps the fact of having worked at the television at the time freed me from my inhibitions in mixing so many elements and allowed me to experiment with the editing. It is perhaps this that gave me a sense of freedom.

Filming the Real

You have repeated several times that you wanted to 'film the real'. Why?

Yes, I wanted to film the things around me, what I could see, what struck me, because I had the feeling, somehow, that fiction involved the imagination – which might or might not be related to the real – but I wanted to question this real which struck me as problematic. So that's why instead of depicting reality in a fictional form, I thought, I'm going to go for it, get straight to the point, and people will be able to recognize the different settings and protagonists, who will really speak. I felt that reconstructing the real allowed me to tackle the problems that people were facing at that time head on.

So cinema has always been a cinema of questioning for you?

Yes, definitely! It's always been a cinema of reflection. It has always been a cinema of questioning, but of entertainment too. The two things have always been present. Right from *Hommage*, there have always been interludes of humour. There is entertainment, but with a reflection behind it.

At what point did you begin to think of yourself as a documentary filmmaker?

In the early days I didn't even really know what that meant. I wanted to make films, I wanted to use the camera to talk about the things around me, to show the life around me, I wanted to make films showing my village. It's as if I were saying to people: 'I'm going to show you, I'm going to take you to discover this or that, I'm going to tell you a story'. That's the way I saw myself as a filmmaker. It wasn't by saying 'I am a filmmaker'. When I tell a story, it needs to be connected to something, it needs to be rooted in a reality. Not a definitive reality, but the one that I see, that I know. Also, the questions that play on me, that interest me, often involve speaking about there where I'm from, about what seems essential to me – questions that strike me as fundamental. It is other people who told me I was a documentary filmmaker. And when I made *Clando*, they said it was a fiction. Yet *Clando* is still very close to documentary in a way. Are these classifications set in stone?

It's not so much classifications that I'm interested in, but rather in how you conceived of your work. Did you used to watch many documentary films at that time?

Not really. And I must say that I often found them uninteresting, because I wasn't interested in knowing, for example, how people made this or that. What interested me, rather, was what you do with that, what is behind it. I have always positioned myself in my films, rather than just wanting to show something. Even in *Lieux saints*, when I show Jules César making the djembe, it is not the act of fabrication alone, but all the symbolism behind it that interests me. So, watching these films, I thought to myself: 'How can you get people to question their environment by showing them films like that?' Because I have always thought of cinema in terms of what people take with them once they leave the cinema. It has always been one of the things I consider essential.

You might thus ask the question what people took away from *Hommage*! I don't know but, for me, *Hommage* was a film that was first and foremost for me, that first of all served to heal me. I was away when my father died, and I wasn't able to go back. I had always had a difficult relationship with him; we used to talk – sometimes we would talk for hours – but without that period of real listening that I would certainly have begun to have later. By my thirties, I would have certainly been able to exchange more easily with him because I would have matured, but, well ... he was no longer there when I began to have a better understanding of the world. As a result, it's a little as if I found myself in the world not having finished my learning process when I was young, and not being able to finish it as an adult, and trying to work out when I would finish it, and perhaps realizing that maybe I wouldn't ever! And therefore that I would remain an imperfect being, and perhaps that through my films I could learn a little bit about the world, about things, always a little bit more.

When did you start discovering documentary works of other kinds? When you started showing your own films in festivals?

I was always curious to see other films and so when I found myself selected in documentary festivals, I went to see the other films and gradually grew closer to people who look at and reflect on the world, seeing their approaches, their ways of working. I found myself in the world of documentary, in the world of independent cinema, of protest cinema – even on a formal level. I found my film family: that of avant-garde cinema, in the sense that all those who made an impression on me, all those who inspired me, were those who didn't respect the official codes. I nourished myself cinematographically on anything that was avant-garde. Already at university, at the film club, I began watching all these 'marginal' films, all the unusual works; that's what I liked. After, when I moved to Paris, I used to go constantly to the Latin Quarter where there was a cinema called the Saint-Séverin, I think, on the little rue Saint-Séverin. It was my favourite cinema. I'd go there and discover the most incredible, strangest films which surprised and shocked me on a formal level. I used to go and watch everything there – out of curiosity. I maybe didn't have the words to describe people's artistic approaches, but I was already fascinated by the fact that people could do a certain number of things. I watched films from Eastern Europe, films by people like Jodorowsky, completely marginal films, everything that was shot on 16 mm, or Super 8 … I saw Miklós Jancsó's films there. I'll always remember one film I went to see there called *Themroc* by Claude Faraldo – wow! – with Michel Piccoli, in which the characters didn't speak; they grunted! It was my greatest pleasure, seeing these unlikely, incredible films in that cinema. That's how I discovered a whole completely weird film culture of iconoclastic films that were wild to watch. I loved them because even if I didn't understand everything, I did enjoy them; I had the impression that these were people with a personal reflection on life who hadn't been formatted by a dominant narrative that left me stone cold. The films that I was into were all particular experiences and some of them were naturally documentaries. I watched documentaries that seemed interminable to me, but at the same time, I enjoyed going to see them because I got the impression that I was seeing new things. And at the same time, I also like commercial cinema, and the well-recognized independent American cinema shown in cinemas – Scorsese, Coppola – all those narrative works that were beautiful cinema. So, I was always torn between greater originality and at the same time a narrative construction that allowed me to address a wider audience.

This meant that when I started making my own films, I wondered how to make something that was personal and at the same time still accessible to others, while constructing a narrative that was as smooth as possible and meaningful. Because, ultimately, I always think that a work needs to say something about the situation of Africa, where we don't have that many narrative spaces. I wanted to inscribe myself within this gaze focused on the world, with tools that were both the simplest possible, and which were close to people. But at the same time, I didn't want a constructed, fictional cinema with a representation of the world that was detached from reality. It was the mix of the two that struck me as interesting. That is how, amidst these tensions, I started developing my cinema.

Are there any documentary filmmakers, or any other filmmakers, with whom you feel a particular affinity, or whose work you admire?

Yes. I have always felt an affinity with Ken Loach, with his fiction films. I always used to think that the day I would make a fiction film, I wanted it in particular to be like Loach's early films, his television films – *Ladybird, Raining Stones* – all those great works that were both social, about ordinary folks, but with such incredible stories. I found his films incredible: not made with great means, but always with remarkable stories. For me, this was the model of fiction film. Moreover, Ken Loach has also made documentaries.

And any other documentary filmmakers?

That's more complicated. In documentary, I first saw Chris Marker's film *Sans soleil* a few years after making *Afrique, je te plumerai* and I really regretted so, because if I had seen it earlier, I would have certainly been able to go much further in *Afrique*. At the time, I had simply set out, navigating with no model. I sometimes felt, in fact, that I didn't really want to have too much of a model because I thought it was better to let things just come out and that they be in a form of coherence that was my own. But *Sans soleil* would have encouraged me to take this exploration further.

You once told me about your attempts when you first started out to meet Jean Rouch. Can you tell the story again?

When I moved to Paris in 1982, I was working at the television and I always had my little camera on me – my little ARRI ST. I used to shoot images that I developed at the TV lab and I started wanting to make films, so my colleagues kept saying to me: 'If you want to make a film, you need to go to see Jean Rouch. He spent a lot of time in Africa and he helps African filmmakers. You have to go to see him.' As France 3 was in the 16th arrondissement at the time, near Avenue Montaigne, it wasn't very far from the Musée de l'Homme [where Rouch worked]. So, during my lunch break, I decided to go one day to try to meet Rouch, as everyone told me I had to meet this man.

Were you familiar with his films at that time?

I had seen his films at the time, which I found interesting, but they didn't move me more than that as they were films that … My knowledge of cinema was … There were some that I didn't like, but everyone raved about them so much that you had to see them – and to consider them a model. So, I went to the Musée de l'Homme once, twice, three times, but he was never there, and I always bumped into this woman who worked in his office. One day she said to me: 'Young man, why, in fact, do you want to see Rouch?' I answered: 'I'm Cameroonian, I want to make films and everybody tells me that if I want to make films I need to meet Jean Rouch'. She looked at me and said: 'Jean Rouch is a very great filmmaker, but as a teacher … I'm not so sure. In my opinion, if you really want to make films that are interesting, you shouldn't meet him. Try instead to find your own direction. It will be more personal.' So, I crept off back out of there!

It was already the time when my idea of going to make films in Cameroon was taking root. While continuing my job, I would go every year. And so I went and shot *Hommage*. My whole reflection when making this film was that I didn't have a model so somehow, I tried to find a sort of coherence with regard to my experiences, my relationship to the people around me, and also the mode of expression that might be the most original. So, I made *Hommage* and the first time that I met Jean Rouch was at the Cinéma du Réel Festival where it was selected. It was after the screening, I was there for a Q&A, and I saw this man, Rouch, stand up and say: 'We have just been given a veritable lesson in cinema!' I was so flustered. And he added: 'When you start a film, you should always know where you are going. That's what I always tell my students: when you know what the ending is, you can quite simply work out how to gradually build up to it. Here, it was perfect, because who could have expected the turn of affairs at the end, the denouement? It's wonderful. Well done, young man!' I was completely astounded. Rouch had said that! And I won the Cinéma du Réel Short Film Award. After, the film was broadcast on TF1, and several other television channels.

But I didn't become one of Rouch's disciples nonetheless, because I still had in mind what that lady had said to me – that I needed to find my own path – and I continued my own quest. Perhaps at the time I ought to have done what a lot of people reproached me for not doing: Film Studies, Sociology Studies at the Collège de France. People wanted me to come and enrol, but at the time I was always very wary. I didn't have the discernment necessary to approach people, take what I needed, nourish my reflection, and continue to keep my independence. So, it was rather ambivalent: I cut myself off from this reflection on documentary in the universities, where people were carrying out this research that could have been beneficial. A lot of people approached me at the time after seeing my first films and wanted me to join them, to develop my general culture. But when you come from where I come from, without having had the opportunities to understand the importance of this form of education, you take a long time to realize it. As a result, I rejected all of that.

It was only much later that I saw Rouch again, a few months before his death. It was in Innsbruck, there was a retrospective of my work, in 2002 I think, and a retrospective of Rouch's films. Rouch was there with his wife, who was also his carer, and when Rouch arrived, someone asked him if he was proud of the heritage of all the films he had made in Africa. To which he answered that of the two filmmakers present, he wasn't convinced that the most African was the one that everyone imagined!

What did you understand by that?

It's not what I understood, but what a lot of people did: that Rouch thought that he was in fact more African than me, that he was the most African director!

The journalists wanted to know what I thought. There had been the famous conflict between Sembène and Rouch, when Sembène said that Rouch filmed Africans like insects. If, by this time, Rouch thought he was African and that he had the legitimacy to film Africans in the way he did because he felt himself to be African, what could I say? Nothing!

Documentary Practice

How do you view the way documentary has developed in Francophone Africa, notably from the pioneering Safi Faye and Samba Félix Ndiaye onwards? Were you familiar with their work when you started making films?

When I started out, they were already there. I was familiar with their work, with the films they made, but it wasn't their work that influenced me. I first of all embraced documentary out of my personal desire to talk about the things around me. But also out of a desire for originality. I wasn't looking to reproduce formulae that worked for others. My very first film *Hommage* was a film I made without wanting either to emulate others, or to distance myself from them; it was first and foremost a personal quest and a desire to find a mode of expression that went against dogma that existed at the time. I was faced with a certain number of questions: how to appropriate the right to speak in order to talk about my environment? I didn't ask myself how my neighbour appropriated the right to speak to address the things around them. I loved cinema, I wanted to speak about the real; I had no model. Samba Félix Ndiaye's films at that time were focused on existing Senegalese patrimony; they weren't really the films that reflected on society that I wanted to make. So, at no time did I follow his approach. I thought Safi Faye's *Kaddu Beykat* (*Letter from My Village*) was a beautiful film, but it wasn't a reflection on the society that I lived in, nor on the urban chaos that was my daily reality. I personally was closer to the world of the writer Mongo Beti. But their films were films that I respected, each of us making the choices that we did, showing the things that interested us. So I had no model at that time – I never have, for that matter – I did not belong to any current or school – not that any existed locally, for that matter, there being only three or four documentary filmmakers in Africa then, including Lionel Ngakane, whose films I had also seen. I saw all these films, but I sought my own path, my own voice, in accord with the concerns I had and with my vision of society.

You later exchanged quite a lot with Samba Félix Ndiaye about documentary.

Yes, Samba Félix Ndiaye – whom I knew personally – and I did discuss documentary, particularly after he had been to Rwanda, and after his 2007 film *Questions à la terre natale* (*Questions to the Native Land*) because he had long criticized voice-overs. At one time – in the 1990s, I believe – people tended to think that what mattered in cinema was the image, and that voice-overs were a facile option. As a result, they were highly contemptuous of the use of voice-overs. But I consider cinema to be both sound and image. I spend a lot of time during the montage working on the sound, not just the voice-over, but also the music and sound effects I choose. The quality of the sound is really important to me. Our discussions were often about the voice-over, then, about the fact that a lot of people thought it was an easy option. So, I really chuckled the day I saw him use a voice-over in *Questions à la terre natale*. I said to him: 'So, Samba, let's talk! Was your voice-over easy to do?' And we talked about it and that was the end of that chapter! But after, what he always used to say to me was that I needed 'to watch my right hook!' That my left one was good, but that I had to 'watch my right hook'. It was his way of saying that I should pay more attention to a certain number of formal elements that in his opinion were not sufficiently present. He thought that my narrative threads weren't sufficiently polished. I didn't agree but, at the same time, that was his opinion and I did hear him. Over time we grew closer because, once he had also worked on writing a text, I think he came to realize that it wasn't as easy as all that to take a camera, to film, then to add a text. And for me, after *Vacances au pays*, which is a film with a lot of voice-over text, I gradually started distancing myself from voice-overs, making them more minimalist, while also trying to make them as poetic and forceful as possible.

What is very interesting is that, with the digital revolution, we have reached a time in which the cinema I was making – that is, a cinema in the first person – has become something accepted, something recognized as, with digital cameras, more and more people have made 'confessional', or 'diary films'.

So, you didn't situate yourself in relation to these first Francophone African documentary filmmakers. As you discovered other documentary practices from around the world, were there any other currents that you felt close to?

There were filmmakers with whom I felt a lot of affinities – affinities in relation to what they contributed, to what they were doing. I felt all the closer to them when I met and talked to them. When I met Johan van der Keuken – unfortunately almost at the end of his life – he had just made *The Long Holiday* (*De grote vakantie*). He had cancer and had travelled the world to see how they treated this illness elsewhere. I showed him *Vacances au pays*, which he really liked, and he said to me – and this is what really interested me – that he didn't know if he hadn't been born in his part of the world, if he had been born in Africa, a continent that was still under domination, what type of cinema he would have made, whether he could he have gone forth in the world and observed others in the way he did. It's true that the empathy he had for others first of all begins with a sort of empathy for those around you, and he wouldn't have been able to observe the suffering and the distress of the people around him in the same way. His films are both the reflection of there where he lived, where he grew up, and his preoccupations as a White Dutchman of his age, and that, that really moved me; not that we all make films according to our own style, but the fact

Photo 21 Johan van der Keuken and Jean-Marie Teno, Perugia, Italy, 1999.

of making films that are very close to the world, and the fact of being someone in this world while trying to show it, to reflect on peoples' condition, to show a form of empathy, a kind of love for people. What I indeed love in the way Johan filmed, what touched me, is that I got the impression that he created something incredible with people, something that you rarely find. At the opposite end of the spectrum I would personally put the kind of relationship you see in the films of someone like Raymond Depardon. Personally, I've never managed to feel that empathy with his characters; even if he talks about the people of his home region, whom he knows, I've always tended to feel very distant from them.

I really liked Johan and we stayed on very good terms. For that matter, I even ended up being in one of his films when he was shooting his film about the photographer – *To Sang Fotostudio* – which was the portrait of an Amsterdam street, with lots of people from different horizons. In the entire street, there were no Africans. And as, even though he was making a documentary, he always added an element of fiction, he said he needed an African; as he loved my African shirts, he called me, and I appear in a sequence of the film!

Thinking about your childhood, your rather unconventional path, and the films and the filmmakers you cite, I get the impression that it is the unformatted that both attracts and resembles you…

Maybe indeed. I don't know what ends up influencing and defining one's choices; life maybe. But in my case, I'm not that sure of myself, so it's clear that my collaborations with people have always been a form of constant quest. When I start a film, I may go in one direction or another; I try to go there where what I discover takes me. Even if I write a project, when I go out and start to shoot, it's like when I start a discussion with someone; I always let the element go as far as possible in the direction it takes, and then after, before the material, my idea may evolve. And that is perhaps why my films are constructed in this way in which my voice, my questioning may vary according to the things that I learn and which take my films in one direction or another. That's why today's formatted writing of projects is a disaster for people like me.

You say you aren't very sure of yourself, yet in your films, your voice is on the contrary very assertive.

Yes, because when I begin, I am not sure of what I am going to discover. Also, I make initial choices and when I make the decision to go in a direction, I do. In general, it takes me a while to find that direction, however; I ask myself a lot of questions, I feel my way forward, I seek, I try, and finally I determine the direction. At times – and this was a big concern of mine for a long time, because I position myself on issues based on the information or elements at my disposal at that given time – I have often thought to myself that if in ten years I learn other things I didn't know before, perhaps I'll seem a bit stupid! But well, that's life. We reason according to what we know. I didn't grow up surrounded by books, or with access to much culture. I didn't go to the best universities. I learn by absorbing things little by little…

You say this was a big concern of yours, but have you ever later watched one of your films and thought you got the main discourse of a film wrong?

No, that hasn't happened to me yet, fortunately, because I get the feeling that by taking the time necessary … one thing that is certain is that my films resemble me. With the films that I make, the questions I ask, I always go a long way in my personal questioning of the things I say. And when I write my texts – it's not someone else who writes them for me – I try as far as possible to seek deep inside for the things I try to say. They are things that I take complete responsibility for, and even in ten or twenty years, or even in thirty if I'm still around, I will still take responsibility for them because, by then, even if there are things I would say differently, it's certain that I don't regret the things I said or wrote in my films' voice-overs.

How would you describe the process by which you construct your films?

It's a difficult moment to talk about my process, because I get the impression that since 2006/2007, I have been going through a period of my work that is really painful in the sense that I get the impression that I am spending much too much time writing, trying to elaborate projects that don't necessarily find the required funding. I think that there ends up being a kind of fatigue, even in the process. I find myself in a situation in which, for example, at pitches, you are asked to present a film project. But everything today is so codified, all the markets are so watertight, that films have to fit into a certain number of slots. It can happen that you may have the best project possible, but if you speak about your subject in a way that isn't the one people want to hear at that moment, you have no chance of finding funding for it. Does that mean that you need to question your process? Is it the things you want to say that need to be rethought, when you pertinently know that the questions you are posing are the continuation of a pertinent reflection on situations that have not improved – on the contrary… These questions that no longer interest anyone are nonetheless still present and have been since Independence, and they deserve that we pause to consider them still, seriously so, until these situations are resolved for the majority. It's important!

After a while, you wonder whether you should do what I did with *Le Mariage d'Alex*, or a film like *Chef!*, which wasn't born out of a process of writing, or films like *Lieux saints* and *Une Feuille dans le vent*, which had no scenario or written project initially; they were films that just started out like that, that I started making, and I just continued working on them until they were finished.

They were films that were born simply out of an idea, a subject, then?

Yes. They are films based on the real, on a situation or an incident that strikes me and that I start to film. As I'm filming the event, ideas and questions fly round my head: why does this incident interest me? What does it evoke? Why? From the answers to these questions and many others that come to mind, the subject of a film is born, a subject that I spend time working on until I'm satisfied. That satisfaction sometimes only comes in the editing room or during the sound mix. Once the subject defined, I think about how to treat it. I also ask myself the question of where I'm speaking from. When I first started out, I didn't theorize that yet, but I always asked the question of who was speaking, where I was speaking from, and how I needed to construct the narrative so that people would understand me. I am of the same generation as Idrissa Ouedraogo; we were both in Paris when we made our first films. He had been both to the VGIK, the Moscow film school, and to the FEMIS [the French national film school], which was called the IDHEC at the time, so he had structure in the way he made his films, and he made them brilliantly. But it wasn't my approach at all. I was more in an intuitive, passionate gesture that found its narrative structure in the subject chosen, or that imposed itself on me. How, in the multitude of narratives that existed, to play with the different elements to construct a narrative about things people don't talk about, or no longer talk about, or which are greatly oversimplified? How to establish for the audience the complexity of a situation? Either you resort only to established forms of narrative – the three-act structure people always talk about – or you ask yourself: 'How can I tell this story to someone close to home, someone who comes from where I come from? What do I need to do so that they can follow me without getting lost?' In short, I try to find endogenous narrative forms. This is just the first stage, and I know it won't be easy, but I think that's how you manage to make something interesting. When I see comedians – there are a lot in Africa – they are incredible storytellers; I always wonder whether we couldn't draw on their way of constructing a narrative that is both funny and efficient. It's funny, for that matter, when I look at my filmmaking path, I have often called on comedians. The voice-overs of my very first film, *Hommage*, were played by two people who did stand-up – Tadie Tuene and Emil Abossolo Mbo – who later became the great actors they are today. My first fiction short film was with Essindi Mindja, who used to do one-man shows. I also worked with Narcisse Kouokam; they are all people who came from a tradition of comic narrative.

But at the same, you find yourself confronted with a major problem: when the funders come from a different cultural zone than the subjects or projects you put before them, they always judge them from there where they are, and according to codes and criteria they know and to strategies of their own. So, you find yourself in a situation in which what is encouraged is often what they are already familiar with and recognize, which leaves little room for innovation; it even discourages innovation. I have even been told that innovation is the very thing that no one wants, that they especially don't want people who take risks. So, I therefore think that maybe with documentary in Africa, we should really look to experimental cinema.

When you look, for example, at the African visual artists who are enjoying an impressive degree of success throughout the world, they aren't people who copy what exists. When I look at the work of Cameroonian artists, such as Pascale Marthine Tayou or Barthélémy Toguo, they are people who, in their field, have created totally personal works. It is them, it's their work, they invented it. If we don't invent, if we don't create, we won't really manage to advance. I think that we should also aim for that in documentary too.

Experimentations, Assemblages

You have often experimented in your films...

Yes, and I still experiment ... In *Une Feuille dans le vent*, for example, when I had no archive images available, when there were no images, I added drawings. Even today, that takes people by surprise. From the very outset, I always felt that anything that is an image can be part of a film. I started right back with *Hommage*, including a painting at the end of the film. Anything that is meaningful visually, I take it. I give it a sense. I take the archives and I give them new meaning and they end up becoming something that people recognize today.

That reminds me of salvage-art, of recycled art, of the practice of artist Pascale Marthine Tayou, whom we see in your film, *La Tête dans les nuages* ... Or of a form of collage. You 'salvage' and you 'collate' different elements in you works.

Absolutely, that's true. It's about salvaging everything, not overlooking anything, and refashioning it. But that is art, that is knowledge, in fact. People create knowledge out of other people's knowledge, which they take, knead and reformulate to express something else, thereby giving it new definitions.

When you were making your first films, was this way of assembling different elements something that came spontaneously?

Yes, it came spontaneously. I have always started out from a specific point. I have a subject, and questions that arise, and I try to find solutions. I think to

Photo 22 Salvage-art: artist Pascale Marthine Tayou in *La Tête dans les nuages*, Yaoundé, 1994.

myself: 'I'll start here and end up there. In the meantime, I'll address this or that.' My question has always been how to show the elements that say that? What elements can I find to show that? How do I go from one idea to the next? What questions do these elements pose me? That is how I have often constructed my films. I constructed them saying to myself: 'So, the situation is like this, and that poses me this question', and from these questions, I set out to seek different elements that will allow me to answer this question, or to find elements that bring me answers. That is how I have often set out, advanced, and found myself in a dead end and had to backtrack to be able to advance again, until I manage, maybe, to find a way out. There are films that I found no conclusion for. With *Chef!*, for example, I didn't find a conclusion. I advanced, I advanced I didn't know where, and I could have carried on advancing more with *Chef!* For that matter, I still need to finish a film that I wanted to make afterwards, continuing the reflection on power in the Bandjoun chieftaincy in Western Cameroon (my hometown); I will finish it one day. It's an attempt to find a response to this question of power: what is the place of this so-called 'traditional' power in the architecture of power today, how do we live with it, what do we do with it, how can we manage to overcome this schizophrenia? Can we continue to live in a country with these two different forms of power without managing to find a real logical bridge between the two, rather than living in this kind of haze?

You juxtapose many elements, including different ways of filming, or different styles: static fixed-frame interviews; street scenes or events that unexpectedly take place and that you capture on the spot, in the heat of the action ... How do you manage these different ways of filming? What takes precedent for you?

All my films are different; each one has been a specific experience. When I set out to make a film, I necessarily set out with an idea. I try to see what different elements I can assemble. Sometimes, I've already filmed some of these elements; other times no, and it's a process that continues until the end of the film. Sometimes, I set out looking for something and, on the way, I come across things, events, that resonate with what I'm working on and which can enrich my narrative. If I have my camera with me, I film. I'm always open to the unexpected, the unplanned, to what just happens, because, right from the start, my cinema has been a cinema that aims to recount the environment that I know, in which I lived, and which, for me, wasn't sufficiently represented. Sometimes I filmed with a camera operator, but it happened that I'd see things I found interesting, that I liked, and that suddenly connected me with the place and made me want to talk, but the time it takes to say to someone else 'look at that', to explain, to ask them to film it, sometimes it was too late; it had gone. If I am alone with my camera and I suddenly see things, daily situations, moments of life that I like, I frame and I film. Sometimes I do it really fast, because the moment I'm trying to capture is furtive. Putting these elements together with others, I can recreate the sentiment that I am trying to convey at that moment. So, in my cinema, the unexpected, the spontaneous are part of the work. When I go out in the street, when I walk, I don't necessarily look for something predetermined. I don't only see what I'm looking for, I see new things that I wasn't expecting and, as a result, I include them. I make a lot of associations in my films, and my voice-over texts link all these different things; that's how I give meaning to what I see, to the things I come across that weren't necessarily things I thought of or imagined. For a while now, and even in the academic field, it is by making associations, finding correspondences, that one manages to enrich knowledge. In my cinema, I always try to make connections in order to see how putting things into relation with one another helps produce new knowledge.

If, thinking back to Samba Félix Ndiaye's remarks, you later realize that the framing of an image you shot on the spur of the moment isn't optimal, or not aesthetically polished enough, is that a problem?

The idea of an image's perfection is in itself interesting. Who defines whether an image is perfect or not? Before, when we were still working in celluloid, the image was supposed to be in-focus, well-framed, etc. In film, you had to take the time to compose a shot, to frame it, because celluloid film was expensive. It was a lengthy process. In video, the process is much quicker. You can shoot with the camera set to automatic and you'll still get a beautiful image. But is it just an image's aesthetic value that matters? Today, you can reframe your shots afterwards on a computer – a lot of people do. Personally, I don't want to do that because it's not what matters to me. For me, it's the emotion. When, all of a sudden, an image speaks to me, when something occurs, for me it's what's in the image, it's the emotion I manage to capture that I'm interested in. And if the golden rules and all the rules of shot composition are not respected, it's not important so long as, at some point, people feel something. What's more, if you take the history of framing, you realize that all the rules that were in vigour at one time ended up being completely contested later. And so, images that were meaningful at one point, that seemed well-framed, can later seem banal, while at the same time conserving the status of archive, which creates a specific relationship with the spectator.

This question of cinematographic codes again takes us back, as you just said, to the question of who defines the codes. It's fair to say that you are, both cinematographically and in your life, someone who doesn't respect codes much – it's a form of freedom, perhaps. But I'm thinking too of Julio Garcia Espinosa's 1969 text: 'For an Imperfect Cinema'. He considered technically and artistically mastered cinema – 'perfect cinema' – often to be a reactionary one...

Absolutely!

...I'm thinking too of the decolonial thinkers, of their questioning Western canons and epistemes ... Is your way of challenging, of subverting imposed canons and codes a political, decolonial gesture, a reflection of your non-conformity, a quest for freedom?

I think a bit of all of that at the same time! If I weren't already, by nature, in my life, in my way of being, someone who sought to contest all these codes, I wouldn't have done so in my cinema. In the group I found myself in when I started making films – that of African cinema, as there weren't many of us – there were very few documentary filmmakers at the time, very few people who approached the real in this way. The real was problematic. The real had already been defined by others. Either we had to accept it, or invent new things which, to get taken seriously, were sometimes very far from the real. But I thought: 'Hold on, we're talking about us and this image that we are giving of ourselves doesn't resemble what I see at all', so why play along by accepting to be the happy-go-lucky, grinning Black boy whom people would be happy to promote, or the angst-ridden intellectual who fits in nowhere, disappears, resigned to his lot? For me, the first most important thing was to contest these representations by proposing others, and by opening up the path for others, saying that wherever they were, they could represent their worlds, their spaces, which are rarely those that the authorities impose on us, both in our home countries and the countries of our exile.

For me, that was the most complete form of freedom. It was to say that if I want to speak about my village, I won't speak about it in the same way as the king's son might, because he sees the village from his position of power; I will speak from my own position, and someone else will speak from yet another position. It's thus a question of opening the space to a diverse range of visions. And for me, it was important to be able to contest all these completely rigid things and to do so in terms of the style, in terms of the narrative – whether unconsciously or not – even if I met others who did the same in other fields – that is, the African writers of the 1970s to 1980s, who were confined by those who control literature to certain spaces. Many of them refused to stay in the place to which they were assigned. In short, it was an approach that came, I think, at the same time as other approaches; there was a form of convergence of these reactions to this assignation to our origins, places or cultures. That is what made African cinema of the 1970s and 1980s so rich and beautiful.

Coming on to montage, when you make a film, you define your subject, then, you think about the questions it poses, you start filming your material, you gather other material, such as drawings or archive footage to make up for the elements you don't have at your disposal and at some point, you find yourself in the editing room. How do you proceed with the montage?

I have my subject, my images, my sounds, and I start by thinking about a voice-over text. Do I need one? This question finds its answer in the position I take regarding my subject: what is my degree of implication? Am I directly, or indirectly, concerned by the story's trigger? The answer to this question will define my implication and the place of my voice-over in the film. It's at this point that I finalize the structure of the narrative and introduce a certain number of effects, which is the fun, mischievous part of the work. It's here that I play with the spectator. If I include a voice-over text, the first major question for me is what is the first word I pronounce? What is the first sentence I say? And why do I say it when I do? What does it mean when I say that? In short, I'm in a form of perpetual questioning. And at the same time, I ask myself where I position myself vis-à-vis the people I don't know, who are going to hear me when I say this or that, and vis-à-vis my film. I establish this relationship between the two through my text, and I begin to advance like that, putting the spectator at ease so they know where I am speaking from, who I am, and what the subject we are going to explore is. And from there, I take them on the voyage that is the film.

For you, is a film really constructed at the editing stage?
No, it starts being constructed well before. For me, it's a permanent construction – in my head, first, making me decide to make a film. There's an idea and when the idea comes to me, I have the matter for a film, having identified several elements that are close to the subject, connected to it, and which help me think and go further in my reflection. So, from the time of formulating the idea until the completion of the film, via the montage and even the sound mixing, I continue to think until the very end. And after, when the time comes to show people the film – because sometimes, when I finish a film I don't know how to present it anymore, because my reflection has evolved so much that I no longer really know what the true starting point of the film was– so when I've finished a film, I have to digest it and reappropriate the film so that I can find the best way to present it so that someone seeing the film for the first time can understand.

What role exactly does the montage play in your films' construction, then?
I started my professional life as an editor so, for me, it's about putting together all the elements so that the story takes form and exists; it's the place where the film comes together. The montage therefore takes a lot of time. To start with, I edit a first rough draft to see how to broach the story, how it might be constructed. From there, based on the images and elements that I have, I ask myself the question of the form, of how to put it all together so it has meaning.

The narrative, the storytelling is really important for you. You said earlier that when you make a film, you above all want to tell a story…
Yes. A film is a story that you tell, that I tell, and begins somewhere and goes somewhere in relation to a subject that interests me. When I define the subject, I think to myself: 'I'm going to start out from there, so how do I construct the different elements?' Like everyone, I sit down, I think, I think about the material and I try to find a sequence for the elements that will constitute the film. I might also suddenly decide to advance, and make elements in the narrative advance

thanks to my voice-over text, in which I can introduce questions, or take the film in one direction or another … It's during the montage that I start to write my text.

You pay particular attention to the sound, the music and the voice in your films. For you, what role does the sound play?

There are so many layers of sound. First, there's the ambient sound that I record at the same time as the images. Then there's the sound that I might add to give the images a specific meaning, to accentuate or attenuate certain tendencies in order to choose in the multitude of possible meanings those that interest me. There is also the music, which adds another dimension to the film, that introduces a distance between the image and the spectator in all senses of the term.

When I use archive images, they often include a soundtrack. Sometimes, in order to question them, I may decide to keep the archive sound; at others, I remove it, replacing it with a soundtrack made up of sound effects, music, or voice-over commentaries.

Generally speaking, the sound can serve as a counterpoint to provide different elements for reading the film; it also sometimes serves to develop what people were saying. A very simple example: in *Bikutsi Water Blues*, I went to a village to interview some women who had formed a collective and it was the husband of one of the women in charge who decided to speak. But as he spoke, his wife had to keep whispering him the answers because he really had no idea! And at one point, he said: 'You'll see when we go to fetch water, things have changed in the village. The men no longer leave the women to work on their own all the time. The men work too, they participate. Particularly by going to fetch water. You'll see. Now men and women go together with their water pots.' Only, when we went to fetch water, he was there, just like that. The women all had their containers. We went up the hill, he let them pass in front, doing nothing. So, when I was editing, I let his interview continue over the image of the women all carrying buckets while he stood there, his hands in his pockets. So, it's always this play between what people say, sometimes pretty demagogically, and what we can see for ourselves.

The Cinematic 'I'

Coming on to your voice-overs, which have become a signature mark of your work, can you describe your path to this first-person voice-over, which you didn't adopt in your earliest films?

When I started making films, I knew I didn't want a 'voice of God' that spoke from who knows where without you knowing where it came from. For me, this voice was highly problematic. That is why in my very first film, *Hommage*, I decided to have two actors play, acting out a conversation. *Hommage* was my own story, it was something personal, but at that time, I didn't have sufficient self-confidence to speak in the first person; I didn't dare. I had no models around me either. I didn't have other examples of the use of the first person. When I saw *Sans soleil* much later, I thought to myself: 'Ah, if only I'd seen this film before, it would have encouraged me'. The two characters I created, who are an image of myself, allowed me to address the issues posed in the film with humour and irony, and to manage the effects of my mise-en-scène. The duality between local and imported culture, the city and the village had been predominant in African cinema from the start. I had the impression that I had both in me. I used to love spending time in the village with my grandfather, but also in the city with my father. The two characters in *Hommage* represent my own contradictions as it were; they are aspects of my own distorted colonial self, of my dual personality. Choosing two characters, one from the village, one returning from the town, and expressing both of their opinions at the same time enabled me to express the internal conflict that has always inhabited me. People only realize at the end of the film that one of the characters is me.

Then, in my first feature film, *Bikutsi Water Blues*, I attempted again to speak. This time, to avoid speaking in the first person, I invented a journalist character in the film who is supposed to be carrying out an enquiry into the question of water access. As I still didn't dare speak in the first person, I created this character who allowed me to be present, to advance the plot, to invite other people to speak, to be the link.

In 1992, in *Afrique, je te plumerai*, you manage to say 'I' for the first time.

Afrique, je te plumerai was conceived as a film in which I was going to totally embrace my subjectivity. Even during the shoot, I looked for a cameraman who would be able – as at the time we were shooting with a 16 mm Eclair Coutant – to put the camera on his shoulder and advance. When we shot the interviews, I asked people to look into the camera lens to create the illusion that the camera was my own gaze. I deliberately worked on that. I wrote my voice-over text in the first person too, only I had so often heard people tell me that I didn't have a nice voice, that my voice wasn't radiophonic, that I had decided to get an actor to do the voice-over. But it happens that I write as if I were talking. So, the voice-over was written the way I talk, with my irony, and when it came to reading the text, it was very hard for someone who wasn't me to bring out the different nuances. It didn't work. Despite the actor's talent and efforts, it didn't ring true. We had hired a recording studio to record, but it was complicated and after three hours, we hadn't even recorded ten minutes. After a while, the editor said: 'You know what you want from your text, why don't you say it yourself?' I had indeed been present during the whole editing process as I was working as a television editor at the time; while she edited, I would say the text to see if it fitted properly, exactly as I was used to doing with the television journalists. I knew my text by heart and all the intonations I wanted it to have at each moment. So, I took the mike and in less than two hours – bearing in mind that the film is ninety minutes long – I had recorded the whole text and, honestly, for me it was like a game. I laughed, I sang ... that was what I considered a voice-over. That's perhaps why this film has its irony, its playfulness, its jubilation, at times its anger, because I felt the things that I wanted to say. I let myself go and I said them. At the same time, there was a certain gravity to it too – that's what made it hard to act. There were several levels of voice – at times reflexive, at times narrative, at times introspective, ironic, playful, sad, joyful – all these tones came through.

When I showed the film in France, people said: 'It's not cinema, it's collage, it's this, it's that', in short, people really virulently attacked the film, or rather its form, but it was a covert way of not addressing the crux of the question, that is, colonization. And as at the same time the film's form isn't particularly classical, as I mix so many different types of image and registers – just as I did too in *Bikutsi Water Blues*, where I already used a form that went in lots of different directions, with a lot of elements mixed together – I thought to myself: 'Ok, as you've decided that what I do makes no sense, then I'm going to continue like that; I must be on the right track!'

And I liked speaking in the first person because it made it easier for me to continue writing and exploring the themes that interested me. So, in my following films, I continued in this direction as the driving impulse of my work is above all what I have to say. When I film, it is my point of view, and this was how I gradually affirmed and improved this first-person voice.

Many thinkers have explained that it is all the more difficult for people who have been colonized, subjected, objectified to appropriate this first-person voice, this subjectivity – and that it is all the more essential that they do.

Absolutely. But it's because of this that my career became what it did! A lot of people reproached me for it, sometimes directly, sometimes indirectly. As my career continued, I had a lot of problems because of my approach and because of the ideas in my films. For *Clando*, the film I made after *Afrique, je te plumerai*, I received funding from the Fonds Sud in France. At that time, the minimum sum given for a fiction feature film was about 600,000 francs. With my film, they couldn't say no, but they gave me half the minimum sum! It made life very difficult for me. I nonetheless made the film with very limited means, but I had to invest all my personal savings because I was determined that they weren't going to stop me from making the film.

Were you conscious at the time you made *Afrique, je te plumerai* of the political gesture that this voice-over, this 'I' represented?

Of course I was. For me, it was important to show the world 'from the point of view of the native that I am', as I say in the film's voice-over. The point was to ask people to do what no one did: to identify with a Black person looking at the world. I thought to myself that the utmost political gesture would be to get people to see through the eyes of somebody they did not want to identify with. That was the first point. And the question of point of view is crucial. As long as people consider you are a nobody, at no point will they want to identify with your point of view. So that was what I wanted to foreground. It was a real political gesture. It was a form of deliberate resistance, from the start. Maybe I was a natural-born resister, a natural-born troublemaker! I did it and people watched this film from my point of view. It moved them, it bugged them, it made them laugh, but I gave myself the permission to do what I wanted, saying to myself: 'If I want to sing, I'll sing! If I want to laugh, I'll laugh! If I want to joke, I'll joke!' As a result, I establish a familiarity, I create a relationship with the spectator which, for me, is the basis of everything.

Still today when I construct my films, I always begin with the idea that I have an hour and a half with people and that they will inevitably wonder who is speaking. I don't want to start by telling them: 'My name is Jean-Marie Teno. I'm going to tell you a story. Are you ready to follow?' They might say no! So, I think to myself: 'Hmm, how am I going to start, to capture their attention and not lose it?' I tell a joke, I ask a question – not necessarily the key question – and then another … and thus it becomes a game. And little by little, people are hooked, and then we can tackle the real issue. That, to me, is cinema! I want us to laugh too, to have a good time together, not for me to take them for a ride, because I hate it when people take me for one, and in the end, you think: 'All that for that!' I am someone who resists, certainly, but I'm also someone who likes the good life, who likes telling beautiful stories, and who doesn't want people to be bored. That's where the poetry comes into it too. I get the impression that when words sound good together, have meaning, or several meanings, several levels of meaning in the words, being able to play with words is also something

I love. I often spend a long time writing my voice-overs because the things I have to say are not things that come spontaneously. They are constructed, written, it takes time to find the concision and justness and the musicality of the words so that they are pleasant to listen to.

You mentioned earlier that you start writing your voice-over texts during the editing of a film.

Yes. That, for me, is definitely one of the best moments to do so, but I'm finding it increasingly complicated these days because I often now edit myself, alone, not out of choice, but due to a lack of means. I'd like to be able to work with an editor, while I focus on writing the texts because it is the moment when I feel the most creative, looking at the images and starting to write, while trying to go always a bit further, perfecting the text as the montage advances.

Your texts, your voice often create an additional layer to all the other layers that make up your films, while also often acting as a counterpoint to the images.

Yes, because cinema is precisely image *and* sound. For a long time, too much primacy was given to the image – the IMAGE! Cinema is images, of course, but it is sound too. I was recently listening to a recording of Jean Eustache, who said that in his films he brought words to the screen. I was really happy to hear that and thought to myself: 'Ah, a true rebel at last!' It's good that people question that diktat at some point. I'm against all diktats! Cinema is both; you can play on this, find different layers. Anything that goes against predetermined, set codes and aestheticism suits me. In the past, it was hard to shoot beautiful images on celluloid; today, with just a telephone, you can shoot wonderful images: the diktat of the image is outdated. So, how to structure the material so that it says something, so that it touches people emotionally? That's the aspect that I love: the emotion. I try to say something of substance, but at the same time, to manage to say it, I need to create an emotion in the spectator because without that emotion, whatever you say has no meaning. And that emotion comes from the way in which the words and images are put together, from how I organize this ballet of images, sounds and music.

Some people reproach you for speaking too much in your films, for not leaving the spectator enough of a place.

Spectators are free not to come! It's like saying to a writer, you write, but you don't leave enough of a place for the reader. There are thousands of ways of writing … I have to say that I don't understand the meaning of this critique.

Your films make no claim at all to the objectivity often associated with documentary; they voluntarily assert complete subjectivity. Considering the evolutions in documentary filmmaking today, is this opposition between objectivity and subjectivity still relevant, or is has it become obsolete?

I find the notion of objectivity completely ridiculous. How is it even possible to make an objective film, and especially a documentary? I don't believe it exists. I, as someone who worked as a television editor for a long time, always found the idea that the television wanted us to swallow – that a TV report is objective – completely preposterous. You can invite several people with different opinions to speak, but from the moment you choose an angle to address a subject, a degree of subjectivity necessarily enters the equation. The very idea of an objective documentary is antinomic, because documentary is precisely someone's vision of a given reality. A person looks, addresses a given reality, and conveys it in their own way, by constructing it into a narrative. How can that possibly be objective? Ten filmmakers would make ten completely different films based on the same reality and using the same elements. So, the notion of objective documentary doesn't exist as far as I am concerned. For that matter, people have so moved on from this notion that they increasingly try to include the fabrication process in their films to clearly show spectators where they are positioned vis-à-vis what they are watching, so that they have keys to better decode this real, taking into account the position of the person who made the film.

Moreover, thanks to recent technological evolutions, where everyone now has their own camera, where anyone can make a film about their own story with very simple tools, the notion of filmic self-portrait, of first-person film, of confessional film, is now widely accepted. Over the past fifteen or so years, there has been a profusion of films talking about oneself, one's family, one's friends and so, necessarily, this phenomenon has emerged in Africa too. The camera has truly become a pen, as Alexandre Astruc famously put it when he referred to the *caméra-stylo*. With your camera, you can make diary films; this is now a very common genre.

That is perhaps precisely the difference with your work: while you have spoken in the first person in all your films since *Afrique, je te plumerai*, you don't really talk about yourself, as an individual. Your 'I' is at times personal – in *Vacances au pays* for example – but it isn't an intimate 'I'; it's above all a collective one.

Yes, I speak in the first person, but as one who is part of a group that was oppressed. This 'I' isn't individual, and certainly not individualistic; it's collective, an 'I' of an entire group that has been subjected – and continues to be subjected – to a certain number of things.

This 'I' makes me a part of a group, and this group might vary several times in the course of a film. I am with the rest of the group of those who are oppressed, and I am also an individual who, from time to time, is impertinent. I am also at other moments with those who revolt; my 'I' fluctuates.

I pose an overarching question while at the same time including myself personally in it. Instead of engaging a questioning of myself and my personal problems, I try instead, through my own journeying, to ask the questions that seem important to me. People in fact know very little about me in my films, even if I'm in them, if only through my voice. I speak more about the country, the problems that are general ones, and I accompany the spectator, like an old friend, on a journey whose outcome I don't necessarily know.

This 'I' is necessarily political, and it is often also polemical because within the group, there are positions that I don't adhere to. I am not indulgent with my compatriots, nor with the group. While belonging to the group, I don't adhere completely to all the group's attitudes, to all its positions. So, it's also an 'I' that sometimes makes people uncomfortable.

Your first-person voice-over also fulfils a variety of functions in your films. Not only do you clearly state where you are speaking from, so that we, the spectators, are aware that everything we see is mediated through your eyes, but your voice also constantly challenges and comments on those images that you show us. At other times you adopt a quite classic narrator role, simply providing information to enhance our understanding of, and/or to decode a situation, but then you always mingle this with your own personal point of view, inviting us to reflect as we join you on this journey that you take us on.

Yes. When I stated in *Afrique, je te plumerai* that I was speaking from the point of view of 'the native', it was important, since we were defined – or over-defined – to say: 'You think we are natives? Ok I'm a native, I accept being a native and I'm going to speak from my native place and my native point of view.' Instead of pretending to challenge that, I preferred to completely embrace the narratives that were projected onto us to better subvert them. So that's when I decided to position myself to take the floor and speak, accepting that I'm a Cameroonian and accepting that we were defeated in the colonial process, because many people were fooled by the whole Independence process, claiming we gained Independence when in reality we didn't. So I decided to embrace that position and, from there, to start addressing issues, not as a content narrator, another 'voice of God', but letting people know where I stand, from which place I speak, knowing pertinently too that there can be many different discourses and voices from the same place where I am. My approach is in fact a claim to diversity by telling people: 'I'm Jean-Marie Teno, I was born here, I am speaking from this perspective'. There are many other perspectives, and sometimes I am challenged by other Cameroonians who claim that what I am saying is not right, but no single person has the 'right' vision or image. But also, as I already said, I tend to claim a collective self, because while I'm the individual speaking, at the same time I'm part of a group who has been defeated, who is still abused, and from within that group, I try to show or express things that people are feeling and seeing from that specific place. My 'I' is not always singular. Sometimes I am just the narrator. I adopt multiple positions. Sometimes I reflect, sometimes I joke, because telling stories is also being able to invite the viewer on a journey, during which we can exchange, communicate. The viewer can follow my thoughts and, if he or she feels at any point that it doesn't work for him or her, that's fine; he or she knows where I started and where I'm heading. I believe that by doing this, I help people to see a different vision, and also remind them that there can be multiple versions of the story.

You are both an individual and part of the group, both an insider and an outsider. Your insider/outsider position can perhaps also be applied to your own family, to the film milieu, to being a Cameroonian living in France, with all that implies vis-à-vis your country of adoption and your homeland ... Maybe this apartness is necessary to be able to see things clearly, to have critical distance...

It is indeed the situation I find myself in and that I can't do anything about, unfortunately. If I knew how to be on the inside, to integrate and to belong to the networks, perhaps I'd be happy to.

But do you think that your viewpoint, your critical distance would be possible if you were?

I don't know. The question is also whether we always need to have a critical eye? Perhaps at some point, all these imperfections are a part of life too, and one can accept that. By constantly criticizing them, perhaps you miss out on life because, for sure, there is no such thing as perfection.

Your cinema is nonetheless a deeply critical cinema.

Precisely, which means that at some point maybe I might need to be less critical so that my cinema becomes a cinema that others more widely embrace! It's a critical cinema, but there are ways and ways of being critical. I have come to realize that my cinema poses all these questions, but how do you manage to articulate a critique while continuing to keep a dialogue going with people?

But being critical isn't necessary negative and alienating; you can be critical in the sense of analysing and questioning.

Yes, mine is a questioning cinema, certainly. People have often said to me: 'You question things just to criticize. What are you proposing?' I have tried telling them that it's not my role to propose a thing. It may well be easy to criticize without proposing anything, but ... I don't know. My dream was always to tell stories and perhaps that all the stories we tell are also critiques of society. If you show aspects of human life, you critique society in a way. If you criticize the existing system in a frontal, direct way, people tend not to listen. So, perhaps, faced with situations such as colonial and postcolonial history, it was normal that I carried out this critical work at that time. But it's perhaps also obvious that the work I need to do now, that I am beginning to do, is more one that takes the critique to a different level, that recounts life. And through the things I recount, to try to introduce elements of reflection about the world.

But the question is often one of means too. We have entered a new mode of production, which consists of making do with the means you have, going off to shoot, and then trying to gradually cobble together some funding. But that poses a whole host of other questions and problems, because, for people like me who come from the age of celluloid, from the days where time was devoted to the editing, to the writing – indeed, as I said before, I write the narration during the montage, constantly throwing my ideas backwards and forwards with the editor to help shape them – the new ways of working mean you are in a sort of complete solitude; if you don't have the money to work with other people, you do everything on your own. Already beforehand, as both producer and director, I wasn't dialoguing with anyone. But with the new tools, in addition to being producer-director, you become camera operator, editor – in short you do everything and you end up in a kind of monologue, which isn't ideal for someone who needs a bit of distance to address complicated issues in a coherent manner. So either I completely simplify the style of films I make, and I don't take on such weighty subjects, or I need to manage to find the means to surround myself with people with whom I can have this exchange and who enable me to construct a reflection and to angle it in a way that other people can follow. So, I am not an artist in the Fine Arts sense, alone in my corner doing things in isolation; I am someone who imagines, who thinks, who reflects, but who works with others to be able to give a film a structure, a form, which might be completely personal, but which is also the fruit of an exchange with several people. So, I begin my creative process, gradually establishing a method to formulate it, and try to find the funding. That is the most difficult phase.

And that phase has changed today?

Yes, it has changed considerably. In the beginning, I made my short films, notably *Fièvre jaune taximan, La Gifle et la caresse, Le Dernier voyage, Mister Foot*, for my own pleasure, for fun. Later, when I began to make films like *Afrique, je te plumerai*, I wrote first, I started out from something concrete, which evolved along the way. There was still a place for singular films and for points of view that came from Africa. I was fortunate enough at that time to be backed by the German television channel ZDF, which funded my projects. In those days, there weren't so many filmmakers – it was the early 1990s. There were not that many people making documentary cinema. There was space for a reflection on Africa. But now, with the number of projects around, it makes things much more difficult.

That's paradoxical, given that the technological evolutions of digital and subsequent reduction of costs ought to have made filmmaking easier. Yet this material facilitation has come at a time when the funders' vision appears to have narrowed, in a sort of antithetical movement.

Yes, there's a dual movement. There is a profusion of images – equipment has become so accessible that everybody can shoot images. But, at the same time, the reflection on the discourse behind these images has dwindled … There is also, unfortunately, a form of standardization. Lots of report magazines, for example, now adopt the first person. Journalists have started saying 'I'; personalization has become the in-thing. But that has nothing to do with the 'I' as I define it. The first person as it is used today in personal narratives is totally different. That is why the work of a documentary filmmaker remains very different to that of a journalist: we focus on a subject, but try to maintain a critical distance, even when speaking in the first person. There is a distance vis-à-vis the subject matter that allows you to find and suggest other analogies in relation to the subject, rather than simply being immersed in a context. From there, it is possible to carry out a kind of accompaniment. That is present in my films too because, when I go somewhere, I go through this immersion process. I go from one character to the next, but at the same time, there is the additional dimension of the voice. It is a personal voice, but adopts a lot of distance, and it's undoubtedly that which comprises the difference between my first-person films and other people's. My films say very little about me personally. At the same time, I hope that people get enough elements from them to clearly perceive and understand the situation we are in.

Is there still a place today for a militant cinema, like that of the first generation of filmmakers in Africa that we talked about earlier?

I don't know if there's still a place. If this place exists, it's for the young people making films today to define it. I get the impression I have followed a path, I have posed a certain number of questions, and I have thought about a certain number of things. Today, maybe I want to ask myself other questions. Over time, I have addressed increasingly complex issues. At present, I am exploring the question of power, which happens to be the ultimate question that my evolving reflection has built up to from film to film. And faced with this question, which is a monumental, complicated one, I'm a bit stuck. It's a subject that writers and academics are addressing too, and which requires a specific dramaturgy. How to tackle the question of power? Why do I make films? It is making me question everything I've done up until now, and that takes time. I want to make a film that is perhaps simpler, or maybe indirectly related, before coming back to that one. And after, I've always said that I want to make a beautiful love story! But at the same time, how do you describe love in a country like Cameroon, how do you recount it, how do you recount people's anguish when the authorities crush reflection, creation and when the ideals we share boil down to so little?

Journeys

Taken collectively, your films constitute a coherent ensemble, or corpus. We can trace a clear development, a continuity of the sorts of issues that you're interested in and articulate, be it access to decent living conditions, like in your first feature-length film *Bikutsi Water Blues* in 1988, to the ties between the state of contemporary Cameroonian society and the country's recent colonial past, to the questions of political repression, of cultural genocide in *Afrique, je te plumerai* (1992), *Chef!* (1999), *Vacances au pays* (2000), *Le Malentendu colonial* (2004) or *Une Feuille dans le vent* (2013).

All my works stem from me looking at my surroundings. The idea for *Bikutsi Water Blues* came from a conversation I had with a doctor in the district where my mother used to live. He told me something that really struck me: that two out of three diseases in the district were the result of unclean water. If the question of giving people access to clean water were solved, two-thirds of his patients wouldn't need to consult. I thought about all the kids in the neighbourhood I'd see who were frequently ill because they drank dirty water. This created a vicious circle, because the kids would then miss school, their education would

Photo 23 Teno on location filming Naana Banyiwa Horne's 2010 return journey and enstoolment ceremony in Akwamufie, Ghana (*Chosen*).

suffer, and they would finally drop out because they got too old to attend anymore. So, we ended up with a vicious circle of water, and a social vicious circle that keeps people down, stuck in the same poor neighbourhoods, not advancing in life, apart from the exceptionally bright ones. I wanted to address this double vicious circle created in society by the poor water system and poor health conditions. It wasn't only a problem in my district; it was a problem in the whole country. I couldn't *not* ask: 'How come we have a problem this huge almost thirty years after Independence? How come no one is tackling this issue, particularly in a country where we have oil, a country rich in natural resources that bring revenue into the country?' That's why I made *Bikutsi Water Blues*, the continuum of which led me to question the issues in *Afrique je te plumerai* because, not finding any adequate answer to my questions, I started to ask: 'What is this culture? What's in the minds of the people running this country? What is it about the history of this country that means that we have rulers who do not even think of providing basic necessities to the people?' That's when I started looking into our colonial history and exploring the questions of abuse, violence, the violence of the state whenever people ask questions, when people ask for what they need, for social services, for all these basic rights that other people enjoy elsewhere. In Cameroon, all these issues are highly political, and from our youngest years, our parents warned us not to get involved in politics as it meant trouble and possibly prison or death. If someone asked: 'Why don't we have a school in this neighbourhood?', they could easily be accused of talking politics, and could get in trouble for it. During the struggles against the colonial system, when people rebelled against colonial oppression, they met with violence, and that violence was learned. People have learned that violence is how a government functions. Right up until today, the Cameroonian government functions with the same colonial mind-set. When people demonstrate to say they want something, the government doesn't invite them to discuss the issue. There's no dialogue, they just send in the police or the army to brutalize or even shoot at a few demonstrators to set an example. We still witness that today.

Another reflection that threads from film to film is that of modernity in Africa – the exogenous modernity imposed from outside versus an endogenous, African modernity.

It's the same question that I pose from film to film because I get the feeling that, for us, the notion of modernity has never been a true modernity, because it is one that was imposed on us and that continues to do us a disservice. It's a term that I find highly complex, this notion of modernity, because it is far too often associated with technological progress, with something that is thought to come from Europe. At the same time, the capacity to reflect on the things that modernity can offer is lacking, so we may legitimately wonder if it is really modernity. So, I would say that this confusion that was sold to us as modernity in Africa to designate everything that is shiny, that comes from abroad, hasn't helped us. I get the impression that when I go back to my village, for example, and see the 'traditional' structures – traditional in inverted commas, because we are constantly caught in this problematic dichotomy pitting modernity against tradition – when I go back and I see most of the structures that existed before in Cameroon, when I see how they functioned, how they were very well organized, and when I see the so-called modern world, with all its chaos and confusion, it is interesting to question the consequences of the superposition of these two organizational systems – the European power system and the endogenous power systems – and the impossibility of addressing this question calmly and clearly in order to create a homogeneous and coherent system from it. The collective body of films that I have made have led me towards this fundamental question. This necessarily involves colonial history, it necessarily involves its consequences and the oppression inflicted by all these heads of state who are still in power, who refuse to give us some breathing space and who deprive people of their freedom in order to continue to maintain them in a situation of constant domination – that is part of the same question.

Male-female relationships within this system, education, the types of schools we have are also part of this question, and all of my films end up being related. It is always this question of how to manage to combine – to fairly combine, in a way that is beneficial to everyone – two systems that were historically imposed on one another.

These themes are highly political. When you first started making films – and even today, some thirty years on – did you consciously think: 'I'm going to make committed films'?

When you say 'committed films', I can't imagine myself speaking to say nothing, or speaking just to talk about the mood I'm in, to make a bourgeois, poetic love story, or anything like that. Especially knowing what people are experiencing in certain parts of the world, I don't see myself making a film that would totally ignore such issues. Nor could I set it in a place where it would just give me the opportunity to show how skilful I am at putting elements together. So, when I started making films, I didn't think: 'I'm going to make committed films'. I was aware that cinema is also entertainment, it's about emotions, but for me, it also had to lead to something, to serve a purpose. I cannot make cinema without emotion, but with the emotion, I also always make films that try to say something meaningful about a person's life, their struggle, their experience. In the Cameroonian context, in the African context, it would be hard for me not to make a film about the different forms of violence people live through, that people experience, at the hand of the state. Or injustices in society between women and men, between the generations. Everything in society that seems to me to be unbalanced is an object that I can use to make cinema. Within that, I try to tell a story, to be engaging enough so that people can follow me on that journey, identifying with the characters portrayed, feeling and reacting to the situation, so that they can understand what is really going on. Cinema is emotion, but also emotion related to a situation, or an experience. And when people are experiencing terrible things, such injustices, the film exposing their situation becomes a committed film.

(Hi)stories, Memory

Right from *Hommage*, and in several of your films, such as *Afrique, je te plumerai*, *Le Malentendu colonial* and *Une Feuille dans le vent*, the question of history is central. Where does this interest in history stem from?

In my films, it isn't so much the question of history that interests me, as how to understand the present if we don't already understand how we got to this point. How to understand the mechanisms that make the present what it is if we don't question where we have come from? So, all my films ask the same question: how to understand the processes that got us here in order to try to find solutions to advance. I am not a historian, I didn't study history, but before a situation like ours where people don't talk, don't recount, where there are no real national historical narratives, where silence reigns, where a heavy lid has been placed on even the recent past, we need to understand at some point what happened in this country. In Cameroon, people have long lived in permanent fear, in silence, and this silence is hard to bear. It's a form of violence. It's a silence that creates a form of immobilism, a silence that stops people from creating, from expressing themselves. So, it's this return to the past in order to understand that interests me and, when you look to the past, you necessarily address history.

In *Une Feuille dans le vent*, Ernestine Ouandié says: 'When history is written, the roaming souls will come to rest'. For you, it seems to be less a question of simply restoring a forgotten chapter of history, but rather of looking at the past in constant dialogue with the present.

With the present, yes. For me, history for history's sake is of no interest. Every time that I explore history, it is always in relation to the present. And it's the present that often refers me back to history to try to make sense of this present and to see how, by looking at the past, we can find a way out of our difficult present. For me, this looking at the past is not about nostalgia. It's a dynamic gaze; I look to history to question the present.

What history were you taught growing up and going to school in Cameroon?

The history taught was one in which there were so many grey areas! We were taught French history. I even learned that my ancestors were Gauls! I belong to the generation that still learned that, even though I saw the coming of Independence. We were so happy, so proud, at that time. We thought that a new chapter of history was about to start. But history can only begin if we are allowed to recount what happened before. But we weren't, because the violence that was still taking place at that time was silenced. And even when people tried to take an interest in what had happened, people would say: 'Oh là là, you absolutely mustn't go meddling in politics or you'll get yourself killed'. Little by little, a sense of terror took hold. And this terror was reinforced by the silence. And this silence meant that we recounted nothing. There was this absence, and when there's an absence, you try to conform to the official discourse. So, people began even to doctor the present, because they didn't want to show the present in its complexity, its difficulties. That is why to me, as a documentary filmmaker, simple observational documentary doesn't sufficiently describe the complexity of the situation. Between what you observe, what you remain on the surface with, and the things implied by what you see, there is a dimension of decoding that, for me, means that the commentary, the text allows me to show, or to reveal the complexity of a situation – by which I mean a text that is worked on until it becomes poetic, because it also needs to be beautiful, strong, to go beyond just being a denunciatory text.

By stating your own position of enunciation in *Afrique, je te plumerai*, you draw attention to the importance of who is talking in documentary. How did you arrive at this awareness of the situated gaze and thus at the desire to question it?

This awareness came from my own questioning. When I used to listen or to watch the news, I'd always asked myself: 'But who is talking?' I asked myself this because the things shown on the news seemed futile to me. They didn't seem to be addressed to people like me. I used to listen to the news talking about the inauguration of such and such a factory, or place… After having seen that once, twice, three times, I began to wonder, given life in a country like Cameroon, whether this was the only news of interest. We heard 10,000 times that the President went to cut a ribbon while making vacuous speeches about the grand works he was going to carry out and knew it would lead to nothing, so I began to wonder: 'How come they don't talk about people's real problems?', which for me, coming from a poor neighbourhood, meant the question of access to public water fountains, to health, to better living conditions – in short, the essential. Or again, for someone like me who walked an hour and a half to secondary school and back, questions of inequality. I was there in the best secondary school in the country with kids who were driven to school by car, who arrived all spick and span while I'd arrive in a sweat, and I used to ask myself: 'Why is the world made this way? What is it in this world that means that some people are born like this and others like that? What did I do wrong not to be born with the same opportunities?' At the same time, my lot was enviable compared to some of my friends whom I left behind in the neighbourhood to go to school, because they didn't even have the opportunity to stick at their studies long enough to enjoy secondary education. I was becoming aware of all these questions of inequality, so when people spoke in the media, I used to think: 'When these people speak, what has it got to do with the neighbourhood that I leave every morning and that is the reflection of the vast majority of the country? Do these people speaking on the radio or the TV care at all about the concerns of the people in the poor neighbourhoods? Why don't they talk about these things?' So, all of that led me to think: 'These people don't speak for me'. And I decided that the day I would speak out, I'd speak about these issues.

My desire to speak about these neighbourhoods, to speak *from* them, grew from that. My awareness of profound injustice too, especially at secondary school where I'd see the place at lunchtime empty of all those who used to go home by car for lunch, while we – there were maybe four or five of us, companions in misfortune! – never knew what, or if, we were going to eat. As soon as one of us had a little money, we would go to the shop on the main street to buy a piece of bread with a smidgen of butter or margarine, and that was our lunch. With a bit of luck, we'd be able to buy a few lumps of sugar to put in water, and that would tide us over. That was when we had the means! When we didn't, we ate nothing. We'd just wait, and at 2.30 pm when the others came back, well, we'd go back into class and sometimes simply fall asleep. It's perhaps also the reason for my anger. Maybe a misplaced anger, because I nonetheless managed to continue and pass my Baccalaureate in the circumstances that were what they were. But at the same time, when I started to want to tell stories, it was the stories of these people that I wanted to tell, and it was above all the stories of these places that I told, not those of children from wealthy families who, for the most part, finished their studies and went straight into positions of responsibility. For them, it was a simple continuation of the system. They had never known anything else. Perhaps I was there to remind them that there were – and still are – people living in poverty in these neighbourhoods.

Much later, when I was working as a television editor, I could see how the news was constructed. I saw the footage coming in, then what was left out or included. We'd receive two minutes of images from a feed somewhere to edit into a 1-minute-30 subject. But the commentaries would never be the same depending on who was talking and the position they were talking from. Some would stick close to what was happening. Others would be radical, with a political agenda, making the images say something quite different. It was fun for me to edit and to see how the same images could tell so many different stories. All this nourished my way of looking at images and made me realize their situated nature. It gave me the freedom, the latitude to be able to construct, or deconstruct, to add still images. It gave me confidence to try things when I was editing that I might not otherwise have tried. It helped me understand the meaning of images, that it's all just a game, that you can play with them, that the whole notion that this does or doesn't work as a cut is nonsense. Indeed, editing has evolved through time, going from the smooth cut, to the jump cut, etc. So, when some people said that the fades aren't smooth enough in *Une Feuille dans le vent*, for example, I just said: 'Well, what does it make you feel when a fade isn't smooth? You feel disturbed. Maybe that was precisely what I wanted, to disturb you.' Editing is not innocent either. So, for me, all this allowed me to show that I could understand that even these images, which existed at a specific time, that are situated, can be used again to tell a different story.

In *Afrique, je te plumerai* you also clearly demonstrate that history necessarily involves a point of view, raising the question of which history is told – and thus of the non-objectivity of history

Absolutely. I knew that I was the one who was going to speak, that this would be my subjective point of view. At the same time, I took this awareness quite far in the sense that I decided that I wanted people to be able to see this history from my viewpoint, because I was sick of always looking at stories and history from other people's points of view, which didn't necessarily correspond with mine. That is why I wanted the protagonists to look into the camera, even if it wasn't me filming, so spectators would feel as if they were seeing the world through my eyes. This consciousness was completely deliberate, then, so that the rest of the world could at last realize that my humanity is also conveyed by the fact that it is me who sees and recounts this history from my point of view, thereby restoring that humanity. And if they weren't capable – but I knew that they were – I would lead them there, seductively, with a smile, because that is my role as a filmmaker; seeing the world from someone else's point of view is what cinema is.

***Afrique, je te plumerai* dates back to the early 1990s. Your approach was very much in keeping with texts such as Gayatri Chakravorty Spivak's *Can the Subaltern Speak?* – and with the reflection developing within postcolonial and decolonial theory…**

That's true. And as a result, when I discovered these texts, I identified with them completely. I hadn't read them before making the film. I didn't theorize all that in writing; it was a theorization that came from my own lived experience, that I applied to my work, that I gradually established within my work.

My cinema is certainly a cinema that challenges, then, a cinema that shifts perspectives and looks at the world from the place of those who don't usually have a say. And when I started using first-person narrative in my films, I wasn't using the first person as Teno speaking, but as a Cameroonian looking at a situation, being in the colonial space and looking at the stories we were told, and reading history from a different place, not from the place of official discourse. The official French discourse completely merged with the official Cameroonian discourse after Independence, as the individuals in the positions of power benefitted – and are still benefitting – from this situation, unlike the vast majority of the population. So, by attacking the state, we attack the colonial master, indirectly. And by attacking both, I ended up between a rock and a hard place!

At what point did you start making this connection with recent colonial history?

When I was studying in the UK, in Portsmouth, and when I came across the Student's Union and discovered the International Socialist Organization! It was at that point that I started making the connection between all these things. For me, it was fascinating – it was more interesting than doing Electronics! It was an extraordinary moment for me. That's when I really started to become aware. But it was an awareness that came – how to put it – in a disorderly fashion. It wasn't a very constructed awareness as, being someone who is a bit of a free spirit and who discovered the world as events unfolded, I continued advancing without any real direction. I didn't fix myself any medium- or long-term objectives. I truly just lived as the mood took me because I never expected to be wherever I found myself! At no time had I wanted to go to Europe. It wasn't my dream to go there – I had no dreams. If I made it to the end of every day in one piece, then I was happy! I had always lived in a form of incertitude. Paradoxically, it's a bit as if I have unconsciously always done everything possible to ruin things so that I find myself in this form of incertitude again – a quest for chaos. I'm aware of that now. The apple doesn't fall far from the tree, as goes the saying.

It became clear to you, then, that the answers to the present were to be found in this colonial history?

You have to remember that I lived through Independence. So, for me, it's something completely obvious. I very clearly remember celebrating our Independence in Cameroon. I remember the huge enthusiasm. I remember all the songs from this period. In 1960, I was six years old – I belonged to the last generation to attend colonial primary school where I learned that our ancestors were Gauls! All of that is part of my living memory. Later, in the early Independence years, we sang all the great revolutionary songs, we shouted our Independence at the top of our voices, thinking that we were going to be happy now. This enthusiasm – which people can't measure the extent of today – came from the fact that we had been colonized; Independence was here, we paraded, things were going to change, we were going to take our destiny in hand. There was such enthusiasm, such passion ... Later, most of my fellow pupils at the Lycée Leclerc – for example, Akéré Muna, who later became President of the Bar, or our supervisor, who later became the censor of the Lycée, then later still the general secretary to the Presidency – they were all people who very rapidly took over control of the country. I can't tell you the number of those who were in the years just above me who later held the highest ministerial ranks ... So, we were completely immersed in colonial history in the sense that, during these early years, up until the 1970s, or even 1980s, anything that went wrong was linked to colonialism. We talked about it a lot. But, as time went by, there were so many people who were assassinated, all the dreams we had were destroyed. And Cameroon in particular was, after all, one of the places where unbelievable massacres were perpetrated, which no one talked about. We followed the trail of Monseigneur Ndongmo, the execution of Ernest Ouandié … I was already old enough to understand what was going on. The silence. All these things marked my childhood and my adolescence. That is why reflecting on all these questions is important. Especially as in Cameroon, everyone behaved as if all that had simply not happened. When the book *Kamerun! La guerre cachée à l'origine de la Francafrique* by Thomas Deltombe, Manuel Domergue and Jacob Tatsitsa came out in 2011, the things it recounts are the things I lived through at that time, without having then all the information that the book reveals. I cannot not be involved in this colonial history, because it completely structured my childhood, my adolescence, my life. And as I was already in rebellion, in revolt, I didn't swallow the official discourse one iota. I was already beginning to challenge it and trying to do everything I could for this history to come to light, so that people would talk about it. And even up until now, we haven't completely managed to analyse all that. It is only very recently that these French and Cameroonian authors managed to start the conversation. And even up until today, we haven't managed to deconstruct everything that was put into place at the time.

Your work also seeks to break this silence. In addition to the trauma of the war of Independence and the political assassination of the independentist leaders Ruben Um Nyobè, Félix-Roland Moumié, and Ernest Ouandié, does the silence that still surrounds these dead figures seem psychologically all the more violent in a culture in which people honour their ancestors, their dead?

I don't know if it's all the more violent … These dead, they were heroes. They were people who significantly contributed to the Independence struggle, even if they have not been properly honoured with statutes or commemorative plaques. But we can ask the question of who we are going to honour if we don't honour those who truly contributed to building our state. We can even ask the question, in a country where the first President of the Republic – there have only been two so far since Independence – is buried abroad because they never let his remains back into the country, what is it that we honour? The remains of Felix-Roland Moumié, who is buried in Guinea, were never allowed to be repatriated either. What place do we accord to the past, even the recent past? Do those who were against those past figures and their history even want people to know about it? Cameroon's leaders don't want their people to even refer to the past. That was one of my biggest problems with *Hommage*. Some people wanted to censor the film in 1984 when it came out because there were images of the first President, Ahidjo, in it. As there had just been an attempted coup d'état and he was involved, people went to the archives and destroyed all the Independence images saying that they no longer wanted to see the first President's face anymore. In every film, they cut his image and destroyed it. How can you honour the dead – even if you are against such and such a figure – by destroying the archives, or by leaving them in such a state of abandon? There is such a culture of mediocrity. It's not because you disagree with someone that you must absolutely destroy all trace.

Also, when you evoke this memory, given that these figures who fought for a true Independence were defeated, how many people want to remember the losers? All the more so as they were described as *maquisards*, as vandals, as rebels – today they'd be called terrorists. As they were defeated, people have done everything to side-line them, not to talk about them, and that is why I say – even in terms of cinema if your style is marginal – that so long as you remain unrecognized by the dominant institutions, or in the dominant vision that manufactures heroes, you don't exist.

Your history works also aim to give these people their rightful recognition, then?

Yes. To stop those who come after from believing – instead of thinking for themselves – 'As so and so isn't recognized, they must be worthless'. I see the same mechanism at play in our cinema. If your work isn't recognized, those who come after prefer to attack you, writing off your work as 'militant' cinema, saying: 'That's not the kind of cinema I want to make, I want to make cinema like those in the limelight', even if the latter doesn't address any essential questions or decode the fundamental issues of the moment. Many simply decode things through the prism of the watching West, which applauds the innocence of this cinema. As a result, you have people who go even further in this obsolescence in their quest for recognition. And so, we are caught in this situation where we are struggling to advance in terms of intellectual reflection, or to engage a reflection on the continent because those coming after us want only to follow in the footsteps of those they think have achieved success and recognition.

Decolonizing the 'Colonial Library'

Coming back to archive material, did that you used in *Hommage* come from the Cameroonian archives?

No. Those archives came from the French Ministry of Cooperation. The Independence sequences were shot for French newsreels at the time, and the

Photo 24 Plaza Cinema, Dakar. *Chef!* screening, 2000.

Ministry of Cooperation had one of these newsreel films in its library. I requested the permission to use the images from the French Ministry of Foreign Affairs, to whom the images belonged.

Why did you decide, right from this very first film, to include archive images?

I wanted to have images of Cameroon in that era. I wanted to have images of Independence, to evoke the joy, the hope, the enthusiasm, the euphoria, to remember that crucial moment when we became free, which was a part of my memory, of my life experience. I remember the singing, the first parades in 1960. I was six at the time. The whole class went to parade and it was an incredible moment. People had been fighting. There had been rebellions. We thought that we were going to be free, that things were going to be better. But after twenty or so years, we saw things go downhill. So, I wanted to address this particular moment. I wanted to show these archive images, but also to question them.

To question them?

Yes, of course. At that time, by editing them into *Hommage*, I was questioning them in a way; later, in other films, differently. When I was a teenager, I didn't question these images; I lived them. It was only twenty years later that I began to, with hindsight, with distance. I also asked what they represented in relation to the present, of course. I'm constantly asking the question of what went wrong.

So, your motivation in *Hommage* was to evoke Independence. What about in *Afrique, je te plumerai*?

In *Afrique, je te plumerai*, I started going deeper into questioning the whole notion of independence, and of violence, so I went looking for the images that existed during the century before Independence.

At the time, very few people talked about or showed these images. I was interested in bringing these images to life, to really show the transition from where we had been to where we had got to. And to understand, for, as I say in *Afrique, je te plumerai*: 'To know where you are going, you need to know where you come from, so that you can build a new future'. So, for me, it was important to return to these places.

I used the archival footage to make people understand the whole state of mind that was still present and hadn't been challenged. I went back to these colonial images because I had the feeling that they were still totally unchallenged. We had moved forward, but no one had questioned this.

The remains of this colonial history, of colonial discourse, were so present, shaping the mental attitudes and the behaviour of so many people. I needed to go back to this and make people aware of that.

Saying you needed to 'go back to this' implies that you already knew these images existed. How did you first discover them?

When I was a kid, they always used to show newsreels before films at the cinema, including these French images with their voice-overs that were never spoken by an African. It was always a White person speaking, the 'voice of God'. When I started making films, I wanted to challenge the notion of that voice telling us things without us knowing whose voice it was.

When I was a kid, the missionaries would also sometimes show some of the old colonial propaganda films to us in school. So, I knew these films existed. I had been in Europe a long time and knew that these French and Belgian archives existed, and I had seen many films using archive images. So, when I started working on *Afrique, je te plumerai*, I went looking for these images. I had to dig them out. I went to the ECPA, the Établissement cinématographique et photographique des armées, in the late 1980s, as I knew that the French army had filmed in the colonies, but I didn't know then the extent of what there was. A lot of other footage came to me randomly.

At the ECPA, I was really lucky to fall on students who were doing their military service and who were only a little younger than I was, so they were very happy to help me. At the time, they were still cataloguing the footage. I told them I was looking for colonial images of Africa and they told me they had plenty, that the army had shot a lot. And they simply helped me by putting aside all these images.

Did their superiors know?

No, they didn't. I was just a young African bloke who nobody knew or cared about. I was nobody!

Later, I was in London at the British Film Institute and I met a woman who told me that there was old Nazi footage with no credits, some of which had been shot in Cameroon. I asked if I could use it, and she said yes. No one was claiming the copyright, so she made a copy and gave it to me, happy that it could be of use.

There were lots of coincidences that year, in 1990. I was at a festival in Leipzig, and I met a group of Brits from Leeds, who ran something called Educational TV and who were the sole owners of archive footage from the Eastern bloc and Russia. I told them I wanted to make a film on colonial history, and they said: 'Oh, we have Lumumba on film'.

So, I kept meeting people by chance and they'd tell me they had footage that I could use. I'd follow up the contact, and they simply gave me a lot of it because there were hardly any Africans interested in these images. They were happy to collaborate with an African wanting to work on these images.

Did you have to pay for these archive images?

Not for most of them. I had no budget to be able to pay, and they were very happy to help me make the film.

The question of accessibility is an important one; would you still be able to access these archive images for free today?

I don't think so. Nowadays, everyone is trying to make money from archives. The BBC has organized its archives, the INA has centralized its archives, everyone. Accessing the archives can be very expensive.

When I obtained that German footage from the BFI, there was a shot of a woman playing with a dog in front of her house. And when *Afrique, je te plumerai* was shown on German TV, a woman contacted me, telling me that she was the woman in the shot, that she was twenty at the time, that her husband was a big German cameraman for the Nazis, who, on his death, had left lots of archive footage that he'd shot in Africa. I went to Berlin to visit the lady – she was 94 or 95 at the time. She was looking for a place to give this archive to. She wanted preferably to give it to an African filmmaker or country. But I didn't react fast enough and she passed away and the archive was no longer accessible any more. It was such a missed opportunity.

Did the Cameroonian authorities shoot any footage of Independence?

Everything that was shot at that time was processed in France. Pathé had all the footage, all the negatives. When I was making *Afrique je te plumerai*, the Cameroonian Ministry of Culture gave me a letter asking that I be allowed to access the stock of Cameroonian news footage, but because they hadn't paid for its storage, Pathé wouldn't let me! And then Pathé handed all these archives over to INA and now INA charges a fortune to access them.

When you first set out to use the archives, did you consciously think: 'I'm going to reappropriate this material to tell my story'? Or did that come about in the process of making the film?

People always say 'reappropriate', but do you reappropriate things that don't belong to you? These images are there. Everybody can use them. It was the representation I wanted to expose, how people were representing us, and I wanted to explore how to challenge this representation. That was why I chose to expose these images, these commentaries, and then subvert them.

Indeed, taking the structure of *Afrique, je te plumerai*, there are three blocks in which you use archive footage. The first time you show it as it is, unmediated, with the original voice-over commentary; the second time, it is shown as it is, but intercut with historians and elderly workers and unionists whose testimonies counter the discourse of the colonial footage; and the third time, you remove the original commentary, replacing it with your own. How did you go about structuring this material at the time?

I didn't consciously set out to structure it like that. I was telling the story and wanted to use elements of the archives to make my point. I started by presenting the discourse of the time, and then had people comment on it.

I get the feeling that, from the start, I've always played with the archive, with how it originally was and my own perception of it. When I was working on the film – it's such a long time ago now – I was trying to delve not only into the memories of my childhood, but also into how I became aware of the whole world. Even in the 1960s, the colonial discourse was still so present because no one had challenged it. It was present in so many aspects and things. To really be able to challenge this discourse, you had to expose it as it was, and comment on what was happening at that time, and then appropriate it. It seemed almost natural, even if I didn't do it consciously. And that's what takes place in the film too. It's also an awakening, which talks about the situation, people's comments, and the revolt and struggle.

When people include archive images in documentary films, it is most often to reconstitute an era, to contextualize what taking place at a given time. In your films, however, you use them, rather, to reveal and deconstruct the ideology at work in them…

Exactly. This tension is part of my very being. As I said earlier, there I was, in a situation in which I was already an anomaly because I wasn't destined to attend the city's top Lycée with all these privileged kids living the comfortable life. Coming from a poor neighbourhood, I was already the odd-one-out. I became aware of these anomalies at a very young age. It is as if this awareness of this dichotomy between what the archive images showed and the reality I experienced had always been there.

Photo 25 One of the first historians of African film, Pierre Haffner, with filmmakers Jean-Marie Teno, Balufu Bakupa-Kanyinda, and François Woukouache, at a film festival in Switzerland, c. 1993/94.

Cinema, for me, has always been something playful. It wasn't something to take that seriously. Haile Gerima said to me one day that he was shocked when he saw *Afrique, je te plumerai* because we used to meet at festivals, and I was always dancing and joking and so he never expected to see someone who seemed so jovial, who wasn't always raising the fist, make such a complex film. I don't know where the film came from. Of course, I was always very conscious of injustice, but I liked playing with things, I loved irony. But when I started making films, it came out serious. As we say in Cameroon: 'Ça sort comme ça sort'; it comes out as it comes out.

The subject of *Afrique, je te plumerai* can hardly be described as anything but serious!

Yes. I made *Hommage* with my small camera, doing everything. I worked like a small craftsman, shooting myself. Being out filming with a 16 mm camera was fun. That's how I liked making films. But when I wanted to make *Afrique, je te plumerai*, it was a film about injustice, about the things that really bothered me. This was almost constitutive of who I was, because when I left Cameroon and came to Europe for the first time, I felt angry knowing how people were living in Cameroon, then seeing life here. I thought: 'Why is it that people live in such poverty? How come some people are born here, and others there? What did they do to deserve that?' All these questions were bugging me. They are very challenging questions. It was what really kept me trying to talk about the place I was coming from, from a perspective of someone who's discovering that this world really sucks.

Coming back to the archives, in a film like *Une Feuille dans le vent*, you confront the problem of the lack of images, using illustrations in the places of images of Ernestine Ouandié's life or of her father, Ernest Ouandié's execution.

I decided to use illustrations as, for me, they constituted a way of going beyond history and memory, and to also turn this into cinema. Ernestine's life was such a tragedy that it goes even beyond history and memory to the human stories behind them. And that's probably a shift in my work, because I've been questioning reality for so long, yet it's incomplete if you don't take into account the human dramas that individuals go through in those periods.

Talking about Ernestine's life puts the human at the centre and suddenly it's not just about oppression. The deeper context is the human being, human suffering, and probably a different approach to dealing with history, because it is people's lives that are affected. We tend to forget that when we talk about 'France', about 'Cameroon', geopolitics or geo-strategy. Going deeply into the core of the consequences for humans, all this becomes more real. It's almost as if it were a quest for me to explore something tangible rather than fighting with concepts. Ernestine's story is tragic. It's a story that everyone can understand. It's important to link colonization to the drama that affects people on a very deep and personal level.

Memory is also always very present in your work. You restore this memory to challenge preconceived ideas. That reminds me of the words of Cameroonian author Patrice Nganang, who described memory as 'the ultimate site of confrontation'. That clearly resonates with your work…

Absolutely, in the sense that in order to challenge the things you've learned, you have to examine them and demonstrate that there are so many inconsistencies in what we were shown and taught, in many of the things that were imposed on us. So, we have, necessarily, to return to the past and undo – or to try to undo – and challenge a certain number of preconceptions, to clearly show people that we are in a system that was totally constructed and that isn't the result of something inevitable. It is no accident that, in many of our states in Africa, education occupies such an insignificant place, because, as soon as people are educated, they are able to deconstruct a certain number of discourses if they so wish, so it's best to keep them as uneducated as possible. And often, the more people are educated, the more they tend to challenge the system – unless, of course, they choose to enter and benefit from the system for their personal advantage.

In your films, you above all construct a counter-memory, which – as already discussed – implies that history isn't objective but depends on who is telling it.

History is indeed not at all objective. The more time passes, the more I realize so. Some years ago, I read a text by Patrice Nganang precisely, in which he develops a quite fascinating reflection on history. In it, he discusses how to translate 'history' in Bamileke languages. He develops a theory about the *nou*, which refers to an event, and the *toli*, which refers to a story. In these Western Cameroonian languages, when people talk about *nou*, it's major, there's a form of astonishment. When people want to recount an event, they say: 'A thing happened', then they tell you what. But much later, if they want you to learn something from this event, it becomes a *toli* – that is to say, they later put this event into a context which, as a result, takes on another dimension and becomes a story. History with a capital 'H', as in a science, isn't a concept that exists as such. People, when they get together, either tell you about an event because it was astonishing, or marking, or they put this event in a context, turning it into a story, but one that serves to argue something, to nourish a reflection, to comment on the present.

So, if I've understood properly, a *nou* is an event, or something that happens, which, if it is later re-told, takes on the status of a *toli*, or in other words a form of history?

Yes. And I get the impression that I – perhaps unconsciously – am inscribed in this thought system. And when I started making cinema, it mirrored that. For me, cinema is about events that have taken place; how, then, do I assemble them, how do I use all the elements at my disposal to transform them into this kind of *toli*? That is why I love telling stories, because it allows me to set a certain number of events in succession, thereby giving them a meaning.

Endogenizing Film Language

Have the narrative structures of oral literature – whose influence on film narratives has been stressed in several studies, including mine in *Africa Shoots Back* – had a particular influence on your films?

Let's put it like this: having grown up in this environment in which I heard people talking, in which words have a meaning, I find the idea that I'd make films without words, without texts, without commentaries completely insane. As cinema is both image *and* sound, I don't see why I would deprive myself of words, especially as you can convey so many things in them. And so, on that basis, orality, the manner of recounting, end up being present and woven into the structures I construct.

Did you listen to storytellers as a child?

Of course! What's more, as kids, we used to tell each other the plots of films. When we couldn't go to see a film ourselves, someone who did go told the others. We spent our time telling each other the plot while we were playing football. As kids, then as teens, we loved playing and would organize matches, often with three teams. Two would play, and once a team had had two goals scored against them, they'd be out and the third would take over, so, while waiting to play, we'd tell each other the film stories. Some kids were very talented storytellers. Sometimes we would disagree, as we didn't always see the film the same way. Sometimes we almost had battles, with each kid telling their point of view. Some would admire the baddies more, and would tell the story from their perspective, others from the point of view of the goodies, so we were already trying our hand at storytelling.

In *Afrique, je te plumerai*, you tell the grandfather's tale. Do you think listening to tales influenced the way you construct your film narratives?

I mainly listened to tales during the holidays when we used to go to the village. There, we used to listen to the elders. I think that when it came to telling my own stories, I needed to find a base from which to tell them. I didn't necessarily specifically remember the stories I'd heard as a child, but it's certain that when you live in an environment in which you often hear people telling stories, it stays with you, unconsciously. And the day I started telling film stories, elements of these tales came back to me. Also, when people recount an event or a story in conversation, you follow all the twists, people digress, and these digressions are stories in their own right that help advance the initial narrative, or issue. Instead of addressing an issue head on and talking only about that, people talk about this and that, recount anecdotes, and then more anecdotes in response to the first, and little by little, the narrative takes shape. It's not necessarily that there are set moments in the day when everyone sits down and someone tells a story. There's not necessarily a formal setting. It's just that people are together and they talk, and stories often serve as metaphors to illustrate or to explain complicated situations. When people tell you a story, it's often to clarify, or to offer a solution to a concrete problem posed at that particular moment. It comes back to the question you asked about history. When you have two people faced with a problem and one says: 'Do you remember when this or that happened?', they take a story which becomes a metaphor for a present situation and which might help resolve it, because people draw on history to find elements of understanding. What I'm trying to say is that when you're having a conversation, and people are astonished or shocked at some point or about something, each will tell a story, and then another, and so on. But all these stories are a form of argument, or metaphors that relate to the problem those people are experiencing in the present – they aim to enlighten this present. So, people draw from the storehouse of all these stories, some of which are well-known, others not, and others again are made up on the spot to make sense of the present situation. So, I think that the way in which people use history is more often to enlighten the present and to help people to better understand situations through stories that take place in an imaginary or an unknown world.

Photo 26 Jean-Marie Teno, post-screening Q&A.

Transmission

Beyond making your own films, you have long sought to promote documentary cinema in Africa. What form has this commitment taken?

It has taken several forms over the years. First of all, we diaspora filmmakers in France created the African Guild of Directors and Producers – la Guilde – of which I was the first president. France, it must be said, is a very curious country because, for ages, several of us filmmakers living here had been trying to organize ourselves and, interestingly, there were always those in the group who did everything to stop an organization from being set up. It took a very long time to finally create a viable association of diasporic African filmmakers. Since the mid-1990s, I think it was, we had been trying to group together to create an association, but it kept derailing because it wasn't in the interest of people in various institutions in France that the filmmakers organize. We fought long and hard for the Guilde to exist.

The Guilde was comprised of several filmmakers who, confronted with the constant introduction of new regulations in funding applications which excluded us a little bit more each time, thought it would be a good idea to constitute a group to pool our energies and to defend what we had in common, in order to be able to exist before the different partners who were defining African cinema, thereby imposing ourselves as an interlocuter. We filmmakers, who were subjected to policies that were put in place without consulting us, needed a structure that would allow us to dialogue with them.

We also wanted to support one another to be able to advance and make films, to have a space of solidarity because we had long had the impression that there was always *one* filmmaker who was *the* great African filmmaker for a few years until, suddenly, one fine day, he or she would disappear and the next new great African filmmaker emerge! So, the idea of the Guilde was to refuse this game, so that all could advance together, to create greater collaboration, a collective effort. Unfortunately, the idea was rather utopian!

We nonetheless started out trying to do things together and it was in this framework that I launched the Côté Doc at the FESPACO. At that time, the Association Ecrans [a Burkinabè non-profit organization working to promote and distribute African film] had launched a short film festival in Ouagadougou called 'Nuit d'Ecrans Côté Court'. In November 2002, they launched the 'Nuit d'Ecrans Côté Doc'. I was their first guest. We talked at length as I also wanted us to do something with the Guilde to promote documentary, which was still the poor relative of African cinema and still didn't have a proper place. I remember, for example, in 2001 that there was such trouble at the FESPACO, with the documentary films being screened in such deplorable conditions, that I thought to myself on arriving at the airport that it would be interesting if these young people, who were organizing their own festival, did something with the Guilde during the FESPACO to give documentary proper visibility. So, I met the Ecrans association members in Ouaga and we agreed that if they really want to exist, it would be better to do so during the FESPACO and that's how the Côté Doc idea was launched. We had three months to pull it off. We contacted people left, right and centre. We contacted Baba Hama, the FESPACO General Secretary at the time, who immediately backed us saying that, as clearly no one knew what to do with documentary at the festival, why not let us take charge and prepare a catalogue of films. We also created an interface between the younger and more veteran filmmakers. The head of the French Cultural Centre was highly enthusiastic too. So, we launched this first initiative. What mattered was extracting documentary from the ghetto that had been shut in at the FESPACO. But there was also something else that I really wanted to do. It was 2003, twenty years since I first came to the FESPACO in 1983, and I had observed the evolution of the festival. In the past, there had been debates after the films, public debates that I found truly wonderful. I had the impression that this dynamic, this relationship that the filmmakers had with the public, was disappearing. So, we made the Côté Doc a place where we could promote documentary, giving it a place of honour, but also a place where we were able to build bridges so that young people, who were increasingly interested in documentary, could meet and exchange with existing filmmakers. The first year was a success. We had a small space to show the films, but the debates that we held in the mornings were one of the most popular, best-attended events of the festival. We secured the backing of the liaison office of the Espace Francophone, and lots of other smaller backers, enabling us to create a space where at last something was happening. The first debates sought to define documentary, to distinguish documentary from reporting. We talked about how to write a documentary, about documentary distribution … we had all sorts of debates. A lot of people came, even those working in fiction – Moussa Touré, for example. Thierry Michel was also very present, who is not only a reputed documentary filmmaker, but also taught in Belgium. It was fascinating. We saw truly new styles emerge. In 2003, for example, I discovered the Cameroonian filmmaker Osvalde Lewat, who makes wonderful, highly committed films that pose truly interesting questions. I also discovered a lot of very powerful South African films.

We ran the section for two editions of the FESPACO, in 2003 and 2005, and it was a great success. But not everyone was happy about this success, and even less so because there was someone like me at the head of this movement who refused to compromise on either the quality, or our discourse. The Guilde, at the time, was meant to exist to defend an ethic, to transmit, to exchange, not for ego clashes. After I'd been president for three years, I wanted there to be a rotation and as Fanta Nacro was vice-president, I thought it would be great if she became president. She became president, but an autocratic one [laughs]! Unfortunately, the Guilde exploded, because we had a bulletin we wrote that came out regularly, one which we trusted each other's articles for, that we trusted the chief editor Mahamat-Saleh Haroun for, whose editorials were never censored. I had decided to write an editorial in which I posed the question, after several years' existence, of whether we had lost sight of our initial objectives. I decided to recall these objectives. Unfortunately, not everyone was happy with that and so they decided to censor my editorial. That's why I left the Guilde. Later, in 2007, the FESPACO decided to end the Côté Doc.

I sense a certain regret, a certain solitude … Do you feel that you ever found a film family?

A huge solitude. But I did find a family, in spite of everything, among those who marked me, who inspired me, those who threw off the established codes. I remember meeting two Swiss filmmakers, Walter Marti and Reni Mertens. When I made *Bikutsi Water Blues*, which got such a slating, it was so painful that I called them and spent three or four days staying with them in Switzerland.

We spent the time together talking and they said to me: 'You know, we have made thirty films between us' – they made films that were so different, so odd – 'and we too have made films that no one believed in or backed, that people ripped to pieces and detested'. I remember, they told me about one of their last screenings. They were in such a situation that they were going from village to village, to places where there wasn't even a cinema to screen their film, and they organized a 16 mm screening in a village church. After the screening, they explained to the audience that a film takes time to make, costs money, and that they had had no backing for this film, so they were going to pass round a hat. The audience put so much money in the hat that they were amazed by this generosity. And they said to me: 'We, at our level, that's what touched us. When you do something, at times artisanally but with conviction, you might not get acclaim, but you do get other forms of recognition because the work you do ends up touching people.' I needed to be around people like Walter Marti and Reni Mertens, to talk to them. That's what gave me the strength to continue.

Much later in 2000, I met Johan van der Keuken. He was someone I loved talking to about the perception of work. He said to me at that time: 'I have made so many films, but at the same time, my films have never really gained

Photo 27 Teno at the world première of *Bikutsi Water Blues*, Carthage Film Festival (JCC), Tunisia, 1988, with festival founder and filmmaker Tahar Cheriaa in the background.

recognition'. In the approximately ten years before we met in Berlin in 2000, the Berlinale Forum had refused all his films. He had decided not to even bother entering them anymore. Until *Amsterdam Global Village* and *The Long Holiday*, he'd stopped distributing his films. When he died, there were retrospectives everywhere! I tried to understand, and I remembered what he'd said to me: 'It's not a choice. When you try to do singular things, you haven't necessarily chosen the simplest path to success.' Singular voices often end up existing or being recognized precisely when they're dying out. But it's complicated ... I don't see myself as belonging to any current, and as I am not a model for those who have come after me either, I sometimes find myself in a delicate situation because a lot of these young filmmakers imagine that, in order to exist or to prove their originality, it is in their interest to denigrate my work to give themselves a form of legitimacy – even without having understood, or sometimes even seeing my films. That accentuates the feeling of solitude.

Over the past decade, documentary has indeed really taken off in Africa. Do you get the impression it has definitively taken root as a form there?

With the new technological means, documentary has definitely taken root, but the question of its visibility needs to be resolved now. Very few documentaries are shown on television in Africa today. Generally speaking, only reports are broadcast, and very consensual reports at that. That's the problem. We still face the major battle of getting television channels to show our films. We perhaps have to explore the possibilities of screening on the internet, but internet is still just a dream because most people can only access internet in cybercafés; very few people have internet at home. So how can we convince the television channels to show more documentaries? It's a battle that can only be fought with the backing of the institutions, one that is very hard to fight on one's own.

What do you think of the emerging filmmakers?

A lot of filmmakers are emerging, but what I find a shame and rather unfortunate is the lack of inventiveness. Often when you see their works, they could have often been made by anybody. Moreover, they are often perfect models of films that people came to shoot in Africa, only this time they are shot by locals. I don't find these models inventive enough in formal terms. It's as if a certain number of genres have become established in documentary, and so long as you stick to these different modes, then that's fine, you make films, end of story. But I sincerely have to say that Rocky-type films, to use an example from fiction – that is, films in which there's an obstacle that needs to be surmounted, and there are a number of stages that have to be gone through to overcome that obstacle, successfully or not – frankly, I find them painful. I'd prefer to watch a fiction film than that kind of documentary. Also, observational cinema in Africa, by Africans, is all well and good, but I personally feel that it refuses, or renounces, going as far as possible in a form of analysis, and I feel that we still haven't analysed and shown the complexity of the continent's situation enough yet. In complex situations, observing is interesting, but … it is to have the luxury of contenting yourself with the situation as it is. All of this means that people are speaking a lot about documentary, but I am not very satisfied with the films I see because they lack both inventiveness and commitment. The points of view aren't committed enough, or when they are, they go a bit over the top … in short, there is a problem still today in the training. That is indeed why I have undertaken to do some training because, at some point or another, we too need to emulate several African visual artists' undertakings to formally find ways to represent local life. Documentary filmmakers also need to try to think a bit more about the representations of life they propose.

Are these younger documentary filmmakers familiar with the work of those who came before? Is there a form of filiation, a transmission?

It depends. When I was invited to the Escales Documentaires festival in Libreville, Gabon, in 2013 to run a writing workshop for aspiring filmmakers, for example, they put on a retrospective of my work and I was quite surprised to see so many young people attend. They were very happy. Some were surprised. They didn't know that this kind of film existed and that motivated them to continue. The Libreville Escales Documentaires indeed hopes to invite more and more school pupils, many of whom attended in 2013. Debates were organized after the films and I was impressed by the level of the questions asked. They watched *Le Malentendu colonial*, for example, and it was incredible. I partook in a debate with the general public and a debate with students and school children, and the latter was truly of a different level! That was encouraging. I realized that, contrary to what people think, young people try to make connections, to understand, even if they don't yet know this history very well. And many of them want to make films too. That is wonderful, especially with the tools they have at their disposal.

In 2017, you set up a training programme in Cameroon. What principal elements do you aim to transmit? What do you aim to get the aspiring filmmakers to reflect on?

They mustn't come expecting a recipe. First of all, I ask them to look around them. I really get the impression that people don't look. It's a bit as if they were afraid to look at what is going on around them. In Cameroon, I'm sometimes shocked to see the subjects proposed, that people look far afield to find. There are so many subjects, so many things going on in our country, but it's as if people refused to see them because they are deemed political. I say to them, look around you. Of course, people are afraid. The last time I ran a workshop for another organization, there were European instructors too who didn't see when there was a subject and who said to me: 'But you can't make a film about that'. I said: 'There is something here, it concerns people, it's their life, their survival, that's where you need to find an entry point to talk about it, to manage to show it, and that's where things become interesting'. Maybe that's why we aren't very present in festivals. I get the impression that in the selections, the subjects that are chosen by those in charge of the different festivals, who have become the gatekeepers, are so-called 'universal' subjects, but which frankly are often not that interesting. Unless it's to show Africa as they imagine it, and not the Africa that we see every day.

Earlier, you described yourself as a craftsman, and I notice that in most of your films, you film long sequences of artisans at work – carpenters, sculptors, hair-dressers – paying particular attention to their manual gestures, or fabrication processes, such as the printer sequence in *Afrique, je te plumerai*. This is a recurrent theme, almost a leitmotif, that culminates in *Lieux saints*, where you film the long sequences of Jules César making a djembe drum. That reminds me of something Fanon says in *The Wretched of the Earth* when he writes about the importance, in the decolonization process, in re-creating the self, of becoming artisans again ... Do you think that this is a conception of cinema that should be explored today?

One of the great debates that traversed African cinema in the 1980s and 1990s was about the professionalization of our cinema. By professionalization, what was meant was how we could better imitate everything that came from elsewhere. Professionalization was always people coming from elsewhere to tell us how we had to do things to be professional – in other words, a form of mimetism. Most of our filmmakers started out by *mégotage* [skimping] as Sembène called it, cadging a bit of film stock here or there, or by working as assistants on film shoots until feeling the need to take the camera and film themselves, to tell their own stories. These pioneers, many of whom started out like that, were those who began to question the hegemonic place of people like Rouch. They weren't necessarily in a form of contestation but proposed other visions, and they did so often artisanally. But right up until now, we are still caught up in this question of the stamp of professionalization ... Since the television has become a kind of open supermarket where you have to make formatted flow-products, there are still works made by individuals who are like brave warriors, but who find very little local backing to allow them to make films that are both locally rooted and have artistic ambition. We can of course talk about Nollywood in terms of local rooting, which has created its own funding processes, and which

Photo 28a Ousmane Sembène and Teno. Milan African Film Festival, 1991.

Photo 28b Souleymane Cissé and Teno. Tübingen International Festival of Francophone Film, Germany, 2013.

produces mass cinema, but I get the impression that most of the time, this remains in a kind of mimetism on a formal level. It's a far cry from the aesthetic or narrative experimentation of people like Djibril Diop Mambéty, for example. All that seems completely forgotten and we are in the realm of the commercial. Yet I feel that we haven't yet exhausted all the narrative forms possible. At the end of *Lieux saints*, I cite Sembène and Mambéty, who gave definitions of the griot that I found both complementary and which can serve as a reference for those who are trying to use this medium to go beyond just making commercial works. If we look back at the FEPACI Charter, which was so discussed and debated in the 1970s and 1980s, it expressed the need to use cinema not only to touch people, but also to encourage them to improve themselves in some way or another by proposing them entertainment, but one also capable of reinforcing their sense of self-respect, of stimulating another level of reflection.

When you foreground Jules César, who says in *Lieux saints* that the djembe is the ancestor of cinema, is it a way of turning more towards endogenous, rather than exogenous influences?

Yes, it's a way of saying that even if things change on a technological level, the processes used are ones that existed in all societies. Jules César says it very well in the film: cinema allows you to convey a certain number of messages; the djembe does too. In his process of making and playing the djembe, he considers it cinema's ancestor. And I think that it's good at some point to show people that you can look at the world without thinking that everything came from elsewhere, that there are a whole host of elements within ourselves that belong to today's world, but which were there already. In every era, there are facets in one's own society that allow you to express, show, say and do things.

Is that an important element in the training of young filmmakers in Africa today?

Yes, absolutely: to tell them that they don't always have to imitate those who come from elsewhere, and that they can delve back into local narratives, into the manner in which our languages are constructed – one could talk about linguistics too – into the ways of telling stories to find new narrative forms.

Does this professionalization – one might also say standardization – empty cinema of its political clout, of the will expressed in the Algiers Charter to raise people's awareness?

Yes. I think that one of the reasons why people try to standardize, to globalize, to define cinema – or to let others define it, above all – is precisely to empty it of any form of protest it might contain, because when cinema addresses ordinary people, when it speaks to them, that means that these people have humanity, they have an existence, they are heroes too. If in Africa, all our stories are simply about the rich, the beautiful, the healthy, that is a problem. Cinema shouldn't be about magnifying values that are negative or repressive for the masses.

With all these efforts to professionalize, we have ended up shutting people in narratives that distance them from their own environments. You can't imagine the number of times I've been told that my cinema is 'militant'. People used to say that when I started out and was experimenting things in 16 mm. Progressively, the critique went from 'militant' cinema to not being 'well-polished' cinema! There is always this need to define you, but with the intention of isolating, side-lining and marginalizing you. So, whenever I met young African journalists who said to me: 'Your cinema is militant', I'd ask them: 'Militant in relation to what?' They've been made to believe that if you talk about them, about their own lives, you are a militant, not that you are talking about the real. The fact of addressing daily problems – their daily reality – becomes 'militant'. What does that mean? It means that 'official' cinema has fulfilled its normalizing mission to fix people in the place that colonization assigned them to in the past. I have always tried to fight against all that. And to do so, I have often called on the figures of the struggle for a true African Independence in my films: Um Nyobè, Moumié, Ouandié, Lumumba, Nkrumah ... For me, it was important to start resuscitating the combat of all these people, who of course were defeated – and I constantly say that – but it's not because they were defeated that we should forget them. These combats are still relevant today. By questioning the world as it is, we continue their combat, even if they lost.

Circulations

Let us end with the question of exile, with your vision as an exile, as you have long lived outside of Cameroon now, even if you go there regularly.

I have always been an exile everywhere I've lived. I have never been at home anywhere, both literally and metaphorically. I don't know where I live. I have never had a home. I long searched for one, and I think that I'm still searching. I went to my parents' village, Bandjoun, and for a long time I thought it was my home, but at the same time, I didn't feel like it was more so than anywhere else. I was born in a little town in southern Cameroon where, at the time, people used to say, referring to Bandjoun, 'Bamileke country', even though we were in the same country. So, having been born in a part of the country where people talked about other 'countries', I was already born an exile in a sense. At that time, you needed a pass to travel to Bandjoun because it was the colonial era, and there was a lot of violence everywhere. I was born in a place, yet knowing that I came from elsewhere and that to go there, you had to go through a whole host of controls. But I still went to Bandjoun, I met people, I tried to get to know the place, I loved it, I wanted to know its culture, its customs, I wanted to make a film about its power structures, but in trying to understand it, I realized that everything that seemed wonderful to me was just a façade … And so, in fact, home … It's a true question. Home is there where I'll find myself … and I am still seeking myself!

You have lived in Europe for years now. Do you get the impression that this geographic and cultural distance has changed or sharpened your vision of Cameroon?

I don't know if it has sharpened or darkened my vision. You have to question your vision at all times. So, I am perpetually questioning. Even if I have a vision, and I see what I see, I always pose myself the question of to what point I'm kidding myself. If I stopped questioning, I'd enter a form of routine which I hope never to enter. I think we need to question all our gazes, our subjectivity at all times. What is fabulous in the world in which we are living now is that people think, write, and that encourages us to question ourselves. For the moment, I'm still fortunate because my questioning in my early films hasn't yet been completely overtaken by new reflections. I'd probably feel terrible if those I articulated at the time had become totally outdated! I continue to read, to nourish myself with all the current reflections about decoloniality, gender, and all the writings on archives and cultural appropriation, both with regard to artistic creation and on a philosophical level … At the same time, there are things that sadden me: the way in which, despite the huge circulation of information, a lot of younger people remain seduced by meaningless things, or really pass by the essential.

In *Clando*, you address the question of departure, of exile, and its corollary: return. It is said in the film that if you no longer know how to advance, go back on your footsteps and make a new departure. Your latest film *Chosen* also addresses the question of return. Today, some twenty years on, do you think this return is possible?

Anything is possible. In the fiction feature that I am also preparing, the protagonist is born in France, knows nothing about Africa, and goes there. She goes there but returns; she doesn't stay. We are in a world in which the colonial system compartmentalized everything. Yet the world before colonization and the emergence of capitalism was a world in which people circulated. For me, it's this circulation that constitutes the richness and beauty of the world. They compartmentalized everything to only let those with capital circulate, those who are able to run this world and its capitalist system. So, I believe that by pulling down these frontiers, these barriers, we will achieve a world of free

Photo 29 Teno on location filming *Chosen* in Awamufie, Ghana, 2010.

circulation and that, to me, is the ideal world. Perhaps we'll never manage, but ours is a world in which people go there where the opportunities lie; that's why people migrate. When you create poverty, when there are wars in the world, it's normal that migration takes place. And as a result of creating wars elsewhere over resources, you end up creating movements of populations that you one day have to answer for.

In his recent book *Politiques de l'inimitié*, Achille Mbembe evoked the 'poetics of the passer-by', calling for us to embrace our status as passers-by in the world, to embrace circulations…

Mbembe's expression is one I adhere to entirely. He thought and formulated that perfectly. I am a passer-by in the world, which might be Cameroon, the United States, or China … but I say one thing, which I always say: I am African. I am an African in this world.

Part III
Appendices

Appendix 1

The Writings of Jean-Marie Teno

Freedom: The Power to Say No[1]

In October 1988, during the screening of my film *Bikutsi Water Blues* at the Carthage Film Festival, I dared to speak about freedom: the freedom to choose a subject matter, the freedom of style, far from the classic, distinct categories of documentary and fiction. The freedom to say out loud what ninety years of oppression had prevented us from saying.

I shall always remember the sarcastic response of some of my fellow film-makers, and one's comment: 'Ideas like that and the film you just made can ruin a career'.

With the upheaval taking place all over the world these past few years, I shall not dwell on such themes here, for they are now out in the streets today. I shall limit my reflection to freedom, the corollary of both personal and collective creativity, and well-being.

Schematically speaking, the world today is divided into two blocks: the North and the South. In the North, as in the South, there are those at the top and those at the bottom. Those at the top are comfortably installed and above all do not want change. Some at the bottom struggle so that everybody may have at least the bare minimum, so that the majority can envisage daily life as something other than a nightmare. When those at the bottom can no longer survive and die like dogs, those at the top shed a tear, collect rice, books, pencils, and call the media to show their ever-so generous solidarity.

Responding to an urgency without attacking the roots of the ill (especially when you have the means to and are in part responsible for them) is a sophisticated form of cynicism. In six-month's time, tanning on the beach, they'll say: 'We were there, we did all we could for them, so tragic, Africa!' And someone will retort: 'But don't forget, we have our homeless too, we have to do something for them'.

---

[1] First published as 'Liberté, le pouvoir de dire non', in FEPACI (ed), *L'Afrique et le centenaire du Cinéma*. Paris: Présence africaine, 1995, 375-78. Translated by Melissa Thackway. © Présence Africaine 1995.

But to those at the bottom who work ten, or even twelve hours a day, how do we explain that they cannot make a decent living from their labour? We can tell them about the current crisis affecting the whole world, but the truth is that if the wages of those at the bottom were better, the profit margins of those at the top would be smaller, and they would have to make do without that second car to drive the kids to school, they would no longer be able to buy themselves a pied-à-terre in Paris (avenue Foch), nor the many houses that they normally have themselves built with tax-payers' money. Selling off Africa's economic patrimony is a game that has lasted for over fifty years, leading us today to situations like those in Somalia and Liberia, which risk spreading to many other African countries. These systems of economic exploitation always rest on three elements: violent repression, state-owned media disinformation, and ruthless censorship. The aim is always the same: to keep the African masses away from the day-to-day handling of their country's wealth, by any means necessary. That also involves an ill-adapted, highly selective education system that leaves the majority of Africans by the wayside, with no training, who are then bombarded with images from abroad, with technicolour dreams, without forgetting to insidiously inculcate them to despise their own image and kind. Even religion is used to justify and legitimate our terrestrial poverty by promising us rivers of milk and honey in the skies above if we are credulous enough and learn to say: 'Yes, Massa, thank you Massa! You are right, Massa, as always!'

Our cinema has emerged in this troubled socio-political context. It must choose its path between a short-term profitability that condemns it to participate in the organized dumbing-down of the continent, and a contribution to the necessary reflection on freedom, at risk of being unpopular. Before this dilemma, it is for each and every one to find the solution that suits them, as analyses of the situation often diverge radically. These reflections and trends ought to enrich our cinema. But unfortunately, cinema is expensive, and we have entered the era of humanitarian aid which does not spare even cinema, while nonetheless taking care to mask itself behind all sorts of well-formulated concepts.

I am not going to attack a certain number of commissions that have been set up in the North to back African cinema, but I am simply going to draw our attention to a tendency towards elitism which, in the long run, will not help cinema organize itself in our countries, but instead will tend to develop an imitation of the European box office and a race for prizes in the various international festival. What can be more pernicious than, on hazy criteria, handing out awards of self-promotion? And all those little comments by experts, in the corridors of the fancy hotels frequented during festivals, who tell you what type of films have more chance of getting shown on TV in the North, and who encourage you to make your film like this or that, and who take leave of you saying: 'Here, have my card. Come and see me in Paris, Brussels, London, Milan or Montreal'.

All those people are the people on high, or work for them; they are friends with the people on high in our lands. Some promise us honey at the third traffic light on the left, or right – it's all the same, as we now know – and others whip us if we do not advance quickly enough precisely in that direction.

Freedom is to take one's time. It is to choose to go backwards, not to budge, or to advance at one's own pace. Freedom is to shoot documentaries, or documents, in Hi-8, or Super-8, especially when everyone else thinks it is demeaning. It is also to refuse to enter this spiral of competitiveness that prevents us from thinking further than our next film.

Freedom, for me, is the power to say no ... with a smile.

Writing on Walls: The Future of African Documentary Cinema[2]

In following the issues and day-to-day workings of a neighbourhood video-club in Ouagadougou, home of the FESPACO and capital of African cinema, my latest work, Sacred Places, *allowed me to question my own work as a filmmaker in Africa, and to consider the direction that cinema is taking on the continent.*

Offering a personal reading of both past and present documentary filmmaking in Africa, this article aims to continue that reflection, raising one of today's most salient questions: that of transmission. As the visionary Abbo reminds us in Sacred Places: *'In the beginning was the word...' But who is speaking? And to say what to whom?*

When I arrived in Ouagadougou for my first FESPACO in 1983, I was struck by the intensity and abundance of debates about African film. In the endless discussions to define African cinema and its future, one of the points that kept coming up was the impression that the first films by African filmmakers were either documentary in style or of documentary value.

This overriding view apparently emerged as most of these first films – *Afrique sur Seine, Contras' city, Borom Sarret*, to name but a few – took place in urban settings, with characters often playing their real-life roles. Moreover, the content of these stories, often rooted in the social and political context of the time, led many people somewhat disparagingly to equate these films with documentaries, at a time when documentary film had not achieved the levels

---

[2] First commissioned in 2010 by the New York African Film Festival, and published online in 2011: http://africultures.com/writing-on-walls-10003 (present version).

of popularity it has gained in recent years with the films of Michael Moore and other European and American directors.

If realism in African cinema led critics to associate narrative films with documentaries at a time when documentary did not have the appeal of fiction film, who can blame African filmmakers for turning their backs on realistic stories set in African cities to embrace stories set in the imagined and idealized village, giving rise to what became referred to as 'calabash cinema' in the 1980s?

Along with Idrissa Ouedraogo and his award-winning films *Yaaba* and *Tilaï*, the most striking example of this to my mind is Souleymane Cissé, who first made *Den Muso*, then went on to make what I consider to be one of the masterpieces of African cinema: *Baara*. Released in 1978, *Baara* is a well-crafted film that has barely aged and can be seen as an example of an African cinema that is both challenging and popular. Cissé went on to make *Finye*, before completing *Yeelen*, one of African cinema's most mysterious, complex and sophisticated films, bringing him the international recognition he deserved and encouraging him to embark on the strange adventure of the film *Waati*, a multi-headed monster that almost sunk his career.

Before Cissé, the very first wave of African filmmakers had successfully appropriated the film medium in their efforts to accompany the social and political struggles of the early years of African Independence. Their works directly and indirectly challenged colonial discourse and offered African audiences representations that promoted dignity and gave them the hope, strength, and confidence to embark on the task of inventing a future in a turbulent and changing world.

The 1960s saw the emergence of masters such as Mustapha Alassane, who went from narrative, to documentary, to animation to address issues that were relevant at that time, and which remain relevant today, fifty years later. One fully appreciates the talent of this man when working, as I currently am, with young avant-garde filmmakers in the USA, who still use 16mm today to reinvent, create, and propose daring metaphors about their lives. In his 1966 film *Le Retour d'un aventurier*, Alassane did just that and more in his little village in Niger, creating a parody of the western to brilliantly and metaphorically address the intrusion of colonial culture in African societies. This is another example of what popular culture can be at its best: inventive, funny, and relevant to the contemporary socio-political situation.

By reappropriating ethnographic codes and blending them with elements of oral narrative, and specifically the griot's storytelling style, Beninese filmmaker Richard de Meideros' short film *Teke, Hymne au Borgou* (1974) paved a path we are still following many years later.

Both Mustapha Alassane and Richard de Medeiros shared a legitimate concern: how to find ways to represent African realities in an accessible form, incorporating African narrative approaches and European aesthetics, but reframing these to serve new purposes. This strategy worked in other art forms too, such as the visual arts and music in particular, with musicians like Manu Dibango or Fela Anikulapo Kuti and Afro jazz. By blending African and Western music styles into what would become the new modern African music, they durably changed African music and found a way to impose it internationally without losing their souls.

Almost ten years older than me, Samba Felix Ndiaye followed in the footsteps of these two pioneering filmmakers, while at the same time developing his own personal style.

Unlike Mustapha Alassane's popular approach to film, however, the late Samba Felix Ndiaye saw himself more as a painter, an artist looking at society, bringing elements together for everyone to see, irrespective of whether the majority of the audience was able to read the relevant connections between them or not.

Samba felt that cinema could stand only for what it was, nothing more. This gave him the ability, the freedom, to step back and achieve a distance that allowed him to make films that I considered observational and at times even a little bourgeois, as I felt they sometimes lacked political edge at a time when I personally considered this crucial in the fight for democracy in Africa.

In all fairness, Senegal in the Eighties was in a far better political situation than many other African countries, even if the situation has since declined. In April 1984, we had a mini civil war in Cameroon; Paul Biya came to power in 1982, and we thought that the twenty-five-year-long nightmare of Ahidjo was over and that the country would move towards democracy. We were deluding ourselves, sadly, and we slid deeper and deeper into the mire. It was in this context of a totalitarian society that I started and continued to make documentary films. One of the goals I set out to achieve was to decomplexify life around me and to present the social and political situation in Cameroon in a comprehensive manner. That is why I choose to narrate my films. In 1992, in *Afrique, je te plumerai*, I adopted first-person narrative for the first time, and I have continued to use it to bring viewers, wherever they are, to look at the world through my eyes, through the eyes of an African. My latest film *Sacred Places* took me into St Léon, a neighbourhood of Ouagadougou, the 'capital of African cinema', to meet Bouba, the video-club operator, Jules-Cesar, the djembe-maker who sees the djembe as the ancestor of cinema, and Abbo, who writes philosophical statements on the neighbourhood walls for everyone to see. Together, these three characters are a metaphor for African film: Jules-Cesar incarnates sound and film's creative aspects; Bouba the image and its constraints; and Abbo is like the filmmaker, writing on the walls of his neighbourhood, hoping for people to come by and read his words.

Many other filmmakers choose to use first-person narrative, such as Zeka Laplaine in *Kinshasa Palace*, adding another dimension of complexity by incorporating themselves in the film as another fictional character – a way of blurring the boundaries of fictional documentary, or an attempt to confuse viewers and leave them wondering where the truth lies in the story unfolding before them. The visual presence of self in films as a narrator and as a character was also present in Mahamat-Saleh Haroun's film *Bye Bye Africa* and in Abderrahmane Sissako's *La Vie sur terre*.

Samba Felix and I often ran into each other at film festivals, or in Paris, where we discussed our work avidly. He repeatedly told me to pay more attention to the form. In retrospect, I realize that my work kept unconsciously answering: 'Forget the form, as long as I truthfully represent my perception of African reality without losing my audience'. Personally, my main concern was to improve my film structures and make my narration as poetic, funny, and engaging as possible without compromising the content.

Samba studied his classics in film school and was fascinated by a Dutch filmmaker, Johan van der Keuken, whom we both knew. In Berlin in 2000, a year before his death, van der Keuken told me that he was fortunate to have been born in a place where the basic issues of democracy had been resolved, and that he was not sure he would have made the same films if he had been born in some of the places he had filmed. This was a kind way of acknowledging my work, even if it was totally different in its approach to his, and I remain grateful to him for that.

Samba Felix Ndiaye and Johan van der Keuken belong to the family of great filmmakers whose empathy for the people before their cameras transpires clearly in their films. They also showed the same empathy to their peers, and especially their younger colleagues, for whom their time and advice was precious. Their absence will leave a long and lasting void.

Despite the disdain for African documentary film that has prevailed up to this date, there are reasons to be cautiously hopeful: 2009 confirmed both the increase in the number of documentary films produced by first-time filmmakers and the number of festivals on the African continent dedicated to documentary film. At the same time, it also saw European cultural institutes, such as the Goethe Institute and the French Cultural Centres, and organizations, such as Africadoc, vying to offer training to young African filmmakers.

This latter situation brought back to mind the words of one African professor from Cheik Anta Diop University in Dakar, whom I met after a screening of *Afrique, je te plumerai*. He commented: 'Your film ends with the affirmation that education is one of the solutions for the future of Africa, but the question is, what education?'

Indeed, one of the recurring problems of cinema on the continent is the absence of transmission from one generation to the next, partly due to the lack of local policies to support film. In such a context, filmmakers rarely have time for anything other than their own daily struggle to create and survive. This does not nurture filiations or long-time collaboration between filmmakers of different generations. Each generation is thus left to fend for itself, and each new generation acts like it thinks it has reinvented the wheel!

With the exception of a few institutions such as Gaston Kabore's Imagine in Burkina Faso, which offers training to African filmmakers from all over the continent, today's training schemes seem to perpetuate a paradigm not dissimilar to the colonial era's civilizing mission: the globalizing mission. Today, for example, the Goethe Institute brings young German filmmakers to Africa to train African filmmakers, as if there were not enough trained filmmakers on the continent to transmit their knowledge to their younger peers. Europeans training Africans to look at and represent themselves raises certain questions, especially if one considers many of these teachers' lack of awareness and sometimes lack of interest in the history of the continent, and particularly the history of African representation.

Isn't it ironic that, fifty years after the first generation of African filmmakers began the struggle to challenge and rectify colonial representations of Africa, Europeans are back to train our youth to look at and represent themselves, often taking as examples and references the ethnographic images they are familiar with, rather than the works of other African filmmakers?

When European organizations such as Africadoc claim to be initiating documentary filmmaking in Africa, what message do they send to their trainees about the legacy of the pioneering documentary filmmakers working on the continent before them?

Have African artists and filmmakers been struggling to introduce elements of complexity in the representation of Africa, to challenge simplistic and essentializing colonial representations, simply to see the return of a new form of cultural colonization fifty years on, in the name of globalization?

Despite the situation I have just described, there is hope. Amidst the numerous productions flourishing all over the continent, some real talents are emerging and their works are opening up encouraging perspectives for the future. Katy Lena Ndiaye (Senegal), for example, whose aesthetic approach is a pure pleasure for the senses, can no doubt be classed as a descendant of the director Samba Felix Ndiaye.

Nourished by her solid journalistic background and a fearless approach to injustice, Cameroonian director Osvalde Lewat has successfully managed in her three films to remind us all that the fight for democracy and change in Africa is still the responsibility of the artist.

In South Africa, the new individual voices of Khalo Matabane and Dumisani Phakhathi are embracing and addressing the complexity of the new South Africa in audacious styles that complement the observational approach of experienced filmmakers such as Francis Webster.

In *From a Whisper*, a sort of fictional documentary that puts some of the realities facing the African continent at the centre of the creative cinematic process, another impressive woman filmmaker, Kenyan Wanuri Kahiu, took a real event – the bombing of the American embassy – and created fictional characters to address the full complexity of Islamic fundamentalism and terrorism. This successful reconciliation of narrative and documentary echoed the approach of pioneering Mustapha Alassane.

Finally, I would like to cite the work of Moussa Touré, who worked as a technician on many of the classics of African cinema before directing his own 35mm features *Toubab-Bi* and *TGV*. In 2000, Touré took a video camera and started travelling the continent, shooting *Poussière de ville* (2001), a film about street children in Congo after the war, followed by the poignant *Nous sommes nombreuses* (2003) on rape as instrument of war and its consequences. Moussa Touré has since gone on to deal with immigration and environmental issues in his neighbourhood in Dakar.

Moussa Touré's work is interesting not only for his relatively atypical cinematic path from narrative film to documentary; his work also raises important ethical questions. When, while shooting *Poussière de ville*, for example, Moussa went looking for the families of his characters, the street kids, he was going beyond the habitual role of the filmmaker vis-à-vis his subject by assigning himself the duty, the responsibility of taking the kids back to their relatives. At the same time, Moussa's films remain difficult to find internationally, even if he does screen them locally: in a sense, it is as if Moussa were writing on walls like Abbo in *Sacred Places*, as most of us are in our local communities.

For me, these two points raise the following key questions, on which I would like to conclude:
- Can the filmmaker, as an artist, allow him/herself to be defined by others who have the means to manipulate and orientate the reading of his/her work, or should he/she be writing on the walls like Moussa in his neighbourhood, at the risk of not being seen further afield?
- Are those who choose to write meaningful things on the walls, for their communities, more likely to survive in the long run, to make a more lasting impact, than those who run after the mirage of a global recognition?

While the walls cannot be moved, today's new forms of internet technology do make it possible to relay those messages, offering a diversity of voices to challenge the standardizing tendencies of globalization. So, ultimately, the question still remains: what messages are we choosing to write on the walls?

Photo 30 Jean-Marie Teno and director of photography Mohamed Soudani on location shooting *Le Dernier voyage*, Yaoundé, 1990.

Filming Alone (extracts)[3]

The answer to the question, 'Why do you film alone?', has varied over the course of my life.

I began filming alone in 1982 when I was learning to use the camera I had just bought. It was a 16mm ARRI ST, with three lenses on a rotating turret. At that time, I was working as a video technician at FR3 (France 3 Television). The news was still made on 16mm, on reversal film stock … I learned to measure the light and to frame in the streets of Paris shooting 30m reversal film reels. The contrasts were high with reversal stock, the latitude for shooting was limited, and you had to be precise because film stock was expensive.

Although I admired filmmakers like Joseph Morder, who made films on Super 8 at the time, my privileged position at FR3 gave me access to the television lab

---

[3] From the 'Filmer seul-e' special edition of *La Revue Documentaire* 26/27 (Paris: 2016), 304-09, in which a number of prominent documentary filmmakers were asked to respond to the question of when and why they shot their own films. Translation by Melissa Thackway.

and 16mm editing suites, which encouraged me to shoot on 16mm, more as a hobby and out of a love of the manual side of celluloid.

[…]

It was with my Arri ST, a Sony tape recorder, and a Minolta CL photo camera – a cheap copy of the Leica CL – that I made my very first film, *Hommage*. The sound was not synchronous, and each time I shot the images, Madeleine Beauséjour, who later edited the film, recorded the corresponding sound.

[…]

This first film was shot when the shooting of another film, *Fièvre jaune taximan* – the story of a taxi driver's day, shot in Yaoundé with a three-person crew comprising a cameraman, a sound engineer and an assistant – was held-up by administrative complications. While waiting to receive the authorization to shoot (which was only delivered after I had left Cameroon), I went to my village, where I started filming life and people going about their daily business.

[…]

Initially, filming was a kind of game for me. There was a whole ritual to respect: loading the film in the dark, without being entirely sure it wouldn't jam. Then there was the feeling of joy when the camera started to roll with no snag. You had to quickly concentrate on the subject you were filming. Had you measured the light properly? Was it the right diaphragm? Who to focus on? Was the subject doing the right thing?

All these questions made your adrenaline pump and you were plunged into an unreal world, the world of cinema that you were never certain to capture properly with your camera. Next came the weeks of waiting – months sometimes – to see the images because there was no film laboratory for developing in Cameroon. And on a zero-budget film, your reels sometimes waited several months in the fridge while you got together enough money to develop and print the positives.

Veiling flare, shots that were too short, shots that were a bit blurred … disappointment sometimes, but also often joy. But come what may, you had to make a film with the material you had. And there began another intellectual, artistic, creative adventure.

With experienced camera operators, the situation is different. You expect everything to be perfect, and sometimes these perfect images are less interesting because they resemble things you already know. They often have the operator's signature, which places the spectator in a comfort zone that one may or may not like.

Having no model, it took me six years to find a form that married my questioning of the state of the world and the place to which I was assigned in this world as an African. The result was *Afrique, je te plumerai*, a film in which I was supposed to be behind the camera – the person filming – and the voice that took the spectator on this journey through time. A film in the first person.

From my first films, which I filmed for pleasure, to *Afrique, je te plumerai*, I worked with numerous camera operators: notably Bonaventure Takoukam (may he rest in peace), with whom I shot several short films; Joseph Guerrin, with whom I made *Bikutsi Water Blues*; Mohammed Soudani (*Le Dernier voyage*); Denis Gheerbrant (*La Gifle et la caresse*); and Robert Diannoux, who filmed *Afrique, je te plumerai*. Robert was a former ORTF [the French national radio and television agency] cameraman, who had travelled the world over with a hand-held Eclair Coutant. That was why I asked him to capture the Cameroonian chaos with a hand-held camera. He agreed to be my point of view for the main shoot. Then, I made another trip to shoot the additional footage, which I shot with an Eclair Coutant equipped with a Zeiss 10-100 F3 zoom and a 9.5. 12, 16, 25, Zeiss wide-aperture series. For these films, I often chose camera operators with extensive experience in documentary film.

The following year, in 1994, I shot *La Tête dans les nuages* in rather specific conditions. Bonaventure Takoukam, my long-term collaborator, was working for Cameroonian television at the time and was not able to get leave to come to work with me. So, he called in sick and we began shooting in the streets of Yaoundé. The next day, an official communiqué went out on national radio ordering him to return to his post immediately, at risk of serious sanctions. So, I continued the shoot filming by myself. When Bonaventure finished work, he would come to join us. Working with Bonaventure, who came from the same cultural environment as me, who understood the stakes, who could anticipate certain situations, gave me a great sense of serenity because he understood the unspoken undercurrents, the dangers, and always found the right words to diffuse situations that sometimes risked degenerating.

In 1995, for my first fiction feature film, *Clando*, I went to film in Cameroon and Germany with Nurith Aviv, who shot the film in S16 with an Aaton. I wanted someone who could give me a raw, almost documentary image, often with a hand-held camera, little light, and, with the exception of Paulin Fodouop, Caroline Redl and Joseph Momo, non-professional actors. A wonderful experience. My model in this genre was Ken Loach's memorable 1970s and 1980s films about the British working class.

As I worked with these DOPs on my films, I always watched and learned a lot, which helped free me from certain technical constraints when the more malleable video cameras arrived on the market.

During my first decade of filmmaking, while continuing to learn different aspects of the profession, I also tried to find ways to talk about things that had been erased from contemporary French history. The choice to work with a camera operator often depended on the film's subject and on the budget available. With a comfortable budget, I would always choose to work with someone for whom shot composition is a profession. The camera operator's questions while preparing the shoot help me clarify my aims and to continue to develop my reflection. For me, a film is something that I work on right up to the final printing of the copies even. How many times did I find myself in the lab with the assistants cutting my negatives to improve the synchronization of certain reels or shortening certain scenes? But that of course is the past; the days of the labs are over.

The transition between film and video was a gradual one. In 1997, I left FR3 television to devote myself entirely to my films, and notably to producing *Vacances au pays*. For that film, I created a mixed 16mm and video set-up for shooting. The long and medium-long shots were filmed on 16mm, and the interviews were filmed on video using a shoulder-mounted camera that took three-hour-long cassettes. That gave me an appreciable autonomy.

When I was on location preparing the film, I happened across the scene of popular justice that I filmed from start to finish, and which became the starting point of the film *Chef!*, the second film that I entirely filmed, directed and produced. This film would not have been possible in the days of celluloid, and I do not think that anyone else could have filmed the event for me. What triggered the act of filming in this specific case was the situation: a teen caught in the act of stealing risked what we commonly call popular justice in Cameroon. I knew from experience that in over 80 per cent of cases, this ended very badly. I decided on the spot to film in order to bear witness to this irrational and dangerous practice. But when things turned violent, I could not carry on filming. I intervened momentarily to save this kid's life.

From film to film, my approach gradually took form. My desire was to look at my country, to decode it, to analyse the behaviour of my fellow countrymen and women in a first-person cinema that went beyond the observational to reorganize the real, using images shot on the spur of the moment that were then re-inscribed in at times story-like, but mainly analytical narratives. I later made two more spontaneous films: *Le Mariage d'Alex* in 2002 and *Une Feuille dans le vent* in 2013.

The video camera allowed me in specific instances to decide to film in order to constitute a sort of visual archive around which I could later construct a film. In *Chef!*, for example, the decision to film was an intuitive one. This intuition was the fruit of my working from the inside and my knowledge of an environment in which I had shot several films and which, at times, triggered a hunter-like instinct, like an ever-ready hunter unconsciously sensing the presence of their prey. With *Le Mariage d'Alex*, I was surprised myself when I discovered some of the scenes between the two wives as I started editing. I had captured a ballet between the three protagonists that revealed the nature of the relations that were taking shape within this polygamous marriage. The shoot itself was at the request of the family, who wanted to conserve a memory of this 'special day'.

The Films of Jean-Marie Teno

Appendix 2

Hommage / Homage

1985, 16 mm, colour/black & white, docu-fiction, 13 min. Production: Jean-Marie Teno (Cameroon).

Synopsis[1]

After a long separation, two friends, one who has remained in his home village, the other who returns from travelling to the city and abroad, evoke with mischievousness and affection their memories and the current state of their village. Mixing poetry and irony, archive and contemporary footage, autobiography and documentary, this filmic conversation addresses colonial heritage, rural exodus, exile, and contemporary Cameroonian social inequalities.

Fièvre jaune taximan / Yellow Fever Taximan

1985, 16 mm, colour, fiction, 30 min. Production: Jean-Marie Teno (Cameroon).

Synopsis

Following a day in the life of Sam, a taxi driver in Yaoundé, the capital of Cameroon, and through the passengers' stories, the film portrays the animated life of this central African metropolis.

La Gifle et la caresse / The Slap and the Caress

1987, 35 mm, colour, fiction, 20 min. Production: Jean-Marie Teno (France).

Synopsis

Ferrouze, a 30-year-old housekeeper, is an immigrant from the Maghreb region. She lives with her husband Abdul in France, an intellectual who has

---

[1] The present synopses are compiled and elaborated from those officially published on Jean-Marie Teno's US website www.jmteno.us/index.html and on the DVD covers of his works.

been unemployed for ten years. On the bus, she witnesses the beginning of a love story between two teens. This pushes her to question her own choices.

Bikutsi Water Blues[2]

1988, 35 mm, colour, docu-fiction, 84 min. Production: Jean-Marie Teno (Cameroon / France).

Synopsis

Thirteen-year-old Moses lives in a poor urban neighbourhood. At school, his teacher regularly invites professionals to come to talk about their work. The class thus gets to meet a radio broadcaster, a sanitary technician, and a musician, Zanzibar, the lead guitarist of the famous Cameroonian band, Les Têtes Brûlées. Together, they address local living conditions. They also learn about the lives of rural inhabitants all over the country and their daily struggle to find lasting solutions to the problem of water. According to doctors, poor water access is responsible for two out of three diseases in these parts that paradoxically do not lack water.

Le Dernier voyage / The Last Trip

1990, 16 mm, colour, fiction, 19 min. Production: Jean-Marie Teno (Cameroon).

Synopsis

Sam is a truck driver. He carries passengers between Yaoundé and Bamenda, two cities 400 kilometres apart. To stave off fatigue, he begins taking illicit pills sold by roadside hawkers.

Mister Foot

1991, 16 mm, colour, documentary, 22 min. Production: Jean-Marie Teno / Channel 4 (Cameroon / UK).

Synopsis

Outside a ministry building in Yaoundé, a young man sells audio tapes, magazines, old sports newspapers and football souvenirs. He is known as Mister Foot.

---

[2] *Bikutsi* is a rhythm from the southern forest region of Cameroon.

Afrique, je te plumerai / Africa, I Will Fleece You

1992, 16 mm, colour/ black & white, documentary, 93 min. Production: Les Films du Raphia (Cameroon / France).

Synopsis

Thirty years after Africa's wave of Independence, the end of the Cold War and the dramatic international political changes in the 1990s inspire a generation of young Cameroonians to take to the streets and challenge the single-party state and its attendant nepotism, corruption and economic failure. In an audaciously free assemblage of archive footage, contemporary images, interviews, documentary, fiction and personal testimony, *Afrique, je te plumerai* mixes past and present to establish a connection between yesterday's colonial experience, the repression and silencing of Cameroon's war of Independence, and the violence and corruption of contemporary Cameroon. In so doing, the film provides a devastating overview of 100 years of cultural genocide in Africa.

La Tête dans les nuages / Head in the Clouds

1994, 16 mm, colour, documentary, 35 min. Production: Les Films du Raphia / WDR / ARTE (Cameroon / France / Germany).

Synopsis

In the streets of Yaoundé, law graduate Jacky desperately seeks a job, before finally becoming a trader, like his parents. Irène Pessonka, a government ministry worker, sells homemade fritters at night to supplement her meagre salary. As for poet and artist Pascale Martine Tayou, he salvages material from the rubbish dumps that invade Yaoundé's streets in order to express the mental anguish that the country's state of chaos engenders. Through these three examples, the film offers a portrait of the difficulties of life in the post-colony and of its inhabitants' resilient resistance.

Clando / Clandestine

1996, 35 mm, fiction, 98 min. Production: Les Films du Raphia /ARTE / ZDF (Cameroon / France / Germany).

Synopsis

Sobgui, a former computer programmer who loses his job after being imprisoned and tortured for partaking in banned political activity, drives an illegal taxi (a 'clando') in Douala, before fleeing to Europe to escape his increasingly suffocating life in his authoritarian country. In Cologne, Germany, Sobgui joins a group of African emigrants. His meeting with the German political activist Irene encourages him to address his trauma and to return home to fight for change.

Chef !/ Chief!

1999, video, colour, documentary, 61 min. Production: Les Films du Raphia (Cameroon / France).

Synopsis

While visiting his home village during festivities in celebration of the former chief, Teno is a chance witness to the near lynching of a teenager, an instance of mob justice in a lawless state. Linking this violent event to his concomitant discovery of a local law that makes the husband the ruler of his wife, and to the imprisonment without trial of eminent journalist Pius Njawe after he wrote an article questioning President Paul Biya's health, the film assembles these at first seemingly unrelated incidents to bear witness to the ways in which the abuse of power permeates everyday life in an authoritarian society. The film thereby offers a reflection on the state of Cameroonian society, its hierarchies, inequalities and repression, while also demonstrating that dictatorship is a system with a logic, a vast machinery of corruption, and a state of mind that pervades an entire population.

Vacances au pays / A Trip to the Country

2000, video and 35 mm, colour, documentary, 75 min Production: Les Films du Raphia / ZDF / ARTE (Cameroon / France / Germany).

Synopsis

As Teno makes the trip to his home village, he questions the illusions of modernity that haunt Cameroonian society and the notions of development that castigate all things local as archaic and worthless. After the ravages of slavery and colonization, the African continent faces another threat: educational systems that perpetuate inferiority complexes and dependence vis-à-vis the West. The film offers a personal reflection on how this self-destructive acculturation establishes a social hierarchy pitting the so-called modern city against the supposedly backward village.

Le Mariage d'Alex / Alex's Wedding

2002, video, colour, documentary, 45 min Production: Les Films du Raphia (Cameroon / France).

Synopsis

A chronicle of a rather particular afternoon during which the lives of three people dramatically change: Alex, the husband, who goes to his in-laws' to fetch his junior wife; Elise, Alex's childhood sweetheart and senior wife, who must accompany him according to custom; and Josephine, the young bride, who leaves her parents to begin a new life. Pressed into service by his neighbour, Teno turns what might have been a typical wedding video into a subtle and intimate portrait of polygamy and its complex power dynamics in contemporary Cameroon.

Le Malentendu colonial / The Colonial Misunderstanding

2004, video/35 mm, colour, documentary, 75 min. Production: Les Films du Raphia / Barbel Mauch Films / ARTE / ZDF (Cameroon / France / Germany).

Synopsis

> When the missionaries arrived, the Africans had the land and the missionaries had the Bible. They taught us to pray with our eyes closed. When we opened our eyes, they had the land and we had the Bible.
> Jomo Kenyatta.

In *Le Malentendu colonial*, Teno sheds light on the complex and problematic relationship between colonization and European missionaries on the African continent. Examining the German missionary societies whose vocation it was to bring Christianity – and by extension, European culture and rule – to Africa, the film looks at Christian evangelism as the forerunner of European colonialism in Africa, and as the ideological model for the relationship between North and South today. The film looks in particular at the role of the missionaries in Namibia on the centenary of the 1904 German genocide of the Herrero people, and how colonialism destroyed African beliefs and social systems.

Lieux saints / Sacred Places

2009, video/35 mm, colour, documentary, 70 min. Production: Les Films du Raphia (Cameroon / France).

Synopsis

Set in St Léon, a poor but lively neighbourhood tucked between the cathedral and the central mosque in Ouagadougou, the capital of Burkina Faso, where, since 1969, the world-famous FESPACO (Pan-African Film Festival) showcases the best of African cinema, the film documents the fight to survive and to maintain one's dignity. Through the daily lives of three characters – Jules César, the philosophical djembe drum-maker and player; Bouba, the manager of a neighbourhood video parlour that also serves as a praying place; and Abbo, a fifty-year-old senior technician turned public writer – Teno examines some of the paradoxes of today's Africa – such as the absence of African films in local film distribution – while also capturing the inventive creativity of the local inhabitants.

Une Feuille dans le vent / Leaf in the Wind

2013, video, colour/black & white, documentary, 55 min. Production: Les Films du Raphia (Cameroon / France).

Synopsis

Breaking the silences that help perpetuate collective and personal trauma, *Une Feuille dans le vent* reclaims forgotten chapters of Cameroonian colonial and postcolonial history, and restitutes the broken lives and untold stories that lie behind it. Executed in 1971 by the Cameroonian authorities, freedom fighter and Independence hero Ernest Ouandié left behind a daughter he never knew. Reopening the Ouandié archive, the film restores his memory through the raw, uncompromising testimony of his daughter Ernestine as she recounts her own scarred and tragic life. The film is a moving reflection on colonialism's profound individual and collective consequences, generation after generation, and poses the questions of history, transmission, trauma, sacrifice and the price of freedom.

Chosen / Le Futur dans le rétro

2018, video, colour, documentary, 89 min. Production: Les Films du Raphia (Cameroon / France).

Synopsis

In July 2010, Naana Banyiwa Horne, a university professor who has been living and teaching in the USA for over 30 years, returns to her home country, Ghana, to be enstooled Queen Mother. Interweaving stories, journeys and exiles, the film mirrors the African-Atlantic circulations of our modern global world. In so doing, it evokes motherhood, sisterhood, group belonging, choices and sacrifice. It is also an existential tale of departures, exile, loss, trauma, and the question of home.

Bibliography

Articles & Chapters on the cinema of Jean-Marie Teno

Harrow, Kenneth W. 'Cameroonian Cinema: Ba Kobhio, Teno, and the Technologies of Power', *Postcolonial African Cinema: From Political Engagement to Postmodernism*, Kenneth W. Harrow. Bloomington & Indianapolis: Indiana University Press, 2007, 66-94.
Izzo, Justin. 'Jean-Marie Teno's Documentary Modernity: From Millennial Anxiety to Cinematic Kinship', *African Studies Review*, vol. 58, 1 (April 2015), 39-53.
Jones, Branwen Gruffydd. 'Le Malentendu International: Remembering International Relations with Jean-Marie Teno', *Alternatives: Global, Local, Political*, vol. 40, 2, Race, De-coloniality and International Relations (May 2015), 133-155.
Nganang, Patrice. 'Deconstructing Authority in Cinema: Jean-Marie Teno', *Cinema and Social Discourse in Cameroon*, ed. Alexie Tcheuyap. Bayreuth: Bayreuth African Studies, 69 (2005), 139-155.
Petty, Sheila. 'Post-Colonial Geographies: Landscape and Alienation in Clando', *Cinema and Social Discourse in Cameroon*, ed. Alexie Tcheuyap. Bayreuth: Bayreuth African Studies, 69 (2005), 159-171.
Prabhu, Anjali. 'Jean-Marie Teno: Creating an African Repertoire', *Contemporary Cinema of Africa and the Diaspora*, Anjali Prabhu. Malden, MA: Wiley Blackwell, 2014, 187-215.
Tchouaffe, Olivier J. 'Colonial Visual Archives and the Anti-Documentary Perspective in Africa: Notes on Jean-Marie Teno's Films', *Journal of Information Ethics*, vol. 19, 2 (Fall 2010), 82-99.
Ukadike, Frank N. 'The Other Voices of Documentary: *Allah Tantou* and *Afrique, je te plumerai*', *iris*, 18 (Spring 1995), 81-94.

Other

Achebe, Chinua. *Arrow of God*. 1964. London: Heinemann, 1986.
Amad, Paula. 'Visual Riposte: Looking Back at the Return of the Gaze as Postcolonial Theory's Gift to Film Studies', *Cinema Journal*, 52, 3, Spring 2013, 25-48.
Anderson, Benedict. *Imagined Communities: Reflections of the Origin and Spread of Nationalism*. London & New York: Verso, 1983.
Anzaldúa, Gloria. *Borderlands / La Frontera: The New Mestiza*. San Francisco: Aunt Lute Books, 1987. Fourth Edition, 2012.
Arendt, Hannah. *The Origins of Totalitarianism*. New York: Schocken Books, 1951.

Assemblée Nationale. 'Jules Ferry (1885) : Les fondements de la politique coloniale', 28 July 1885, accessed 8 July 2018, www2.assemblee-nationale.fr/decouvrir-l-assemblee/histoire/grands-moments-d-eloquence/jules-ferry-28-juillet-1885.

Aufderheide, Patricia. 'Public Intimacy: The Development of First-Person Documentary', *Afterimage*, 25, 1, July-August 1997. 16-32.

—— *Documentary Film. A Very Short Introduction*. Oxford: Oxford University Press, 2007.

Bakari, Imruh & Cham, Mbye, ed. *African Experiences of Cinema*. London: BFI Publishing, 1996.

Baldwin, James. *Giovanni's Room*. New York: Dial Press, 1956.

Barlet, Olivier. *Les cinémas d'Afrique des années 2000: Perspectives critiques*. Paris: L'Harmattan, 2012 / *Contemporary African Cinema*. Trans. Melissa Thackway. East Lansing: Michigan State University Press, 2016.

Barthélémy, Pascale. 'L'enseignement dans l'Empire colonial français : une vieille histoire ?', *Histoire de l'éducation*, 128 (2010), 5-27.

Bhabha, Homi K. *The Location of Culture*. London & New York: Routledge, 1994.

Bloom, Peter J. *French Colonial Documentary: Mythologies of Humanitarianism*. Minneapolis: University of Minnesota Press, 2008.

Boucheron, Patrick. 'Quelles frontières', *La Nuit des idées*, Institut Français Paris, 27 January 2016, accessed 19 July 2019, www.lanuitdesidees.com/fr/archives/quelles-frontieres/.

Cazenave, Odile & Célérier, Patricia-Pia, ed. 'Le Documentaire francophone africain et afro-diasporique : État des lieux, pratiques et pistes de lecture', *Nouvelles Études Francophones*, 33, 1, 2018.

Césaire, Aimé. *Discours sur le colonialisme*. Paris: Présence Africaine, 1955 / *Discourse on Colonialism*. Trans. Joan Pinkham. New York & London: Monthly Review Press, 2000.

Chakrabarty, Dipesh. *Provincializing Europe: Postcolonial Thought and Historical Difference*. Princetown & Oxford: Princetown University Press, 2000.

Chamoiseau, Patrick. *Texaco*. Trans. Rose-Myriam Réjouis & Val Vinokurov. London: Granta, 1997.

Cherki, Alice. 'Fanon au temps présent. L'assignation au regard', *Politique africaine* 143: *Mobiliser Fanon*. Paris: Karthala, 2016, 145-152.

Chion, Michel. *The Voice in Cinema*. Trans. Claudia Gorbman. New York: Columbia University Press, 1999.

Cissokho, Aboubacar Demba. 'Samba Félix Ndiaye : Dites simplement la vérité' (6 November 2010), *Le grenier de Kibili*, 6 November 2015, accessed 22 January 2018, https://legrenierdekibili.wordpress.com/2015/11/06/samba-felix-ndiaye-dites-simplement-la-verite.

Crosta, Suzanne, Niang, Sada & Tcheuyap, Alexie, ed. 'Documenting the African Experience; Documentary Filmmaking in Africa', *Critical Interventions*, 11, issue 3 (2017).

Curtius, Anny. 'Zabou la pacotilleuse fissurée : diaspora, folie, catastrophe climatique et civilisationnelle dans Timbuktu d'Abderrahmane Sissako', *Congrès 2018 du CIÉF*, La Rochelle, 6 June 2018.

Dahlgreen, Will. 'The British Empire is "something to be proud of"', *YouGov*, 26 July 2014, accessed 9 July 2019, https://yougov.co.uk/topics/politics/articles-reports/2014/07/26/britain-proud-its-empire.

de Bromhead, Toni. *Looking Two Ways. Documentary Film's Relationship with Reality and Cinema*. Aarhus: Intervention Press, 1996.

De Groof, Matthias. 'Rouch's Reflexive Turn: Indigenous Film as the Outcome of Reflexivity in Ethnographic Film', *Visual Anthropology*, vol. 26, 2 (2013), 109-131.

Deltombe, Thomas, Domergue, Manuel & Tatsitsa, Jacob. *Kamerun ! Une guerre cachée aux origines de la Françafrique, 1948-1971*. Paris: La Découverte, 2011.

Derrida, Jacques. *Archive Fever: A Freudian Impression*. Trans. Eric Prenowitz. Chicago & London: University of Chicago Press, 1995.

de Sousa Santos, Boaventura. 'Beyond Abyssal Thinking: From Global Lines to Ecologies of Knowledges', *Revue XXX*, 1 (2007), 45-89.

—— 'Epistémologies du Sud. La ligne abyssale entre la sociabilité métropolitaine et la sociabilité coloniale', *Colonial Abyssal* conference, Fondation Calouste Gulbenkian, Paris, 5 April 2018.

De Souza, Fabiana. 'Réactualiser l'archive, réécrire l'histoire : des pratiques artistiques décoloniales', *Revue Asylon(s)*, 15, February 2018, accessed 9 February 2018, www.reseau-terra.eu/article1406.html.

Diawara, Manthia. 'Oral Literature and African Film: Narratology in *Wend Kuuni*', *Questions of Third Cinema*, ed. Jim Pines & Paul Willemen. London: BFI, 1989, 199-211.

—— *African Cinema: Politics and Culture*. Bloomington & Indianapolis: Indiana University Press, 1992.

—— *African Film: New Forms of Aesthetics and Politics*. Munich/London/New York/Berlin: Prestel Verlag/Haus der Kulturen der Welt, 2010.

Djebar, Assia. *Idiome de l'exil et langue de l'irréductibilité*. German Publishers and Bookstores Peace Prize / 'Prix pour la Paix' acceptation speech, 2000, 5 May 2003, accessed 23 May 2016, http://remue.net/spip.php?article683.

Dorlin, Elsa. *Se défendre. Une philosophie de la violence*. Paris: Zones, 2017.

Dovey, Lindiwe. 'African Film and Video: Pleasure, Politics, Performance', *Journal of African Cultural Studies*, vol. 22, 1 (2010), 1-6.

—— *Curating Africa in the Age of Film Festivals*. London & New York: Palgrave Macmillan, 2015.

Ellerson, Betti. 'African Women and the Documentary: Storytelling, Visualizing History, from the Personal to the Political', *Black Camera*, vol. 8, 1 (Fall 2016), 223-239.

Escauriza, Bettina. 'That which will become the Earth: Anarcho-Indigenous Speculative Geographies', *Journal des Anthropologues* 152-153 (2018), 83-106.

Espinosa, Julio García. 'For an Imperfect Cinema', 1969. Trans. Julianne Burton, *Jump Cut* 20 (1979), 24-26.

Fanon, Frantz. *Les Damnés de la terre*. 1961. Paris: Gallimard, 1991 / *The Wretched of the Earth*. Trans. Constance Farrington. New York: Grove Press, 1968.

Fauvelle, François-Xavier & Perrot, Claude Hélène, ed. *Yves Person : Historien de l'Afrique, explorateur de l'oralité*. Paris: Editions de la Sorbonne, 2018.

Faye, Safi. 'Jean Rouch jugé par six cinéastes d'Afrique noire', propos recueillis par Pierre Haffner, *CinémAction* 17 (1982), 63-64.

FEPACI (Pan-African Federation of Filmmakers). 'The Algiers Charter on African Cinema, 1975', *African Experiences of Cinema*, ed. Imruh Bakari & Mbye Cham. London: BFI Publishing, 1996, 25-26.

Foucault, Michel. *The Order of Things: An Archaeology of the Human Sciences*. New York: Pantheon Books, 1971.

Fronty, François & Kifouani, Delphe, ed. *La diversité du documentaire de création en Afrique*. Paris: L'Harmattan, 2016.
Gabara, Rachel. '"A Poetics of Refusals": Neorealism from Italy to Africa', *Quarterly Review of Film and Video*, 23, (2006), 201-215.
—— 'War by Documentary', *Romance Notes*, vol. 55, 3 (2015), 409-423.
—— 'From Ethnography to Essay. Realism, Reflexivity, and African Documentary Film', in *A Companion to African Cinema*, ed. Kenneth W. Harrow & Carmela Garritano. Hoboken, NJ: Wiley Blackwell, 2019, 358-378.
Gabriel, Teshome. 'Thoughts on Nomadic Aesthetics and Black Independent Cinema: Traces of a journey', *Blackframes: Critical Perspectives on Black Independent Cinema*, ed. Mbye B. Cham & Claire Andrade-Watkins. Cambridge, MA: The MIT Press, 1988.
Garritano, Carmela. *African Video Movies and Global Desires: A Ghanaian History*. Athens: Ohio University Press, 2013.
Gassama, Makhily (ed.), *L'Afrique répond à Sarkozy : contre le discours de Dakar*. Paris: Editions Philippe Rey, 2008.
Gauthier, Guy. *Le documentaire : un autre cinema*. Paris: Nathan, 1995.
Godard, Jean-Luc. *Jean-Luc Godard par Jean-Luc Godard*, ed. Alain Bergala. Paris: Cahiers du Cinéma/Editions de l'Etoile, 1985.
Goerg, Odile. *Fantômas sous les tropiques : Aller au cinéma en Afrique coloniale*. Paris: Vendémiaire Editions, 2015.
Gikandi, Simon. *Maps of Englishness: Writing Identity in the Culture of Colonialism*. New York: Columbia University Press, 1996.
Givanni, June. 'African Conversations: An Interview with Djibril Diop Mambety', *Sight and Sound*, vol. 5, 9 (September 1995), 30-31.
Grosfoguel, Ramón. 'Decolonizing Western Uni-versalisms: Decolonial Pluri-versalism from Aimé Césaire to the Zapatistas', Trans. George Ciccariello-Maher. *Transmodernity: Journal of Peripheral Cultural Production of the Luso-Hispanic World*, vol. 1, 3 (2012), 88-102, accessed 10 August 2017, http://escholarship.org/uc/item/01w7163v.
Hall, Stuart. 'New Ethnicities', *Black Film, British Cinema*, ICA Documents, 7 (1988), 27-31.
—— 'Cultural Identity and Cinematic Representation', *Framework*, 36 (1989), 68-81.
—— 'The Question of Cultural Identity', *Modernity and its Futures: Understanding Modern Societies*, ed. Stuart Hall, David Held & Tony McGrew. Cambridge: Polity Press, 1992, 273-326.
—— 'When Was "the Post-Colonial"? Thinking at the Limit', *The Post-Colonial Question: Common Skies, Divided Horizons*, ed. Iain Chambers & Lidia Curti. London & New York: Routledge, 1996, 242-260.
—— 'Constituting an Archive', *Third Text* (Spring, 2001), 89-92.
—— with Schwarz, Bill. *Familiar Stranger: A Life Between Two Islands*. London: Allen Lane, 2017.
Harrow, Kenneth W. *Postcolonial African Cinema: From Political Engagement to Postmodernism*. Bloomington & Indianapolis: Indiana University Press, 2007.
—— *Trash: African Cinema from Below*. Bloomington & Indianapolis: Indiana University Press, 2013.
—— 'Manthia Diawara's Waves and the Problem of the "Authentic"', *African Studies Review*, vol. 58, 3 (December 2015), 13-30.
Hegel, G.W.F. *The Philosophy of History*. Trans. J. Sibree. 'Introduction' C.J. Friedrich. New York: Dover Publications, 1956.

Hessel, Stéphane. *Indignez-vous!* Montpellier: Indigène Editions, 2010.
Higbee, William & Lim, Song Hwee. 'Concepts of Transnational Cinema: Towards a Critical Transnationalism in Film Studies', *Transnational Cinemas,* vol. 1, 1 (2010), 7-21.
Higgins, MaryEllen. 'The Winds of African Cinema', *African Studies Review*, vol. 58, 3 (December 2015), 77–92.
hooks, bell. *Talking Back: Thinking Feminist, Thinking Black*. Boston, MA: South End Press, 1989.
—— 'Marginality as a Site of Resistance', *Out There: Marginalization and Contemporary Cultures*, ed. Russell Ferguson, Martha Gever, Trinh T. Minh-ha & Cornel West. Cambridge, MA & London: The MIT Press, 1990, 341-343.
—— *Black Looks: Race and Representation*. Boston MA: South End Press, 1992.
Imbert, Henri-François. *Samba Félix Ndiaye: cinéaste documentariste africain*. Paris: L'Harmattan, 2007.
Juompan-Yakan, Clarisse. 'Hollande reconnaît la repression française au Cameroon', *Jeune Afrique,* 9 July 2015, accessed 12 September 2018, www.jeuneafrique.com/245223/politique/hollande-reconnait-la-repression-francaise-au-cameroun-les-reactions-de-mbembe-et-tatsitsa.
Kaufmann, Miranda. *Black Tudors: The Untold Story*. London: Oneworld Publications, 2017.
Kisukidi, Nadia Yala. 'Laetitia Africana – philosphie, décolonisation et mélancolie', *Ecrire l'Afrique monde*, ed. Achille Mbembe & Felwine Sarr. Paris/Dakar: Philippe Rey/Jimsaan, 2017, 51-69.
Kodjo-Grandvaux, Séverine. 'Effets de miroir : penser l'Afrique, penser le monde', *Penser et écrire l'Afrique aujourd'hui*, ed. Alain Mabanckou. Paris: Seuil, 2017, 60-71.
Kracauer, Siegfried. 'Photography', *Frankfurter Zeitung,* 28 October 1927. Trans. Thomas Y. Levin. *Critical Inquiry*, vol. 19, 3 (Spring 1993), 421-436.
Luste Boulbina, Seloua. *L'Afrique et ses fantômes : Ecrire l'après*. Paris: Présence africaine, 2015.
Maillard, Matteo. 'Ateliers de la pensée #2', *Le Monde Afrique,* 14 November 2017, accessed 9 August 2018, www.lemonde.fr/afrique/article/2017/11/14/ateliers-de-la-pensee-2-la-grande-priorite-est-d-abolir-les-frontieres-de-l-afrique_5214792_3212.html.
Mansfield, Nick. *Subjectivity: Theories of the Self from Freud to Haraway*. New York: New York University Press, 2000.
Mazrui, Ali. *World Culture and the Black Experience*. Seattle & London: University of Washington Press, 1974.
Mbembe, Achille. 'African Modes of Self-Writing', *Identity, Culture and Politics*, vol. 2, 1 (January 2001), 1-39.
—— 'Afropolitanism', 2005. *Africa Remix: Contemporary Art of a Continent*, ed. S. Njami. Trans. Laurent Chauvet. Johannesburg: Jacana Media, 2007, 26-29.
—— 'Nicolas Sarkozy's Africa'. Trans. Melissa Thackway. *Africultures,* 7 August 2007, accessed 11 July 2019, www.africultures.com/nicolas-sarkozys-africa-6816.
—— *Politiques de l'inimitié*. Paris: Editions La Découverte, 2016.
—— 'L'Afrique qui vient', *Penser et écrire l'Afrique aujourd'hui*, ed. Alain Mabanckou. Paris: Seuil, 2017, 17-31.
Mercer, Kobena. 'Recording Narratives of Race and Nation', *Black Film British Cinema*, ed. Kobena Mercer, ICA Documents 7. London: Institute of Contemporary Arts, 1988, 4–14.

―― *Welcome to the Jungle: New Positions in Black Cultural Studies*. New York & London: Routledge, 1996.
Mignolo, Walter D. 'Delinking', *Cultural Studies*, vol. 21, 2 (2007), 449-514.
―― 'Geopolitics of Sensing and Knowing. On (De)Coloniality, Border Thinking, and Epistemic Disobedience', *Transversal*, vol. 1 (2012), accessed 2 April 2019, http://eipcp.net/transversal/0112/mignolo/en.
Miller, Christopher. *Theories of Africans: Francophone Literature and Anthropology in Africa*. Chicago: University of Chicago Press, 1990.
Minh-Ha, Trinh T. 'Documentary Is/Not a Name', *October*, vol. 52 (Spring 1990), 76-98.
Moure, José. 'Essai de définition de l'essai au cinéma', *L'Essai et le cinéma*, ed. Suzanne Liandrat-Guigues & Murielle Gagnebin. Seyssel: Editions Champ Vallon, 2004, 25-40.
Mudimbe, Valentin Y. *L'odeur du père*. Paris: Présence africaine, 1982.
―― *The Invention of Africa: Gnosis, Philosophy and the Order of Knowledge*. Bloomington & Indianapolis: Indiana University Press, 1988.
Nancy, Jean-Luc. *A l'écoute*. Paris: Editions Galilée, 2002
Ngũgĩ, wa Thiong'o. *Decolonising the Mind: The Politics of Language in African Literature*. London: James Currey, 1986.
Niang, Sada. 'Fiction and Documentary African Films: Narrative and Stylistic Affinities', *Critical Interventions*, vol. 11, 3 (2017), 228-235.
Nichols, Bill. *Introduction to Documentary*. Bloomington & Indianapolis: Indiana University Press, 2001.
Petty, Sheila. 'Keynote speech', *Documentary Filmmaking Practices in Africa* Conference, University of Toronto, 19-20 January 2017.
Pfaff, Françoise. 'The Uniqueness of Ousmane Sembene's Cinema', *Ousmane Sembène: Dialogues with Critics and Writers*, ed. Samba Gadjigo. Amherst: University of Massachusetts Press, 1993, 14-21.
Prabhu, Anjali. *Contemporary Cinema of Africa and the Diaspora*. Malden, MA: Wiley Blackwell, 2014.
Quijano, Anibal. 'Coloniality of Power, Eurocentrism and Latin America'. Trans. Michael Ennis, *Nepantla: Views from South*, vol 1, 3 (2000), 533-580.
Ranger, Terence. 'The Invention of Tradition in Colonial Africa', *The Invention of Tradition*, ed. Eric Hobsbawm & Terence Ranger. Cambridge UK: Cambridge University Press, 1983, 211-261.
Rascaroli, Laura. *The Personal Camera. Subjective Cinema and the Essay Film*. London & New York: Wallflower Press, 2009.
Ricci, Daniela. *Cinémas des diasporas noires : esthétiques de la reconstruction*. Paris: L'Harmattan, 2016.
Roger, Patrick. 'Colonisation : les propos inédits de Macron font polémique', *Le Monde*, 16 February 2017, accessed 6 July 2018, www.lemonde.fr/election-presidentielle-2017/article/2017/02/16/pour-macron-la-colonisation-fut-un-crime-contre-l-humanite_5080621_4854003.html.
Rushdie, Salman. *The Satanic Verses*. New York: Viking, 1988.
Said, Edward. *Reflections on Exile and Other Essays*. Cambridge, MA: Harvard University Press, 2000.
Sawadogo, Boukary. *Les cinémas francophones ouest-africains (1990-2005)*. Paris: L'Harmattan, 2013.
Sembène, Ousmane. 'Filmmakers and African Culture', *Africa* 71 (1977), 39-41.

Sharpe, Christina. *In the Wake: On Blackness and Being*. Durham, NC & London: Duke University Press, 2016.

Taylor, Clyde. 'Searching for the Postmodern in African Cinema', *Symbolic Narratives / African Cinema: Audiences, Theory and the Moving Image*, ed. June Givanni. London: British Film Institute, 2000, 136-144.

Tcheuyap, Alexie, ed. *Cinema and Social Discourse in Cameroon*. Bayreuth African Studies, University of Bayreuth, 69 (2005).

Thackway, Melissa. *Africa Shoots Back. Alternative Perspectives in Sub-Saharan Francophone African Film*. Oxford/Bloomington/Cape Town: James Currey/Indiana University Press/David Philip, 2003.

—— 'Crossing Lines: Frontiers, Circulations, and Identity in Contemporary African and Diaspora Film', *A Companion to African Cinema*, ed. Kenneth W. Harrow & Carmela Garritano. Hoboken, NJ: Wiley Blackwell, 2019, 444-463.

Todd, Zoe. *The Decolonial Turn 2.0: The Reckoning*, 15 June 2018, accessed 18 June 2018, https://anthrodendum.org/2018/06/15/the-decolonial-turn-2-0-the-reckoning.

Ukadike, Nwachukwu Frank. *African Cinema: Narratives, Perspectives and Poetics*. Port Harcourt: University of Port Harcourt Press, 2013.

Vergès, Françoise. 'Approches postcoloniales de l'esclavage et de la colonisation', *Mouvements*, vol. 3, 51 (2007), 102-110.

—— *Le ventre des femmes : Capitalisme, racialisation, féminisme*. Paris: Albin Michel, 2017.

—— *Un féminisme décolonial*. Paris: La Fabrique Editions, 2019.

Vieyra, Paulin Soumanou. *Le Cinéma africain des origines à 1973*. Paris & Dakar: Présence Africaine, 1975.

Yange, Paul. 'Achille Mbembe: Je classe Um Nyobè au premier rang des martyrs africains de l'indépendance' (interview), *Grioo*, 25 June 2007, accessed 13 September 2017, www.grioo.com/info10756.html.

YouGov. 'Survey Results', *YouGov*, 2016, accessed 07 August 2018, https://d25d2506sfb94s.cloudfront.net/cumulus_uploads/document/95euxfgway/InternalResults_160118_BritishEmpire_Website.pdf.

Index

Abossolo Mbo, Emil 125, 137, 150
Academy of Motion Picture Arts and Sciences, Teno's membership of 3
Achkar, David 26
Africa Fête music festival 126–7
African cinema/documentary 4–5, 11, 14, 22, 33, 30, 38–9
  aesthetic experimentation of 18, 26, 37, 195, 205
  autobiographical voice 23, 62
  blurring of fiction and documentary 13–14, 24–6, 127, 136, 206, 208
  depoliticization of 41, 130–1
  first-generation/pioneering filmmakers 5, 14n, 21–2, 26, 37–8, 132–4, 145, 147, 150, 167, 204–5, 207
  incorporation of African narrative approaches 22–4, 204–5
  professionalization of 131, 134, 193, 195–6
  realism/artistic representation of reality in 12–15, 19–20, 24, 26, 29, 204
  socio-political contexts of 19–20, 30, 38–9, 135, 204
  Western legacy 15, 38
  see also technological evolution; Teno, Jean-Marie, oeuvre
African Guild of Directors and Producers (la Guilde) 187–9
African societies deemed 'traditional' 17&n27
Afrique, je te plumerai 1, 5–6, 32–4, 43, 51–4, 56, 58–62, 66, 74, 143, 158, 210–11
  attacks on/negative responses to 77, 159
  juxtaposition of archival footage in 35, 67&n37, 68p–69, 70, 76, 86–8p, 91, 181–2
  legacy of colonialism as key theme 44, 64, 77, 83–4, 86–7, 88p–9, 90, 159–60, 163, 167, 174
  situated gaze in 158–9, 171–2
  theme of Cameroon's troubled independence era 35, 53, 90, 179, 183

  see also first-person voice-overs in Teno's films
Afrique sur Seine 19, 21, 203
Ahidjo, Ahmadou 48, 90, 177, 205
Akomfrah, John 26
Alassane, Moustapha 136, 204–5, 208
Algeria 42, 65–6n35, 83n30, 87n44, 98
Amad, Paula 17&n26
Anderson, Benedict, concept of 'imagined communities' 96n12
Anzaldúa, Gloria 52n33, 86n42, 94, 109
apartheid regime 80
  anti-apartheid struggle 53, 79p, 124
archive 84–5 *see also* colonial film archive
Arendt, Hannah 79
Association Ecrans 188
Aufderheide, Patricia 12–13, 61–2
authoritarianism 43–4, 49, 54, 109, 137
Aviv, Nurith 102p, 211

Banyiwa Horne, Naana 105, 106p, 107–8, 168p
Barlet, Olivier 4n7, 41, 60
Beauséjour, Madeleine 125–6, 138, 210
belonging, cultural 6, 25, 46, 58, 95–7, 107
Beti, Mongo 44, 145
Bhabha, Homi K. 94&n6
Bikutsi Water Blues 6, 32, 119p, 159, 189, 211
  Carthage Film Festival screening 190p, 201
  health/socio-economic theme 43–4, 167–8
  invention of journalist character 57–8p, 158
  music/sound in 43–4, 157
Biya, Paul 44, 48, 53–4, 76, 205
Bollywood 42, 67, 118
border crossings 93n4, 94, 96, 107–108 *see also* cinematic transnationality; exile and return
Boucheron, Patrick, *histoire-monde* 95&n9
British Council 120–1, 211
British empire/colonialism 15, 41, 48

Burkina Faso 31, 126, 188, 207 *see also* Pan-African Film and Television Festival of Ouagadougou
Bwana Magazine 126, 129p

Cabral, Amilcar 19, 73
Cameroon 2, 21, 31, 78, 144, 167, 192
   Bandjoun (Teno's home town) 44, 49, 63, 67, 98, 100, 152, 196–7
   Douala 87, 100–101, 102p, 104, 119p
   social inequality/injustice in 54, 84, 116, 121, 123, 170, 172–3, 183, 207
   quest for modernity 62, 100
   repression of UPC party 35, 48, 53, 76, 80–1, 90–1, 115
   Sangmelima 118
   Yaoundé 32p, 62, 64, 67&n37, 97–9, 116–17, 119p, 120–2, 152p, 209p, 210–11
   see also under Teno's exploration of socio-political/historical contexts
censorship 16, 24, 53, 86, 118, 136, 175, 177, 189, 202
Césaire, Aimé 79&n26, 98
'Cinema Novo', Brazil 19
Chakrabarty, Dipesh 75&n18
Chamoiseau, Patrick 71
chaos 51, 54, 145, 169, 175 *see also* violence as theme of Teno's work
Chef! 6, 33, 43, 51, 53, 67, 149, 152, 178p, 212
   exploration of power relations/violence in 44, 49–50p, 51, 59, 152, 167, 212
   theme of resistance 53
Cherki, Alice 83&n30
Chion, Michael 59–60
Chosen 2, 6, 33, 43, 46, 66, 94, 106p, 168p, 197–8p
   insider-outsider perspective 97–8
   journeys/exile and return as central to 105, 107–8, 197
cinéma vérité 17–18
   influence on Teno's work 24
cinematic 'I' *see* first-person voice-overs in Teno's films; subjectivity, Teno's embracing of
cinematic transnationality 31, 93n4, 94
   and Bhabha's concept of 'third spaces' 94&n6
   in Teno's films 5, 93&n4, 95–6, 108
   see also exile and return
circulations 6, 94–7, 100, 110, 197–8
   rooting as corollary of 82, 97, 107, 193
Cissé, Souleymane 14n18, 31, 37, 83n31, 194p
   Baara 126, 131, 204
   Teno's encounter with 131–2

Clando 1, 6, 43, 46, 102p–3, 117, 141, 160
   Sobgui's quest for self-knowledge 40, 51, 53, 98n18, 100–1, 104–5
   transnational linking of spaces in 94, 100–101, 104–105, 197
   theme of violence/resistance 51, 53, 83
colonial film archive
   accessibility of 85, 179–81
   distortions/erasures in 91, 211
   ethnographic gaze 16–18, 20
   exclusion of African filmmakers 16
   film as propaganda medium in 13, 15–18, 85–6, 134, 179
   Laval Decree 16&n21
   Nazi footage 180–81
   racial stereotyping in 41, 94
   relation to political power 84
   see also decolonial history-memory films: revisiting history/deconstruction of colonial archive in; voice-of-God narrative approach
Colonial Film Unit 15
colonialism/colonization
   'boomerang effect' of 79
   Christian evangelization as forerunner of 78
   cultural genocide of 44, 100, 167, 207
   dehumanization/non-being of colonized 41, 52, 57
   land appropriation under 94
   ongoing legacies of 43–4, 118, 196
   racial superiority theories to justify 72&n5&7
   restriction of movement under 96
   see also French colonialism; German colonialism; historic representations of colonialism
coloniality of power 48–9, 57, 78
Curtius, Anny 52

Dakar 23–4, 208
   Cheick Anta Diop University 73, 206
   Discours de 73
   Plaza Cinema 178p
de Bromheid, Toni 12–13n, 34
decolonial history-memory films 5, 19n36, 23, 39, 43, 71, 73–4, 98, 110, 170–1
   from point of view of 'the native' 64, 76, 85, 160, 163, 173
   revisiting history/deconstruction of colonial archive in 84–7, 88p–9, 90–2, 171–2, 177–82
   see also memory as theme of Teno's films
decolonial theory/thinkers 2, 30, 49, 57, 154, 174

Index

decolonization process 19
   importance of self-narration in 62–3
   and quest for/reconstruction of identity 5, 63, 193
De Groof, Matthias 18, 21n39
democracy 43, 100, 206
   'fake' 53
   fight for 58, 63, 69p–70, 205, 207
Derrida, Jacques 84–5
de Sousa Santos, Boaventura 52&n32
De Souza, Fabiana 65, 86&n42
détournement 85&n39
development, lack of 43, 135
Diannoux, Robert 66, 211
Diawara, Manthia 74
diary films 146, 162
Dikongue-Pipa, Jean-Pierre 37&n4, 118
distribution of African films 30–1, 38, 42, 46, 74n15, 93n4, 188–9, 191
Djebar, Assia 38n4, 98, 108
documentary/cinematic codes and rules 22
   Teno's resistance to 24, 54–5, 142, 151, 154
Dorlin, Elsa 65n32
Dovey, Lindiwe 31n5&6

elitism in cinema 202–203
Escales Documentaires Festival 192
Espinosa, Julio Garcia 19n36, 55, 154
Escauriza, Bettina 75
Établissement cinématographique et photographique des armées (ECPA) 85–6, 179–80
ethnographic approach 15, 17, 23
   ethno-fiction 18
   move away from 16, 18, 20–4
   see also voice-of-God narrative approach
Eurocentricism 49, 71, 78, 80, 91
European rationalism *see* Eurocentricism
exile and return as theme of Teno's films 5–6, 25, 31, 46, 93n4, 94–96, 105, 107–8, 155, 197–8
   insider-outsider perspective 97–8, 164
   see also belonging, cultural; cinematic transnationality

Fanon, Frantz 19, 30, 48, 63, 73, 83n30, 93&n2, 95, 100–101, 109, 193
Faye, Safi 20, 25, 37&n4
   Kaddu Beykat 23–4, 145
Fièvre jaune taximan 138, 166, 210
filiation 46, 97–100, 107–8, 192, 207 *see also* transmission, intergenerational/filial
Film essai/essay film 26

first-person voice-overs in Teno's films 5, 35, 49, 50–2, 56, 58–60&n16, 63–4&p, 66, 78, 81, 83, 149, 155–6, 161
   as challenge to omniscient colonial voice-over 56–7, 67, 68p–9, 87, 88p–9, 157, 160, 163, 174, 205
   critical distancing effect of 59–60, 67, 85, 90, 96, 98, 146, 164–6
   resonating with collective 'we' 62, 100, 162–4
   use of irony in 2, 44, 54, 59, 66–7, 77, 86–7, 90, 98, 158–9, 183
   see also subjectivity, Teno's embracing of
First World War 48, 86
Flaherty, Robert 12–13, 17
Fodouop, Paulin 103p, 211
Folly, Anne-Laure 26
Foucault, Michel 17n25, 64–5
French Cultural Centre 188, 206
French colonialism 15, 41–2&n21, 48, 53, 65–6n35, 76, 85, 91, 115–16
   'civilizing' mission of 16&n21, 72, 86–7, 207
French national film school (FEMIS) 22, 122, 150
Francophone auteur/arthouse cinema 30–1&n5, 34, 38, 60
funders/funding issues 54–5, 77, 130, 149–50, 160, 165–6, 187, 193

Gabara, Rachel 1n3&4, 18–19&n33
Gabriel, Teshome, concept of 'nomadic cinema' 25, 97
Ganda, Oumarou 19–20, 37
gender dynamics in Teno's films 5, 43–5, 170
Gerima, Haile 57, 132, 183
German colonialism 48, 77
   Berlin Conference 15, 78
   Herero resistance/genocide under 48, 77–9
Ghana 2, 36, 66, 80, 91, 105–6p, 107–108, 168p, 198p
Gikandi, Simon 76n23, 94, 104
globalization 133, 135, 195, 207–8
Godard, Jean-Luc 12
Goethe Institute 206–7
Griaule, Marcel 16–17
griot storytelling codes 25n47, 39, 54, 75n22, 77, 195, 204
   infusion of African cinema with 40–1, 204
   see also oral history/literature
Grosfoguel, Ramón 72n5
Guinea 51, 176

Hall, Stuart 41, 48, 57, 63, 71, 83, 85, 91, 97
   'position of enunciation' 2
Haroun, Mahamat-Saleh 26, 189, 206

Harrow, Kenneth W 5, 11n3, 38
Hegel, GWF 72–3, 95
Henni, Samia
    de-propagandizing the archives 87&n44
Higgins, Mary Ellen 30
historical representations of colonialism 1, 15, 19, 41–42&n21&22, 71–3, 196, 207
    silencing/negation of the colonized 56–7, 71, 73, 85, 87
    see also memory: history and
hooks, bell 1, 3, 56, 58, 74, 86
Hommage 5–6, 24–5, 32, 43, 46, 57, 150–1, 170, 178–9, 183
    attempted censorship of 176–7
    awards for 138, 144
    as personal quest 125, 136–8, 140–1, 145, 158
    transnationality as leitmotif in 46, 93, 96–7, 100
    use of path leitmotif 7p, 36
Hondo, Med 37, 74, 126
humour/playfulness in Teno's films 25, 54, 66, 124, 137, 140, 150, 159, 183, 206

identities
    redefined post-colonial 5, 19, 95, 108, 193 see also decolonization process
IDHEC see French national film school
Imbert, Henri-François 21n40, 22
imperialism 1, 20, 135
indigène 65n32, 93
    Teno's appropriation of term 64–5&n32
irony see under first-person voice-overs in Teno's films

journeying as theme of Teno's films 6–7p, 29, 33–4, 52, 62, 97–8, 100–101, 105, 107–108, 163–4, 168p
    see also exile and return as theme of Teno's films

Kaboré, Gaston 31, 126, 129p
Kamete, Bishop 78–9p
Kamwa, Daniel 31, 118, 136
Kisukidi, Nadia Yala 57, 76n23, 96
Kodjo-Grandvaux, Séverine 63, 97

La Gifle et la caresse 166, 211
La Tête dans les nuages 6, 34, 43, 53, 117, 151–2, 211
    metaphor of uncontrollable body 51
Le Dernier voyage 139p, 166, 209p, 211
Le Malentendu colonial 6, 33–4, 43, 53, 79, 167, 170, 192

    theme of agency/resistance in 53, 167
    theme of history and memory in 77–8
Le Mariage d'Alex 6, 33, 43, 149
    domestic power relations at play in 44–5p, 53, 212–3
leitmotifs in Teno's work 7p, 29, 35, 90, 93, 107, 193
    artisans at work 46, 97, 193
Lewat, Osvalde 189, 207
Lieux saints 6, 17, 33, 39, 44, 47p, 64n29, 141, 149
    Abbo's public writing as metaphor 33, 35, 46–7p
    analogy of Jules César's craftsmanship 33, 35, 46, 141, 193, 195
    Bouba's cine-club 33, 35, 46–7p, 205
    use of music in 35
    see also Sacred Places
Loach, Ken 143, 211
local economies 22, 43, 46
Lumumba, Patrice 83&n31, 180, 196
Luste Boulbina, Seloua 57, 71&n4

Macron, Emmanuel 42n22, 77n24
Makharam, Ababacar Samb 37, 132
Maldoror, Sarah 37&n4
Mali 16, 31, 131
Mambéty, Djibril Diop 37, 39–40, 127, 195
    Contras' city 127, 203
Marker, Chris 130
    Sans Soleil 143, 158
Marti, Walter 189–90
Mazuri, Ali 62n23
Mbembe, Achille 57, 62–3, 76n23, 83, 95–6, 198
memory
    archeology of 5, 74
    collective 39, 54, 75, 79–80
    history and 5, 71, 73, 78, 184
    tension between knowledge and 85
    wounded 52
memory as theme of Teno's films 39, 54, 43, 61, 70, 73, 75, 85, 100, 184 see also decolonial history-memory films
Mercer, Kobena 43
metaphor 35, 51, 63, 101, 105, 133, 186, 196, 204–5
Mignolo, Walter 49, 73n12, 86n42
migration/migrant experiences 6, 40n15, 93n4, 94, 96, 100, 104, 124, 131, 198
Miller, Christopher 92
Mindja, Essindi 53–4, 138, 150
Minh-Ha, Trinh T 13–14, 67, 93n3
missionaries, role in colonial Africa 53, 77, 117, 179
    Rhenish Mission Society 77–80

Index

modernity 43, 62&n23, 74, 98
   acculturation and 44, 99–100
   duality between 'tradition' and 137, 169
   sham/pseudo- 100, 130
Monga, Célestin 53
Moumié, Félix-Roland 83–4, 176, 196
Mudimbe, V.Y. 65, 71
   concept of 'colonial library' 6, 85, 177
Musée de l'Homme, Paris 17, 20n37, 143

Namibia 79–80, 124
   Lutheran Church 53, 77–9p
Nancy, Jean-Luc 3
narrative structure in Teno's films 142–3, 150
   blurring of fiction and documentary genres 2, 24–6, 32–3, 43, 137, 141
   shift from linear to non-linear 32–4, 59, 75, 77, 100, 107
   rejection of formatted writing 54, 142, 148–50
   use of dialogue/conversation 25, 57, 61, 97, 137–8, 158
   see also first-person voice-overs in Teno's films
Ndiaye, Iba 22
Ndiaye, Katy Lena 207
Ndiaye, Samba Félix 25n46, 136, 145, 154, 205–7
   relation to Senghor 23
   narrative voice 22–3, 146
neo-liberalism 41, 130–1, 135
Nganang, Patrice 52–3, 64–5n30, 184
Ngũgĩ wa Thiong'o, concept of 'decolonizing minds', 19
Niang, Sada 19, 25n46
Nichols, Bill 12–13, 26, 33–4
Niger 19, 204
Nigeria see Nollywood film industry
Njawe, Pius 44, 53
Nkrumah, Kwame 19, 51, 73, 83, 105, 196
Nollywood film industry 30–1n6, 42&n23&24, 193
notions of the real 1, 4, 12–14, 17–18, 25
   Teno on 34, 41, 56, 90–91, 127, 136–8, 140, 150, 155, 196

oral history/literature 5, 39, 72, 75, 77, 204
   allegory/metaphor as narrative characteristic of 77, 104, 186
   influence on Teno's narratives 39–40, 75, 90, 97, 107, 156, 160, 165, 185–6, 204
   see also griot storytelling codes
orature see oral history/literature
Ouandié, Ernest 35–6, 80–81, 83, 176, 183, 196
   Kembo Samba's drawings of execution of 80, 91–2p, 183
   see also Une Feuille dans le vent
Ouandié, Ernestine see Une Feuille dans le vent
Ouedraogo, Idrissa 31, 127
   Teno on Yam Dabo 133
   Yaaba 46, 204

Pan-African Federation of Filmmakers (FEPACI) 38, 132
   Algiers Charter 19n36, 37, 127, 195
   Niamey Charter 127
Pan-African Film and Television Festival of Ouagadougou (FESPACO) 31&n6, 44, 46, 126, 128p–9, 131, 136, 203
   debates/discussions on role of cinema 127, 130, 132–3, 203
   launch of Côté Doc 188–9
   Teno's criticism of 130
Pan-Africanism 96, 105, 130
Paris 1, 17, 23, 202
   Images d'Ailleurs Festival 1
   Teno in 122, 125–6, 138, 142–3, 150, 206, 209
patrimony 145, 202
Peck, Raoul 26
Person, Yves 72n6
polygamy 44, 53, 213
post-colonial Africa
   new elites 48, 63, 66, 116, 135
   Teno's filmic analysis of 2, 48–9
power/power relations 5, 43–4, 152–3, 167
   North-South asymmetries in 29, 77–8, 93n4, 94, 201
   see also gender dynamics in Teno's films
Prabhu, Anjali 25, 29, 37n3, 38–9, 61
precolonial African societies 17, 96–7
pro-democracy demonstrations see democracy: fight for

Quijano, Anibal 49&n29, 73n12

racism 95, 104
   SOS-Racisme 126
Ranger, Terence, concept of 'the invention of tradition' 17n27
Rascaroli, Laura 60, 63n28
representational context of African cinema 4, 11–12, 15, 75n18, 127, 192, 204
   contested 18–19, 41–2, 26, 134, 207
   importance to Teno 33, 93–4, 126–7, 136, 155, 181
   and Western hegemonic historiography 15, 38, 41–3, 45, 84, 94–5

resistance 56
  art as form of 4–5, 17n25
  as theme in Teno's films 46, 52–5, 58, 74–6, 86, 108, 110, 160
  see also humour in Teno's films: as form of resistance
return *see* exile and return as theme of Teno's films
Ricci, Daniela 94n5
'roaming souls'/ghosts in Teno's films 82–3, 171
Rocha, Glauber 19–20
Rouch, Jean 16–18, 20–21n39, 23, 143–5, 193
  Teno's meeting with 138, 143–5
Rwanda 23, 146

Sacred Places 203, 205, 208
Said, Edward 61, 96
Sembène, Ousmane 19, 31, 37, 39–40, 126, 132, 135, 194p, 195
  Borom Sarret 19, 37n4, 101, 127, 203
  Ceddo 22, 74&n15
  conflict between Rouch and 20–22, 145, 193
  'father' of African cinema 20, 39
  Mandabi 19, 37n3, 54
Senegal 19, 21–3, 31, 74n15, 145, 205, 207
  government censorship in 24
  see also Dakar
Senghor, President 22–3, 74n15
Sharpe, Christina 57-8
Sissako, Abderrahmane 26, 52n30, 206
Sita-Bella, Thérèse 21
slave trade 62n23, 65n32, 72, 78, 87, 95n9
Soudani, Mohamed 209p, 211
sound design in Teno's films 146, 157, 161
  expressive rather than realistic 35, 90–91, 101, 104–5, 161
  multi-layered/polyphonic 32, 34–6, 59, 60–1, 157, 161
  use of music 35–6, 43–4, 58, 67, 87, 91, 99, 117, 157
  see also first-person voice-overs in Teno's films
South Africa 80
  documentary filmmakers in 189, 208
  see also apartheid
South West Africa *see* Namibia
Spivak, Gayatri Chakravorty 54, 174
subalterns/subaltern theory 2, 54, 65, 75n18, 91, 174
subjectivity, Teno's embracing of 2, 5, 24, 33–4, 56, 58&p, 59, 61, 66, 75, 158–60, 162, 197
  as decolonial gesture 5, 57–60, 64, 77, 90
  see also first-person voice-overs in Teno's films
symbolism/symbolic meaning in African cinema 22, 24
  in Teno's films 35, 51, 62, 78, 83, 94, 97–8, 100–101, 104, 108, 138, 141

Takoukam, Bonaventure 102p, 211
Taylor, Clyde 62n23
Tayou, Pascale Marthine 151–2p
Tcheuyap, Alexie 60n16
Tchouaffe, Olivier 84, 85
technological evolution 12, 122, 162
  digital era 14, 31n6, 146, 166
  internet 191, 208
television 22, 34, 42, 56, 66, 77, 85n39, 131, 143–4, 166, 193, 211
  ARTE 34
  lack of documentary screenings on 191
  Teno's editing work in 24, 122–3, 125–6, 136, 140, 159, 162, 173, 209, 212
Teno, Jean-Marie
  activism/socialism of 121, 124, 175
  cinematic influences 123–4, 141–3, 147–8, 158
  early experiences of colonial violence 115–16
  early memories of cinema 117–18, 185
  early filmmaking experiences 125, 136, 143, 209–10
  influence of grandfather on 77, 99–100, 137, 158
  on exile 196–7
  on feelings of solitude 189, 191
  on filming/film shoots 209–213
  on freedom 201, 203
  on future of African documentary cinema 203, 206–208
  on training young filmmakers 192–3, 195, 206–207
  personal contradictions/duality 97, 99–100, 137–8, 158
  relationship with father 24–5, 100, 116–17, 120, 122, 137–8, 140–1, 158
Teno, Jean-Marie, formal education 144, 172
  Ecole Polytechnique, Yaoundé 121–2
  INA scholarship 122
  Portsmouth Polytechnic scholarship 120–1, 124, 175
  schooling/Lycée Leclerc 62, 97–9, 116–17, 120, 123, 175, 182
  University of Valenciennes 122, 125
  Yaoundé University 120
Teno, Jean-Marie, oeuvre 4, 43

autobiographical voice 23, 26, 33–4, 56, 62, 97, 99, 136–7
blending of documentary modes 33, 54–5, 154
character-based approach 33, 53, 96–7, 104, 107
contestation/challenge in 1, 43, 54–6, 59, 75, 84–5, 91, 95, 104, 109, 154–5
editing process 86, 122–3, 125–6, 138, 140, 150, 155–7, 159, 161, 165, 173, 179, 209–10, 212
experimental/avant-garde approach 25, 38, 77, 90–1, 125–6, 140, 142, 151–2, 196
notions of freedom in 2, 26, 34, 43, 54, 96, 108, 110, 154–5
use of juxtapositional montage in 34, 43, 54, 67&n37, 85–7, 90, 98, 101, 153, 155–7, 161, 165
Teno's exploration of socio-political/historical contexts 33, 38, 43, 48, 78, 108
Cameroon Independence struggle 3–5, 24–5, 29, 33, 43, 48, 50, 52, 59, 62, 64, 80, 84, 172, 174–5
foregrounding of impact on individual/collective psyche 80–4, 167–8
questioning of/counter discourse to imposed colonial historiography, 5–6, 39, 43, 46, 48, 54, 58–60, 62, 64, 71–5, 77, 80, 84–5, 91, 98, 123, 140, 165, 169–72, 174–6, 178–9, 181–2, 196
Third Cinema 19&n36, 39
Touré, Moussa 189, 208
transmission, intergenerational/filial 46, 98–100, 134, 192, 203, 207
of trauma 82–3
see also filiation; oral history/literature
transnationality see cinematic transnationality
Tuene, Tadie 125, 137, 150

Um Nyobè, Ruben 83&n32, 176, 196
underdevelopment see development, lack of
Une Feuille dans le vent 2, 6, 33, 43, 46, 52, 84, 97, 149, 151, 170, 173, 212
Ernestine Ouandié's testimony 35–6, 51, 53, 61, 80–1&n29, 82&p, 83, 90–1, 105, 171, 183–4
intertwining of public and private history in 77, 80–1, 183–4
metaphor of broken body 51
theme of transnationality/journeying in 94, 97
theme of war of independence 35, 90, 167
polyphonic narrative form 61
use of leaf-shot leitmotif 35, 82–3
use of mixed media in 80, 90–2p, 183
see also Ouandié, Ernest
Union of the Peoples of Cameroon see Cameroon: UPC party
United Kingdom (UK) 124, 175
United States 17, 80n27, 198, 204
Gainesville 105, 107–8

Vacances au pays 6–7, 27, 34, 43, 46, 52–3, 56, 67, 105, 117, 146–7, 162, 167, 212
cultural legacy of colonialism as key theme 44, 52, 98–100, 167
theme of journeying/returning in 33, 40, 62, 93–4, 97–8, 100
van der Keuken, Johan 147&p, 148, 190, 206
Vergès, Françoise 74&n17, 75–6n23
Vertov, Dziga 12, 17, 85n39, 130
Vedder, Heinrich 79–80
Vieyra, Paulin Soumarou 19, 21, 132
as head of Actualités sénégalaises 22
violence as theme of Teno's work 5, 43, 49–50p, 51, 54, 67, 70, 76, 83, 170
colonial 17, 67, 68p –9, 70, 86–7, 90–91, 94, 167–9, 179
gender-based/family 44, 49, 80–1
metaphor of broken body 51–2
political 58, 168–9, 176
psychological 44, 49, 80, 176
voice-of-God narrative approach 15, 22, 24, 56
Teno's rescinding/challenging of 60, 85–6, 137, 158, 163, 179, 181–2

Witt, Michael 85n39
Wouassi, Félicité 127, 138

xenophobia 95, 130

ZDF German TV channel 77, 166

www.ingramcontent.com/pod-product-compliance
Lightning Source LLC
Chambersburg PA
CBHW080837230426
43665CB00021B/2862